I0793072

IMAGES
of Modern America

# Christmas in San Diego

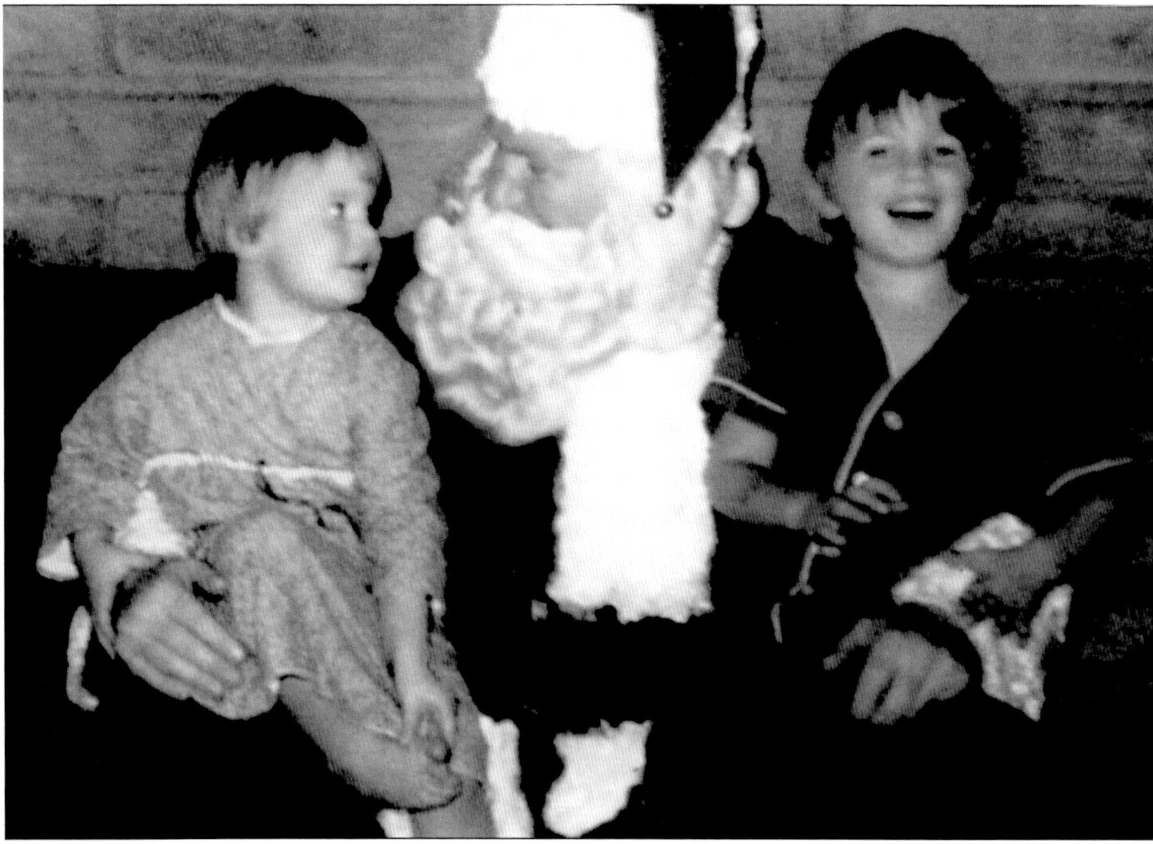

**Classic Quote.** "Yes, Virginia, there is a Santa Claus," wrote Francis Pharcellus Church in the *New York Sun* on September 21, 1897. "He exists as certainly as love and generosity and devotion exist . . . "

**On the Front Cover:** Clockwise from top left:
Santa and the beach bunnies (Courtesy of Chuck Whitmarsh and Phil Prather), Mick Ward as Irish Santa (Author's collection), Balboa Park's 30-foot Christmas tree (Courtesy of Del Cerro Baptist Church), Beefcake Santa on the guitar (courtesy of Drum Macomber), and Santa in a lifeguard chair (Courtesy of Beach & Bay Press)

**On the Back Cover:** From left to right:
Over-the-Line Santas at the beach (Courtesy of Robert J. Trombley), Santa extending a warm welcome (Author's collection), and the Balboa Park Christmas lights (Courtesy of the Balboa Park Conservancy and Richard Benton)

IMAGES
of Modern America

# CHRISTMAS IN SAN DIEGO

Bill Swank

ARCADIA
PUBLISHING

ISBN 978-1-4671-3455-2

Published by Arcadia Publishing
Charleston, South Carolina

Printed in the United States of America

Library of Congress Control Number: 2015951547

For all general information, please contact Arcadia Publishing:
Telephone 843-853-2070
Fax 843-853-0044
E-mail sales@arcadiapublishing.com
For customer service and orders:
Toll-Free 1-888-313-2665

Visit us on the Internet at www.arcadiapublishing.com

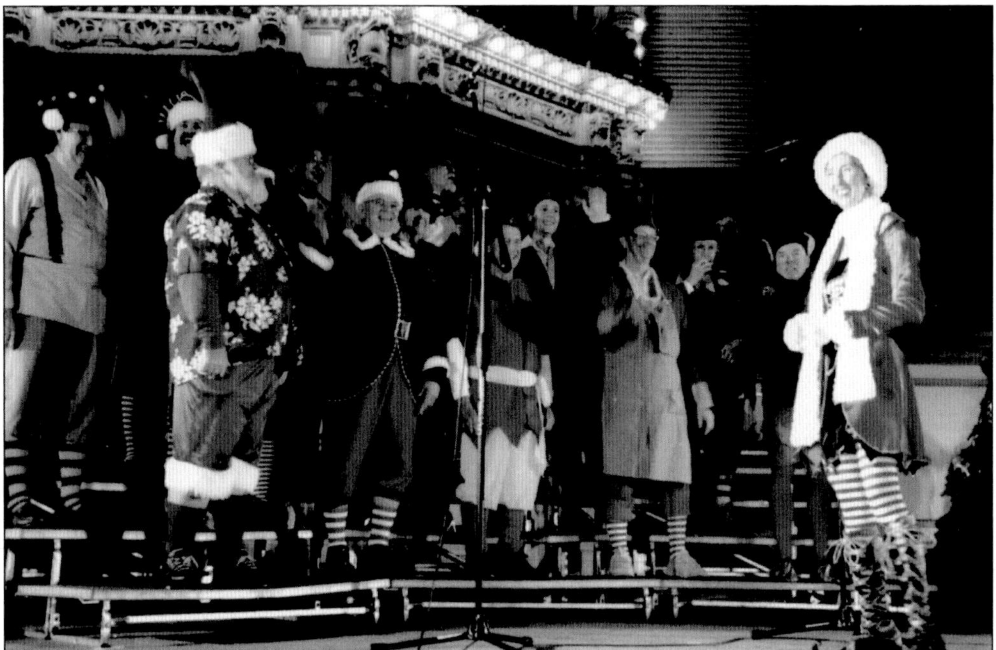

*This book is dedicated to those who bring joy to the world—like the Sun Harbor Elf Chorus and its director, Kathleen Hansen (right).*

# Contents

# ACKNOWLEDGMENTS

Because the sun smiles on the southwestern corner of the United States year-round, "White Christmas" is not a San Diego tradition. The first page of each chapter in this book features a specific year where the local temperature was 70 degrees on Christmas Day. For that, the author tenders his acknowledgment and appreciation to our meteorologists, climatologists, and weather record-keepers.

It took over a year to complete this project. During the research process, many people generously contributed their stories, ideas, and photographs. Without the help of others, this book would not have been possible. In a way, the tree was bare until the following elves helped decorate it.

Thanks are due—in alphabetical order—to Mary Allely, Corrina Allison, Richard Amero, Suzanne Andersen, Walter Andersen, Wendy Barker, Larry Baumann, Doug Beckham, Pat and Mike Bessie, M.L. Bey, Ernie Bonn, Lori Boucher, Gabe Bradford, Curt Benedetto, Richard Benton, June Bernesser, Phil Brigandi, Adrienne Brown, David Bruce, Paul Burlingame, Scott "Burner" Burnworth, Fabiola Camacho, Sheila Chatterjee, Anne Clifford, the Cool San Diego Sights blog, Alana Coons, Linda Costello, Charlie and Margaret Coval, Rick Crawford, Glen Crooks, Jason Cruz, Pam Davis, Sharon Davis, Al Demoran, Mara Derakapet, Sara Dick, Sarah Dickey, Arthur B. Dodge, Ralph Drew, Paul Ecke III, Richard Eckfield, Encinitas Undercover, Andrea Feier, Deana Findlay, John Fry, Tom Fudge, Gina Garcia, Nina Garin, Wendy Gay, Ted Giannoulas, Lisa Comrie Gibson, Robert Gigl, Elizabeth Gillingham, Nick Golden, Ken Groom, Helen Halmay, Larry Halstead, Joe Hodnicki, Morgan Hurley, Jake Jaccard, Pat James, Alyssa Jones, Alex Jung, Bobby and Thais Jungblut, Ann Kerr, Don King, Rich Kirsch, Don Kojis, Annie Korn, Cynthia Kovalesky, Suzi Woodruff Lacey, Bill Lansville, Heather Laslo, Cassie Lee, Nicole LeBlanc, Terry Leeds, Janis Legzdins, Bob Lehman, Lee Lescano, David Lewis, Sandé Lollis, Bruce Lowe, Drum Macomber, Petra Maes, Adam Martinez, John McCoy, Peti McHenry, Kevin McKay, Julia Meier, Michael Mishler, Eric Minella, Sam Modica, Jo Moreland, Derek Moses, Bob Moss, Michelle Mowad, Todd Mowbray, Patrick Mulroy, Sheila Mura, Gretchen Newsom, Mei Chan Ng, Shannon O'Dunn, Mary Oswell, Roger Pena, Marcelina Peraza, Debbie Petruzzelli, Phil Prather, Rita Gaffney Price, Miriam Raftery, Lauren Rasmussen, Kate Reeve, Roberta Rose, Ann Rosser, Peter Rowe, Jeff Ruetsche, Todd Salovey, Suzanne Sannwald, Elizabeth Schlappi, Randy Seaver, Rachael Shay, Julia Simms, Steve Sloan, Joyce and Mary Jane Smith, Margaret Smith, Snowman, The family of Bekki Stewart, Chris Stone, Jeri Lynne Swank, Raymond Swank, Pete Tapia, Kristin Tinderholt, Todd Tobias, Danielle Thomas, Susan Tran, Robert Trombley, Eileen Turk, Suzan and Tony Valdez, Charlie Velazquez, John Vigil, Kellie Vogt, Susan Walter, Victoria Ward, Tim Wayne, Ellenjoy Weber, Phillip L. Wenz, Tom and Kathie Wellington, Kathy Whelan, Chuck Whitmarsh, Leomia Wilson, Theresa Wulf, Nathan Young, Lucille Youngquist, and Barbara Zaragoza.

Special thanks are extended to my stepson, Tim Wayne. One day, while working on this book, the text disappeared in the blink of an eye. I sat in numb disbelief. A year's work had vanished without a trace. Then Tim, a computer genius, found it. Thank you, Tim!

Unless otherwise noted, all photographs are from the author's collection. Sadly, some prominent celebrations and traditions are not included in this book, as they are either commercial, declined to share pictures, or simply did not respond to repeated attempts at contact.

# INTRODUCTION

*Swank is a tall, burly, white-bearded guy. You need more description? OK, imagine Santa Claus' younger brother.*

Peter Rowe, *San Diego Union-Tribune*

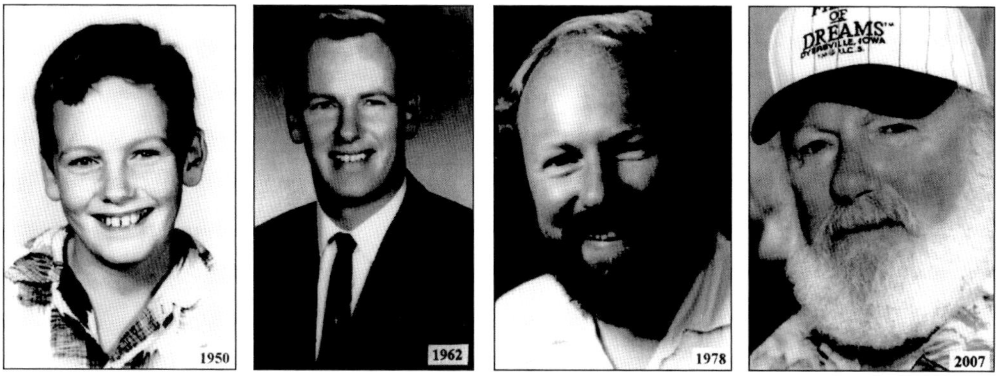


*The author is pictured here at various stages of his life: (from left to right) in 1950, 1962, 1978, and 2007—showing his evolving resemblance to Santa Claus.*

I didn't know I'd end up looking like I do, but when you are a mature gentleman with a full white beard, rubicund cheeks, and an ample belly, Santa-for-hire entrepreneurs, photographers, and "real bearded" Santa organizations seek you out. I never saw myself as Santa Claus. Specifically, I couldn't imagine selling myself as a mall Santa or private party Santa. Santa is special, and I'm one of those people who think Christmas is too commercialized. Wearing the red suit wasn't for me.

Until something magical happened.

One evening, while loading my plate at HomeTown Buffet, I felt something on my leg. I looked down and saw a little Mexican girl with both arms wrapped around my leg. She looked up and said, "I love you, Santa."

My heart melted.

A woman standing nearby asked if that happened often. I told her that the older I got, the more it happened.

Within a year, my wife and I were at a neighbor's party. Two women approached me to ask me a question. They represented the Community Christmas Center Committee in Balboa Park, and they needed a new Santa Claus.

When my kids were small, we regularly visited the life-sized Christmas story dioramas that the Community Christmas Center Committee maintains at the Organ Pavilion. This was a rare opportunity to become part of a traditional, noncommercial celebration of the Christmas season.

I have been their volunteer Santa since 2002.

The focus of this book is on unique San Diego Christmas traditions, celebrations, and the many wonderful San Diegans who enjoy sharing their Christmas cheer and spirit with others.

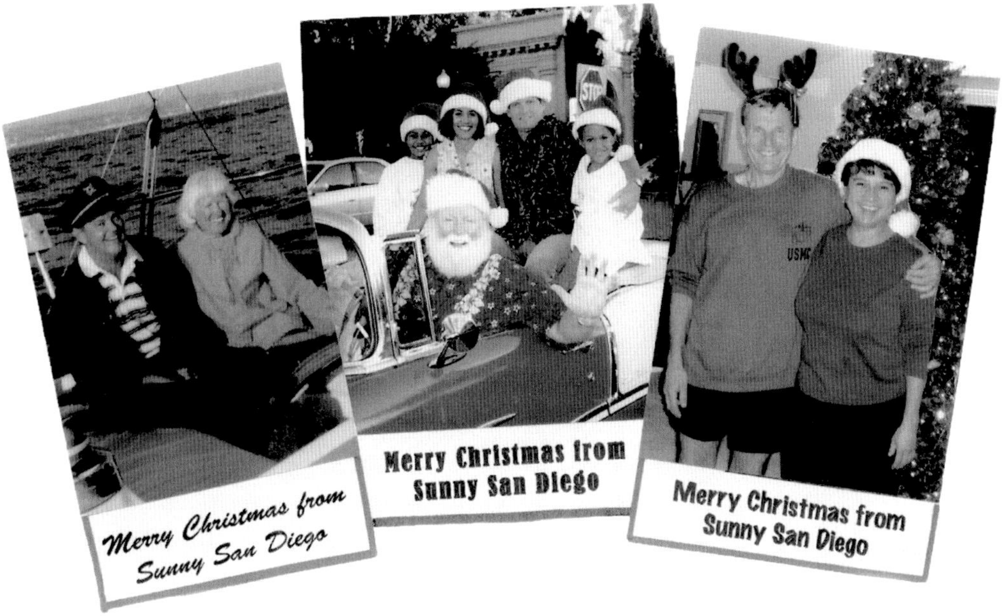


SNAPSHOTS OF SAN DIEGANS ENJOYING CHRISTMAS. Pictured are Wendell and Jean Lisle, the Noble family (Rachel, Kelly, Ron, Nathaniel, and Santa), Paul and Christy Gerencser.

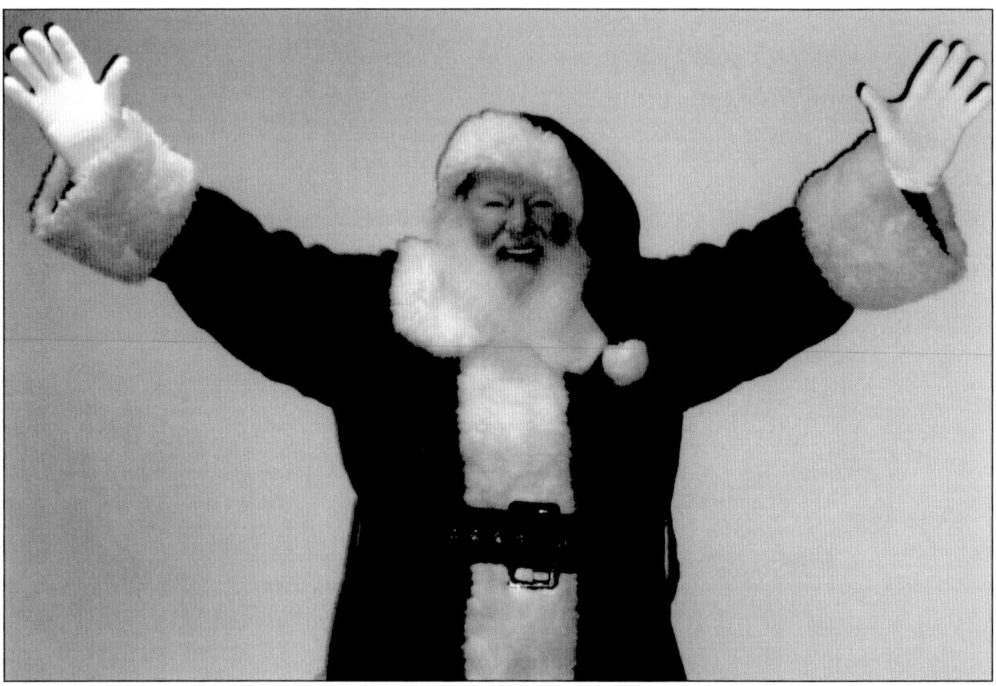

MERRY CHRISTMAS. Santa Swank is pictured spreading Christmas cheer.

# *One*

# History

*Merry Christmas from Sunny San Diego*

*December 25, 1894    Temperature: 70 Degrees*

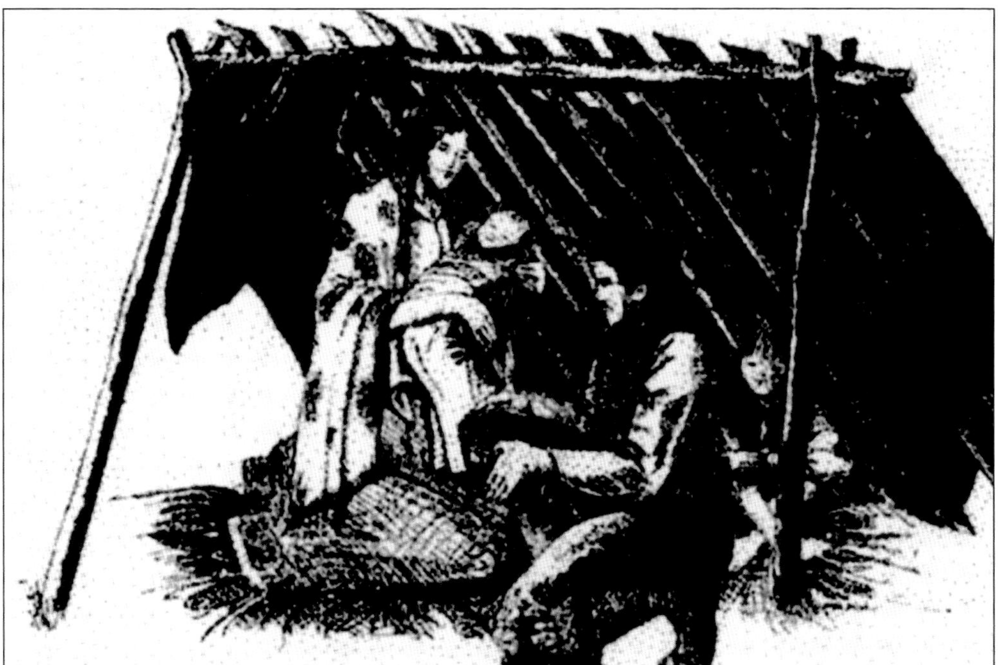

THE CHRISTMAS BABE. On Christmas Eve, 1775, while Capt. Juan Bautista de Anza was leading a group of 240 settlers and soldiers from Sonora, Mexico, to Monterey in Alta California, a soldier's wife gave birth to a baby boy in Coyote Canyon, near Borrego Springs. Appropriately, the child was named Salvador, which is Spanish for savior.

Don José Antonio was equally amusing in his character, and was ever on the alert seeking for some new device for my gratification. It was nearly time for the religious festival of "la noche buena," and he directed the customary exhibition of the "*pastores*." They were rehearsing night after night, till at length Christmas arrived, and I had an opportunity of beholding the ceremony of midnight mass and the subsequent performances.

**La Pastorela.** The first Christmas celebrations in San Diego were church plays known variously as *Los Pastores*, *La Pastorela*, and *El Diablo en la Pastorla*. Their Spanish origin focused more on the conflict between good and evil than the birth of Christ. The central characters were the angel Gabriel and the fallen Lucifer. Alfred Robinson, a Yankee merchant from New England and the author of *Life in California*, wrote this detailed description of an 1830 performance of *Los Pastores* in San Diego.

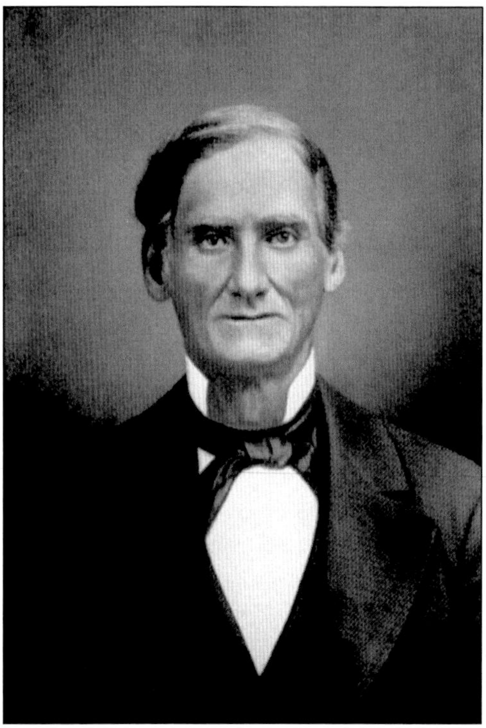

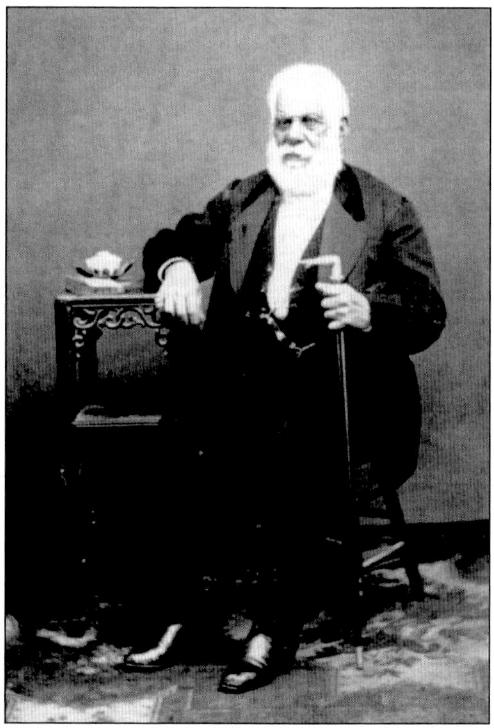

**Christmas Day, 1838.** Guests were enjoying *La Pastorela* in the home of Juan Bandini (left) when their holiday was disrupted by troops of Gov. Juan Alvarado. Future California governor Pio Pico (right), who was playing the role of the devil, was among five men taken prisoner and later released.

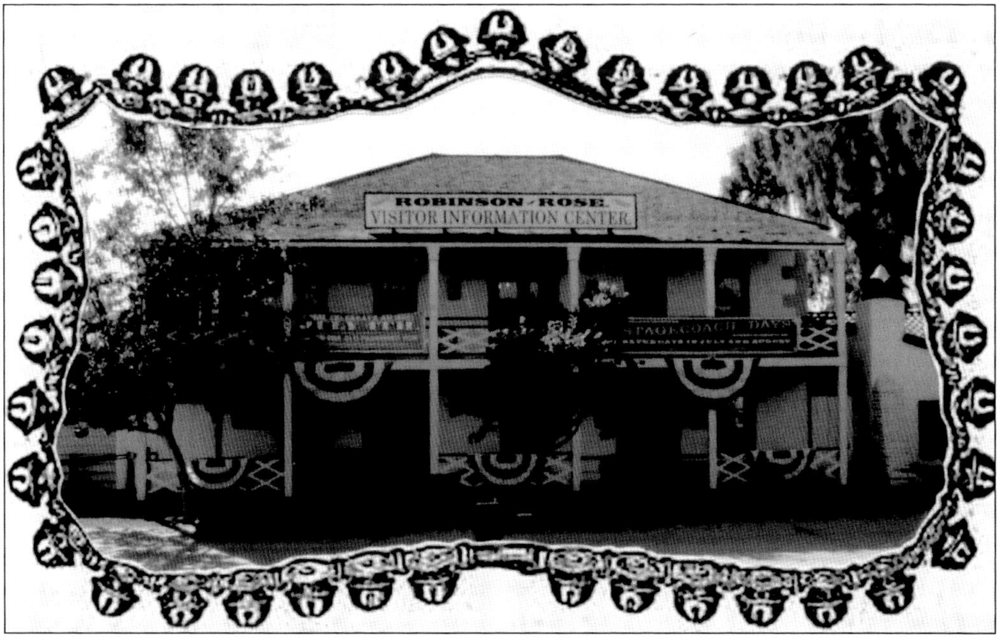


STILL AIR TORMENTED BY JINGLE BELLS. The earliest published news account of Christmas appeared on December 10, 1853, in *The San Diego Herald*. The annual Fiesta of the Patrona ran from December 8th to December 25th that year. Apparently, the Grinch was a cub reporter for the short-lived *Herald*. The article noted, "the still air was tormented by the jingle of bells." The *Herald* was published in the Robinson House, shown here after being reconstructed in Old Town State Park.

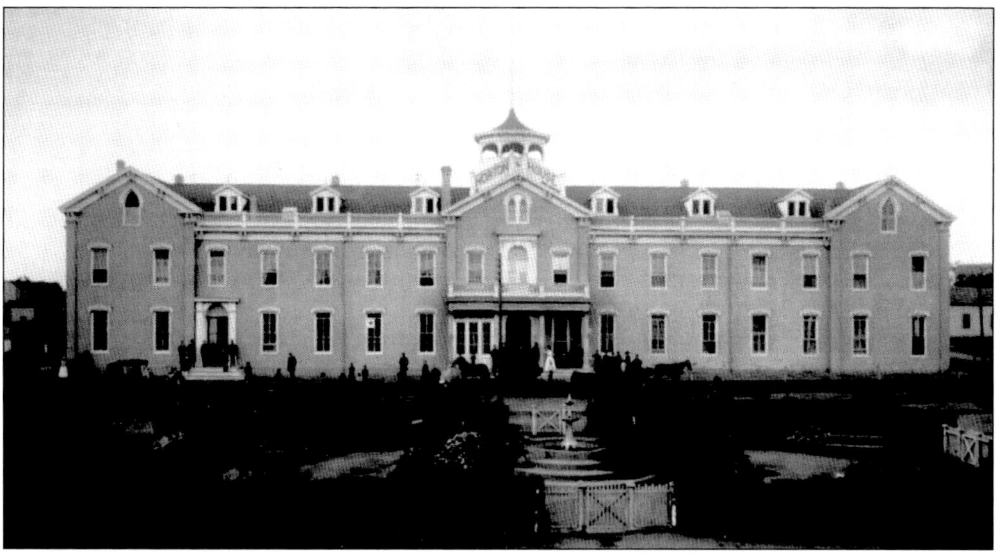

"CHRISTMAS—HOW IT WAS CELEBRATED." Under this December 27, 1871, headline, *The Daily Union* reported, "A number of guests at the Horton House (pictured) spent the evening preceding Christmas in the parlor with the intention of bidding each other a 'Merry Christmas' at midnight. As soon as the clock struck twelve an interchange of Christmas salutations took place, and immediately thereafter those assembled proceeded to the dining room which had been made ready for the purpose, and indulged in a dance."

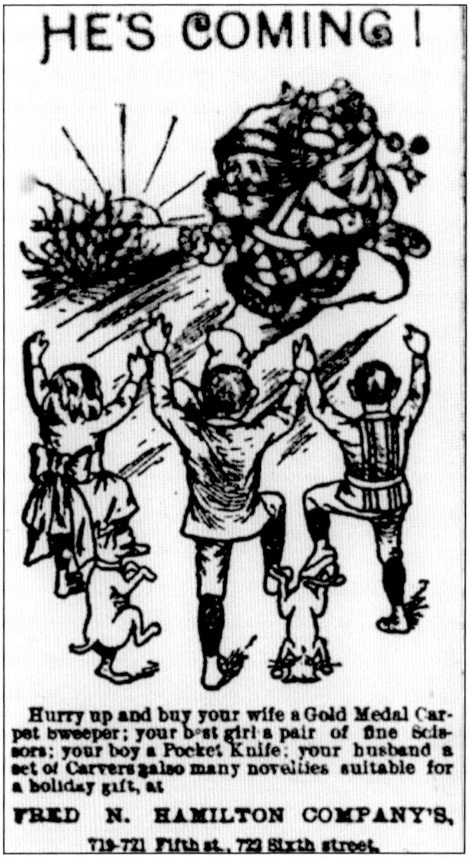


**He's Coming.** The ad may have proclaimed the pending arrival of St. Nicholas, but there were few published sightings of Santa Claus during the 19th century. He did visit County Hospital on Christmas Day, 1882, and gave "a few picture books" to a young boy with a broken leg. In 1892, Santa "freely dispensed fine French candies and nuts" at the Great American Importing Tea Company, on Fifth Street, to "good children when accompanied by their parents." It was reported in 1899 that Santa arrived at the Hotel del Coronado by automobile. (Courtesy of the *San Diego Union*.)

**Christmas Dreams.** This poem appeared in the December 20, 1890, issue of the *Coronado Mercury*: "At Ten. Childhood's sleep has wrapped her round, Shut out ev'ry sight and sound, And of Santa Claus she dreams—Bright and clear the vision seems. At Eighteen. Christmas Eve this maiden sees, While she slumbers at her ease, Leaves of joyous mistletoe, Dancing, gaslight, and a beau." (Courtesy of the *Coronado Mercury*.)

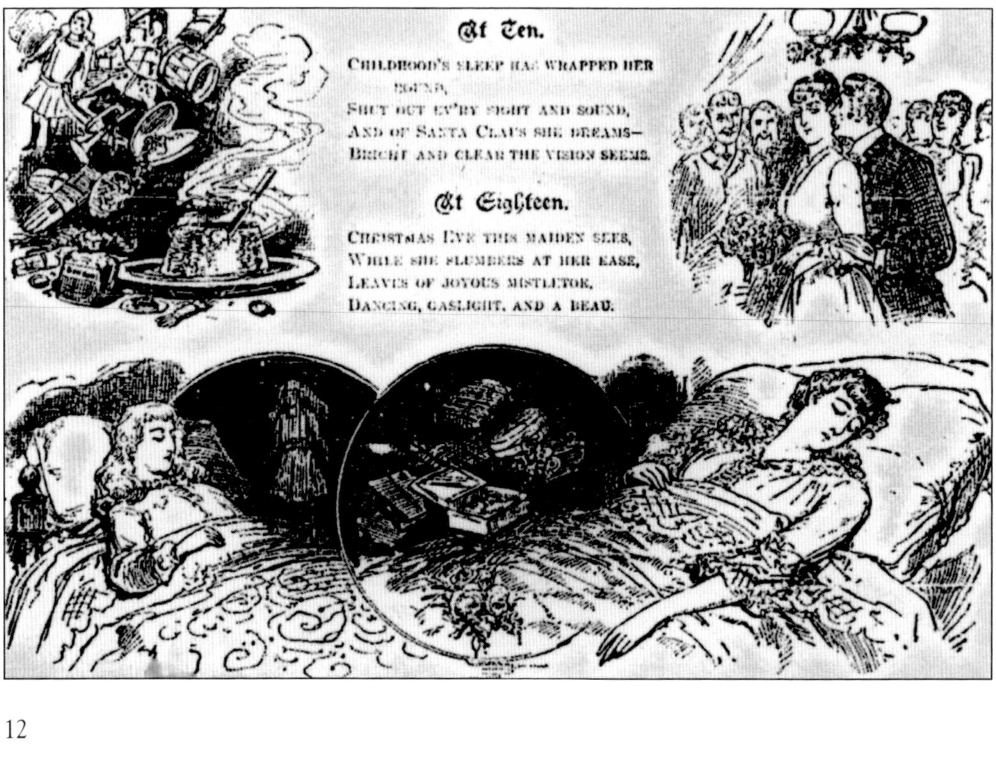

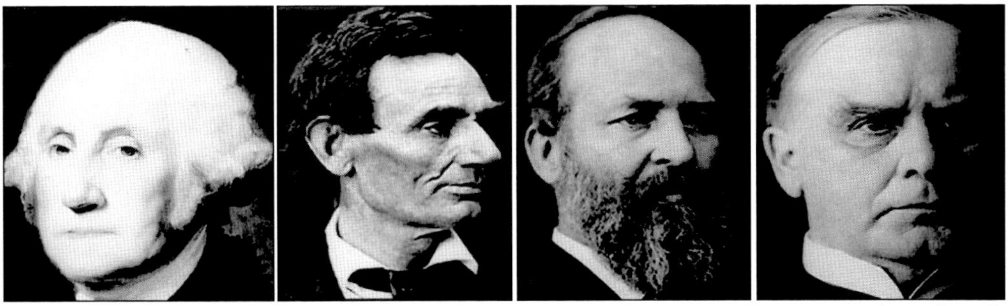

**"FINEST DISPLAY EVER SEEN HERE."** The headline of a 1901 *San Diego Union* article said it all. Alongside "an unusually attractive half a hundred dressed mutton carcasses" at the Bay City Market, there was a display created by "versatile genius Fritz Schmitz." Framed by green holly wreaths with red berries were portraits of Presidents Washington, Lincoln, Garfield, and McKinley. The renderings were carved from lard. "Just lard from the hog of commerce, that's all." Surely, nothing quite conveys the Christmas spirit like lard carvings of three assassinated presidents.

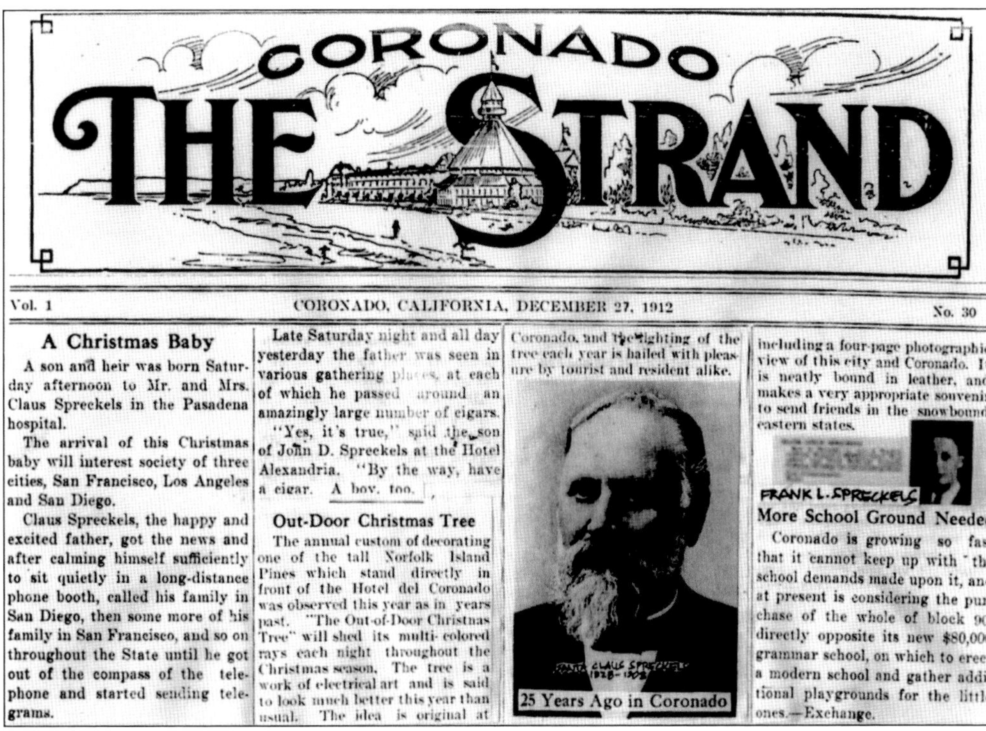

CORONADO

THE STRAND

Vol. 1 — CORONADO, CALIFORNIA, DECEMBER 27, 1912 — No. 30

**A Christmas Baby**

A son and heir was born Saturday afternoon to Mr. and Mrs. Claus Spreckels in the Pasadena hospital.

The arrival of this Christmas baby will interest society of three cities, San Francisco, Los Angeles and San Diego.

Claus Spreckels, the happy and excited father, got the news and after calming himself sufficiently to sit quietly in a long-distance phone booth, called his family in San Diego, then some more of his family in San Francisco, and so on throughout the State until he got out of the compass of the telephone and started sending telegrams.

Late Saturday night and all day yesterday the father was seen in various gathering places, at each of which he passed around an amazingly large number of cigars.

"Yes, it's true," said the son of John D. Spreckels at the Hotel Alexandria. "By the way, have a cigar. A boy, too."

**Out-Door Christmas Tree**

The annual custom of decorating one of the tall Norfolk Island Pines which stand directly in front of the Hotel del Coronado was observed this year as in years past. "The Out-of-Door Christmas Tree" will shed its multi-colored rays each night throughout the Christmas season. The tree is a work of electrical art and is said to look much better this year than usual. The idea is original at Coronado, and the lighting of the tree each year is hailed with pleasure by tourist and resident alike.

25 Years Ago in Coronado

including a four-page photographic view of this city and Coronado. It is neatly bound in leather, and makes a very appropriate souvenir to send friends in the snowbound eastern states.

FRANK L. SPRECKELS

**More School Ground Needed**

Coronado is growing so fast that it cannot keep up with the school demands made upon it, and at present is considering the purchase of the whole of block 90 directly opposite its new $80,000 grammar school, on which to erect a modern school and gather additional playgrounds for the little ones.—Exchange.

**CHRISTMAS BABY.** The lead article in the December 27, 1912, *Strand* hailed "A Christmas Baby," born heir to Ellis and Claus Spreckels—son of John D. and grandson of Claus. The couple named the boy Frank Leslie. He would graduate from Harvard in 1935. The paper spoke of an "Out-Door Christmas Tree" that still stands outside of John D. Spreckels' Hotel del Coronado. (Courtesy of the *Coronado Strand*.)

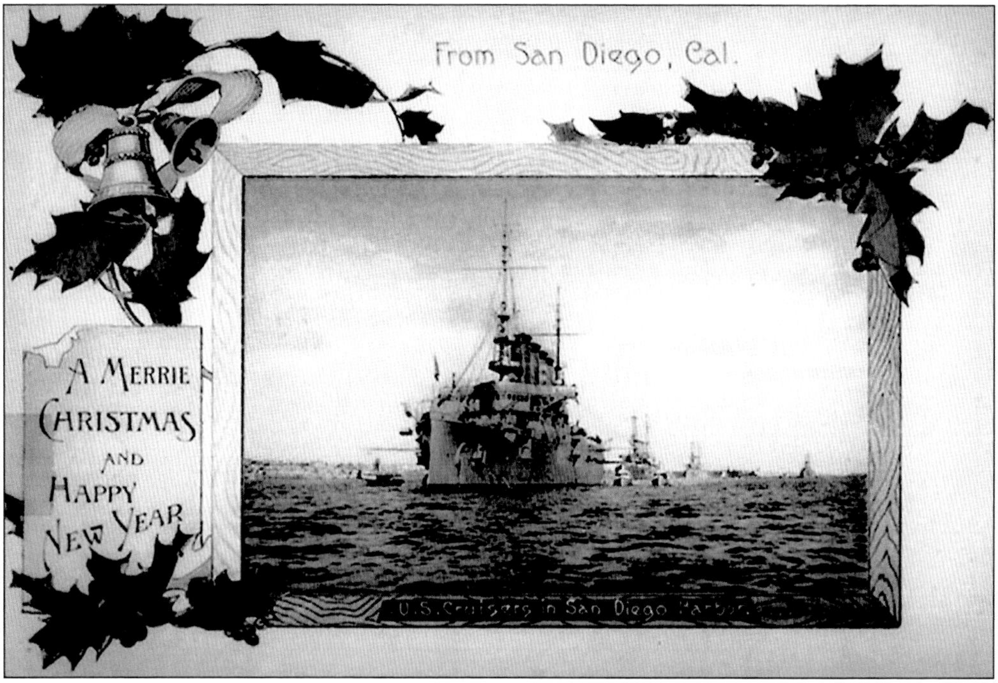


**Merrie Christmas from Dago.** In the old Navy, San Diego was called "Dago." With the passage of time, the term has disappeared from sailors' vocabularies, but this Christmas post card features the Navy cruisers USS *Pennsylvania*, USS *Colorado*, and USS *California* in San Diego Bay. When the Navy decided to name battleships exclusively for states, these ships were renamed USS *Pittsburgh*, USS *Pueblo*, and USS *San Diego*.

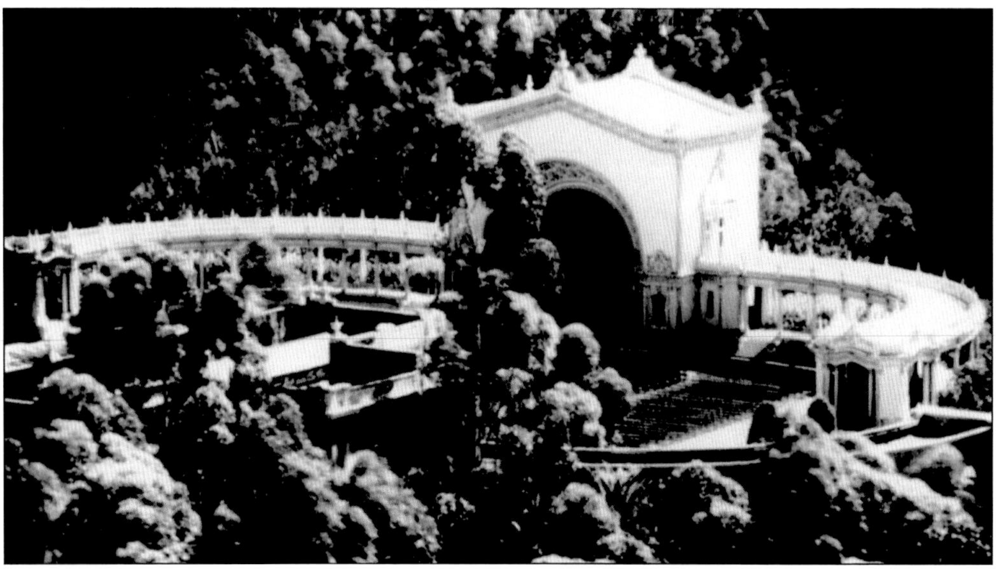

**Christmas in Balboa Park.** As part of the 1915 Panama-California Exposition in Balboa Park, a 60-foot Christmas tree from Cuyamaca was placed at the Spreckels Organ Pavilion. Its branches held stockings filled with toys and candy. On Christmas Day, the stockings were given to 4,500 San Diego children. It was the first citywide Christmas celebration since *La Pastorela* was performed in Old Town in the 19th century.

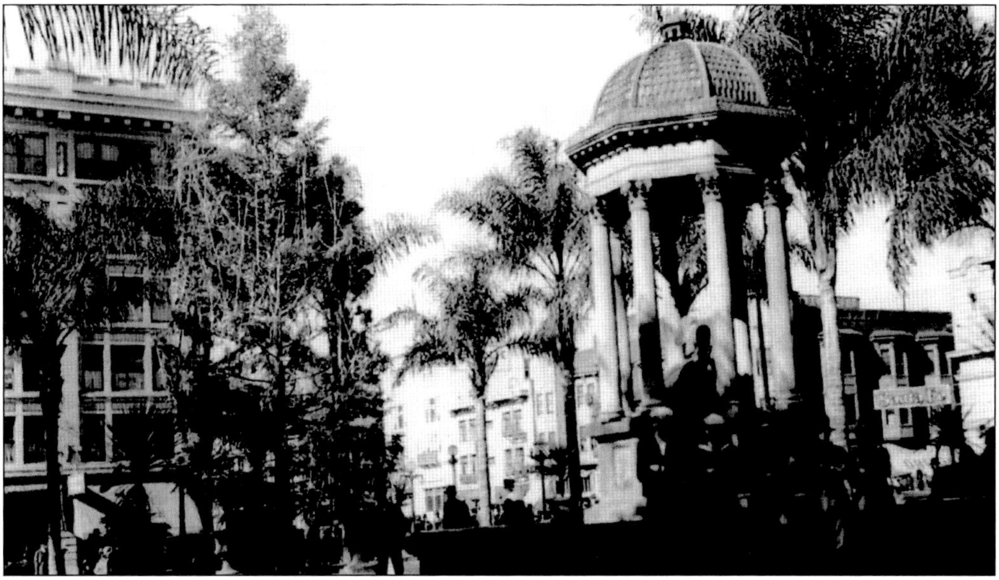

**HORTON PLAZA, CHRISTMAS, C. 1920.** Ernest Crevier was 17 years old in 1919, when he hitchhiked from New England to San Diego. He lied about his age and joined the Navy. At Christmas, he and a shipmate had their picture taken beside some soldiers in front of the Broadway Fountain, at Horton Plaza. On January 7, 1913, water in the fountain froze when the mercury dropped to 25 degrees. It was the coldest day on record for San Diego. (Courtesy of Peti McHenry.)

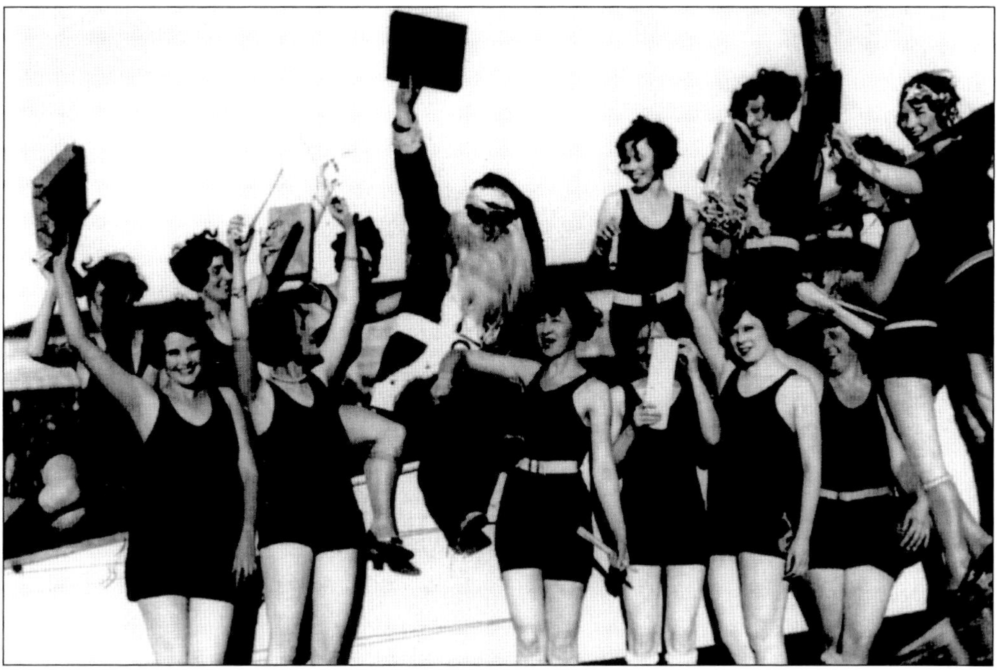

**SANTA CLAUS AND THE BEACH BUNNIES.** In 1925, Santa's two-seat biplane landed on the sand by the amusement center in Mission Beach. Bathing beauties wearing the latest fashion in revealing swimwear quickly surrounded Claus. In the 1920s, proper attire to stroll along the wooden boardwalk included a coat and tie for gentlemen and long dresses for the ladies. (Courtesy of Chuck Whitmarsh and Phil Prather.)

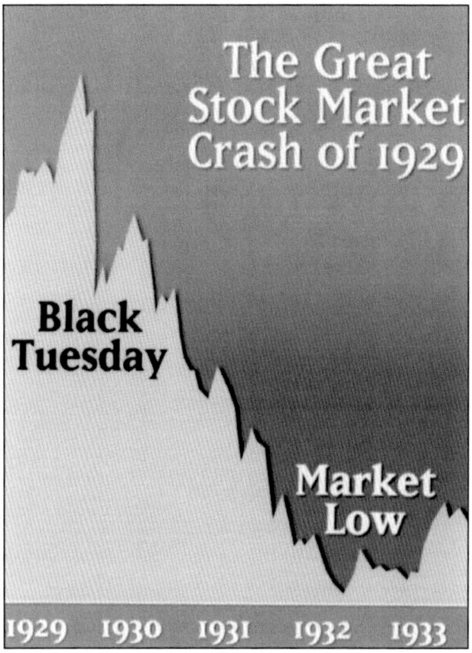


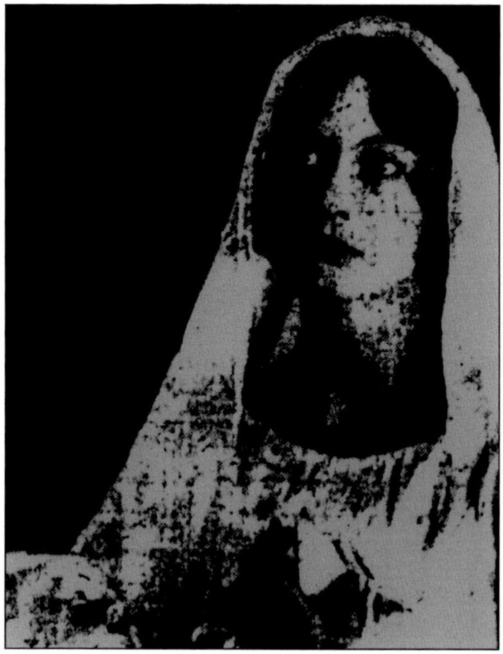

**Black Tuesday Cancels Christmas in Balboa Park.** As a result of the stock market crash in late 1929, the annual Organ Pavilion Christmas celebration was cancelled. The Yule was observed intermittently in Balboa Park during the Great Depression and was abrogated when the park was converted to a Navy base during World War II. Christmas would not return to the Organ Pavilion until 1953. Religiously themed paintings, such as the Madonna and Child at right, were staged as living tableaux at the Organ Pavilion from 1923 into the 1930s. The identity of the models was a closely guarded secret. (Courtesy of Harry Bishop, San Diego Union.)

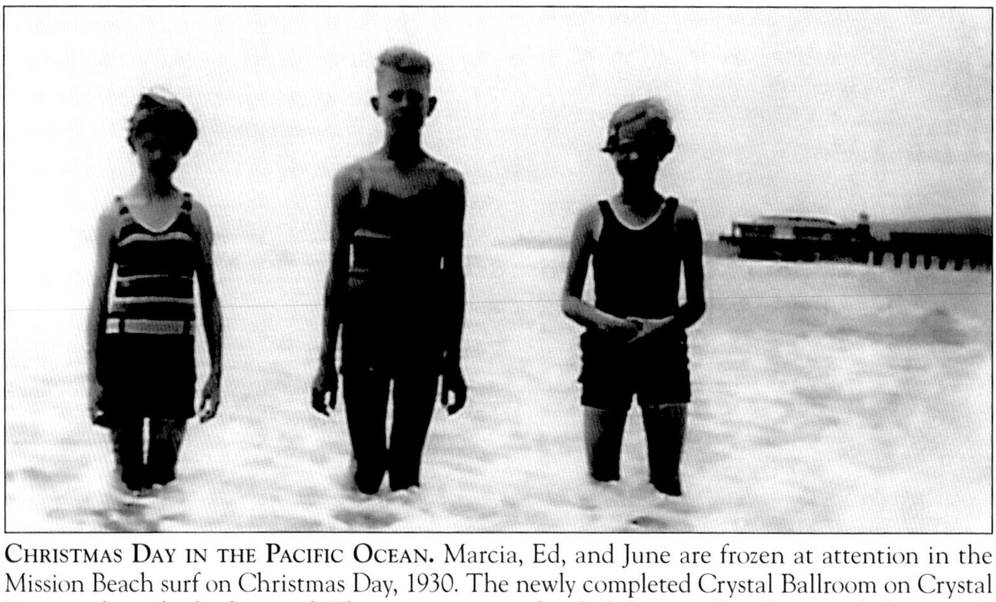

**Christmas Day in the Pacific Ocean.** Marcia, Ed, and June are frozen at attention in the Mission Beach surf on Christmas Day, 1930. The newly completed Crystal Ballroom on Crystal Pier stands in the background. This image proves that kids have endured parental photograph poses for at least 80 years, but at least June is trying to force a cheerful Christmas smile for the relatives back East.

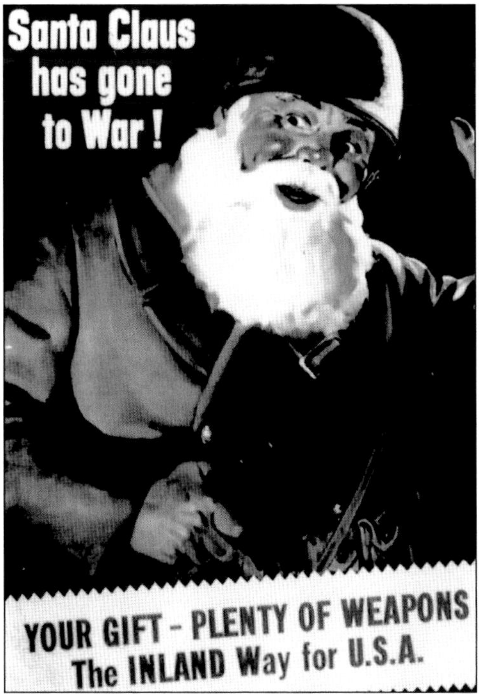


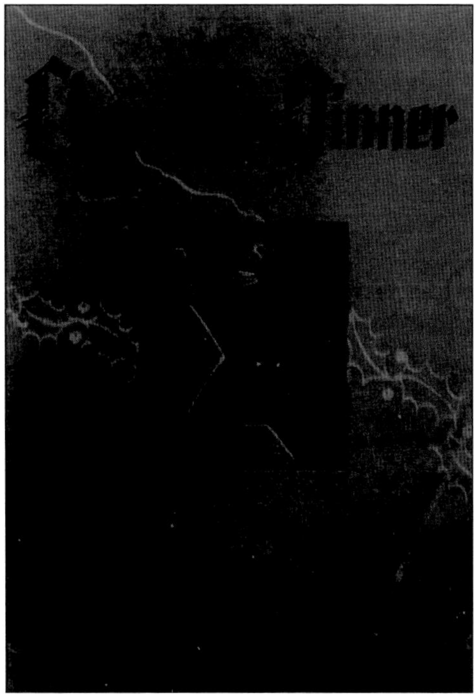

**SANTA GOES TO WAR.** Patriotic wartime posters must be considered within the context of the times. Christmas dinner in a 1943 foxhole wasn't quite the same as Christmas Dinner at the US Naval Repair Base—known today as the Thirty-second Street Naval Station.

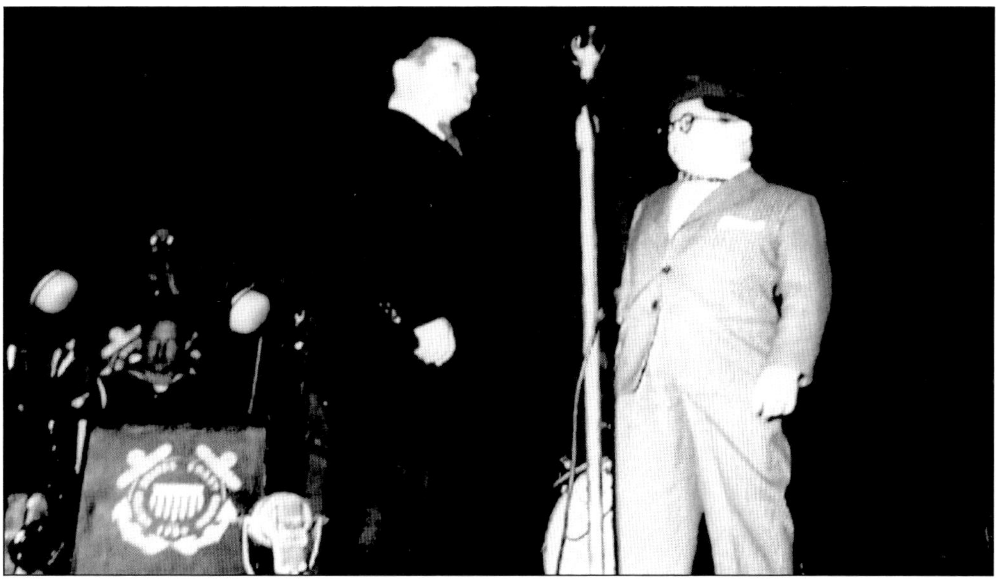

**1944 USO CHRISTMAS SHOW.** Bob Hope's USO Camp Show traveled to San Diego to entertain the troops during the war. Frances Langford, unaware of Navy terminology, was baffled the first time sailors laughed at her haunting rendition of "You Go to My Head." This photograph shows either "Say No More" Joe Mathias or "Hello There" Eddie Ware—top bananas at the Hollywood Burlesque Theater—performing their special brand of risqué humor for the boys at the US Naval Repair Base.

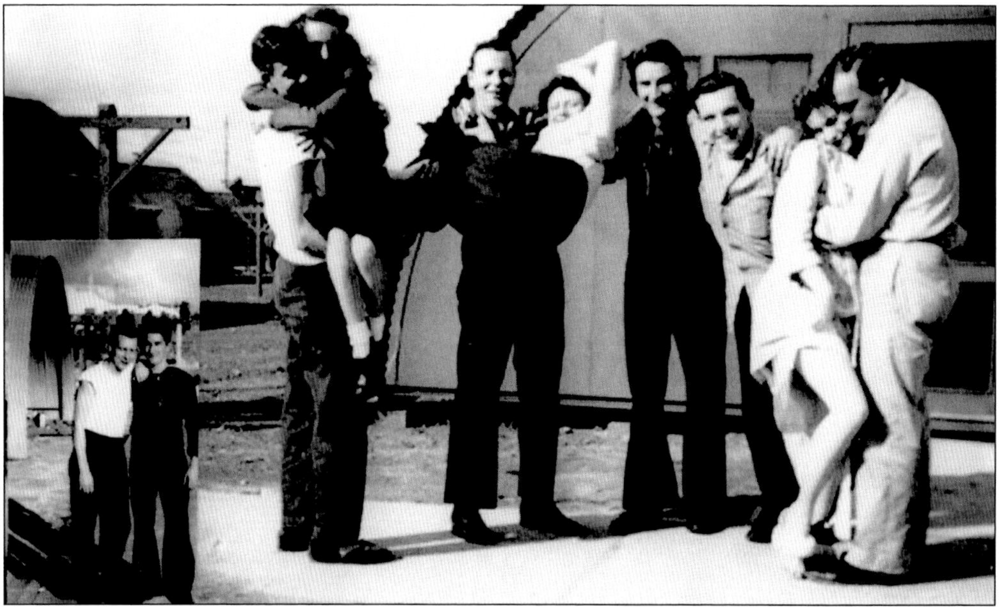

**THE JOY OF PEACE.** Here, World War II sailors in San Diego celebrate a joyous 1945 Christmas outside Quonset huts with their wives and sweethearts. From left to right are Bill Thomas, Blanche Hight, Bob Thomas, Lorraine Marney, Herbert Vaughn, Bill Coates, and Peggy and Jim Hight. Bob Thomas and Herbert Vaughn are visible in the insert. (Courtesy of the Jesse Marney Collection, USS *Allen M. Sumner* DD-692.)

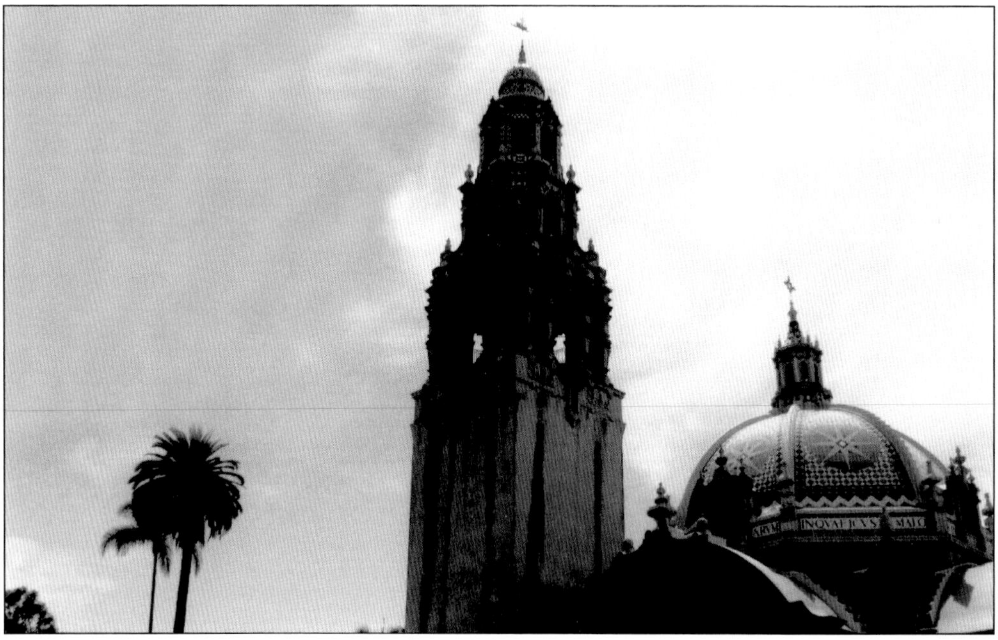

**CALIFORNIA TOWER IN BALBOA PARK.** The California Tower features a beautiful carillon that was given as a Christmas gift to San Diego. A commemorative plaque reads, "The Ona May Lowe Carillon—Given in her honor by her son, Frank M. Lowe, Jr., Christmas 1946 and Commemorating the Peace, September 2, 1945. Replaced in her memory Christmas 1966 with a 100-bell symphonic carillon, Dedicated April 30, 1967."

**Christmas Party in Balboa Stadium.** In 1950, television's biggest star, Hopalong Cassidy, rode into Balboa Stadium aboard his white horse, Topper, for San Diego's Christmas party. That year, Hoppy was featured on the first illustrated lunchbox, which made up a portion of over $70 million in merchandising. The western hero, who drank only sarsaparilla, presented cards of his "ten commandments" to the well-behaved little cowboys and cowgirls in the stands.

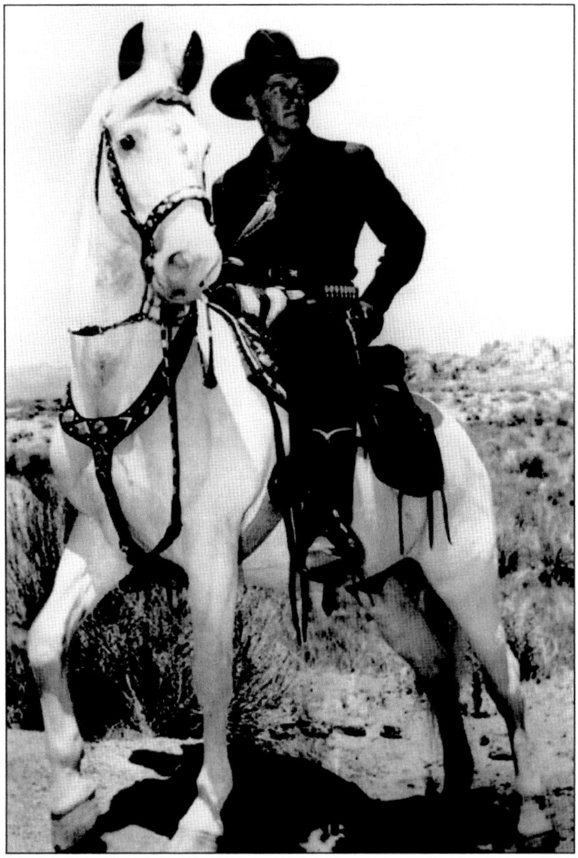

**Civic Center Yule Manger Scene Opened.** Janabelle Feyerherm (left) and her little sister, Shirley Ann, are shown in 1951 viewing the Yule manger display at the Civic Center, on Pacific Highway. The display was lit nightly during the holiday season. These same figures can still be seen in the Community Christmas Center Nativity diorama, which moved to the Organ Pavilion in 1953. (Courtesy of the *San Diego Union*.)

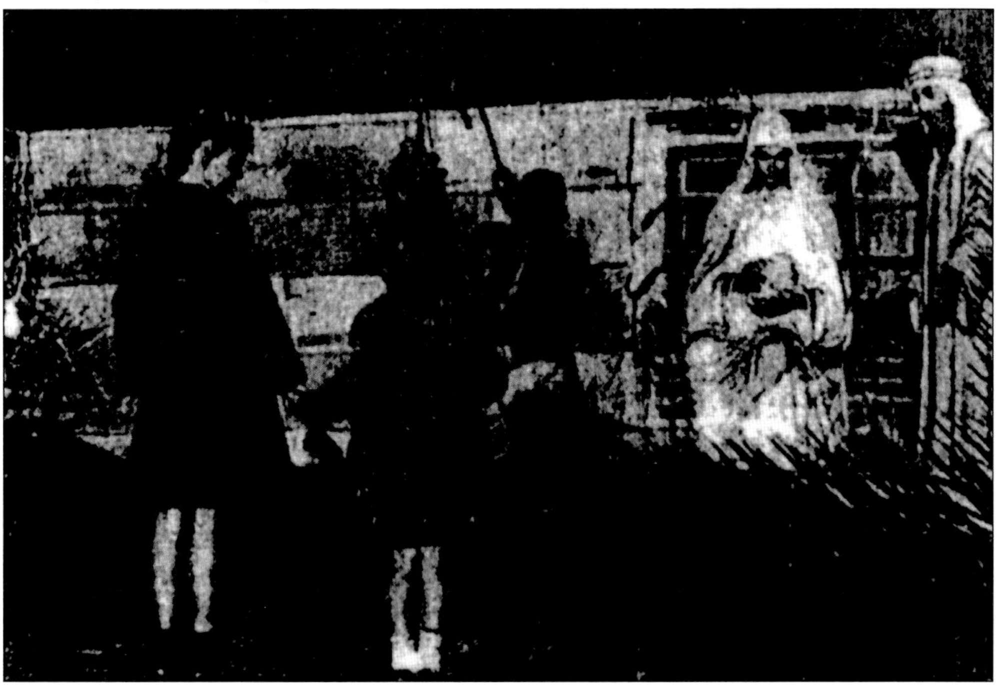

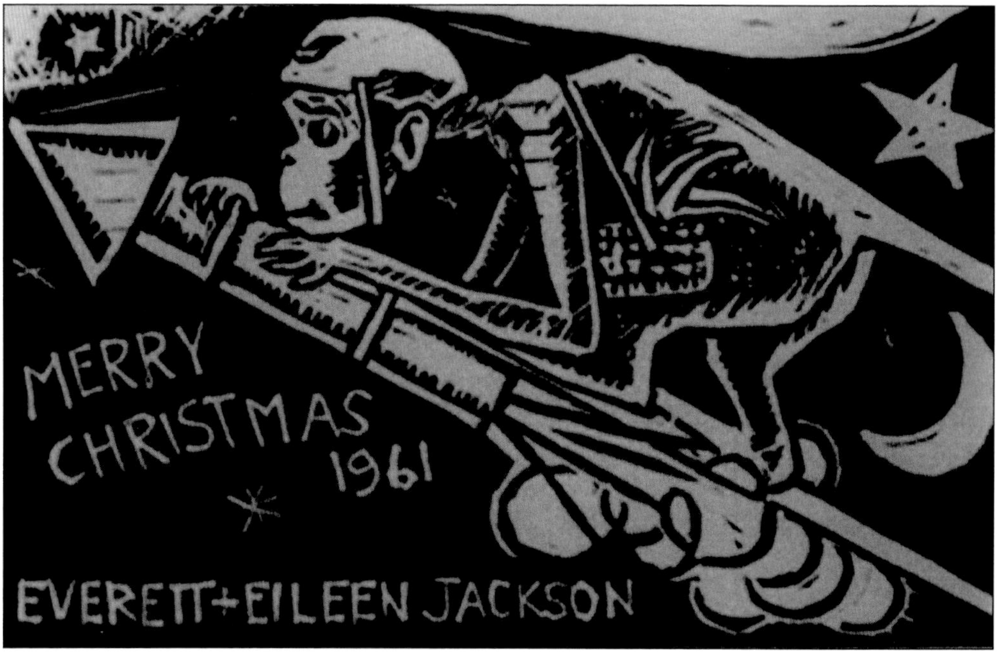


**EVERETT GEE JACKSON'S 1961 CHRISTMAS CARD.** Everett Jackson was one of San Diego's most approachable and respected artists. He taught art at San Diego State College for over 30 years. Jackson began creating poignant linocut Christmas postcards during World War II and maintained the tradition until the 1970s. His playful, 1961 card honored either Ham or Enos—the first American chimps in space. (Courtesy of the San Diego State University Library.)

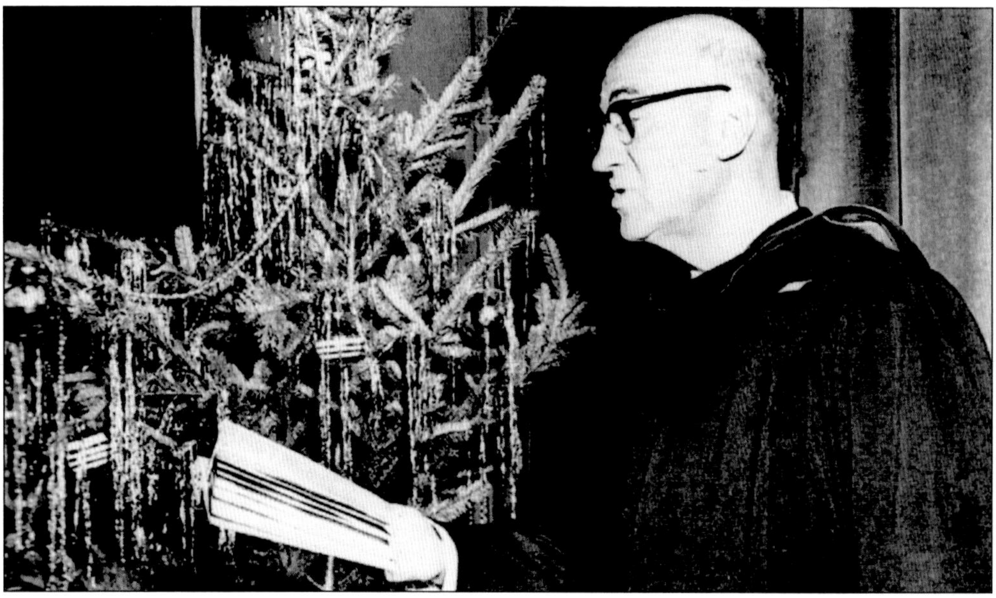

**E. KINGSLEY POVENMIRE.** In 1936, San Diego State College speech professor E. Kingsley Povenmire began the Montezuma Mesa tradition of reading Charles Dickens' *A Christmas Carol*, which lasted until the late 1960s. Prior to the dawn of television, audiences enjoyed listening to a classic tale read by a melodic voice with proper inflection. It was an era when kids and adults could close their eyes to imagine characters, settings, and action. (Courtesy of Del Sudoeste, 1962.)

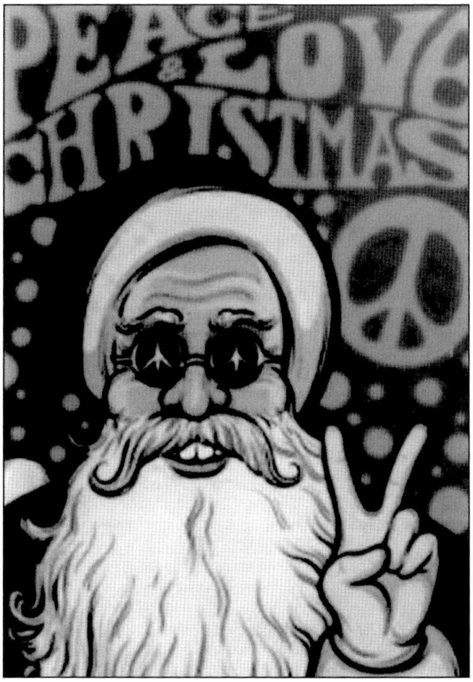


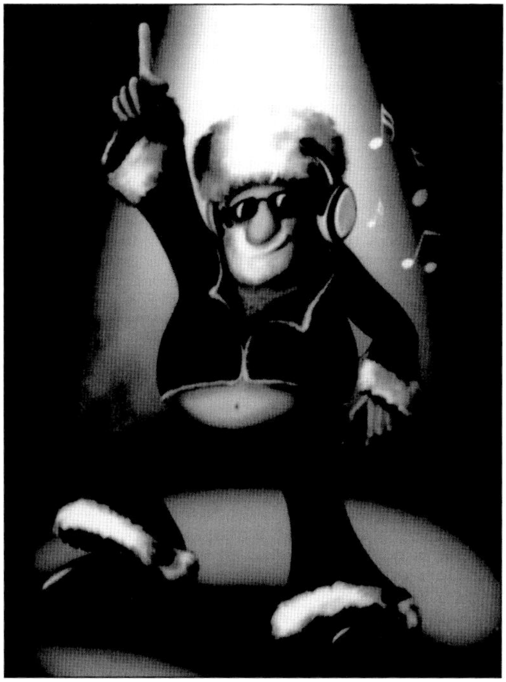

**HIPPIE SANTA AND DISCO SANTA.** By the 1960s and 1970s, the times—and Christmas—were "a-changin'." A 1969 headline announced that Balboa Park was "turned on" for the holidays. Some believed that the 1970s would become an "age of post-materialism," but the polyester decade is remembered in pop culture as the disco era. Materialism didn't die and its lasting effects on Christmas are staggering.

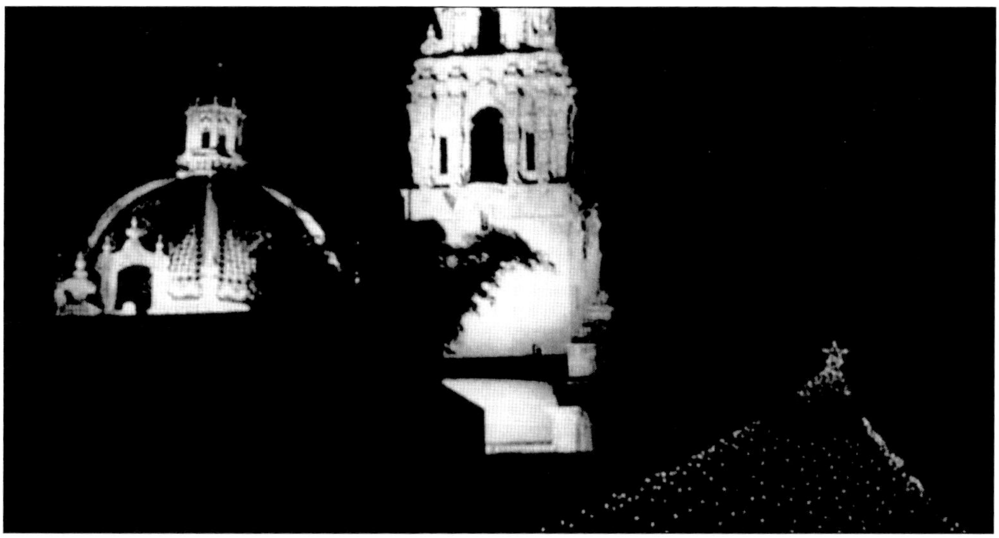

**CHRISTMAS ON THE PRADO.** In early 1978, arsonists destroyed the Aerospace Museum and Old Globe Theater in Balboa Park. To stimulate business, 10 cultural organizations organized a two-night event: Christmas on the Prado. The highlight was a performance of Dylan Thomas' *A Child's Christmas in Wales* on "the charred proscenium of the burned-out Old Globe Theater." It was the Globe's first production since the March fire. The play targets the noncommercial side of Christmas. (Courtesy of the *San Diego Tribune*.)

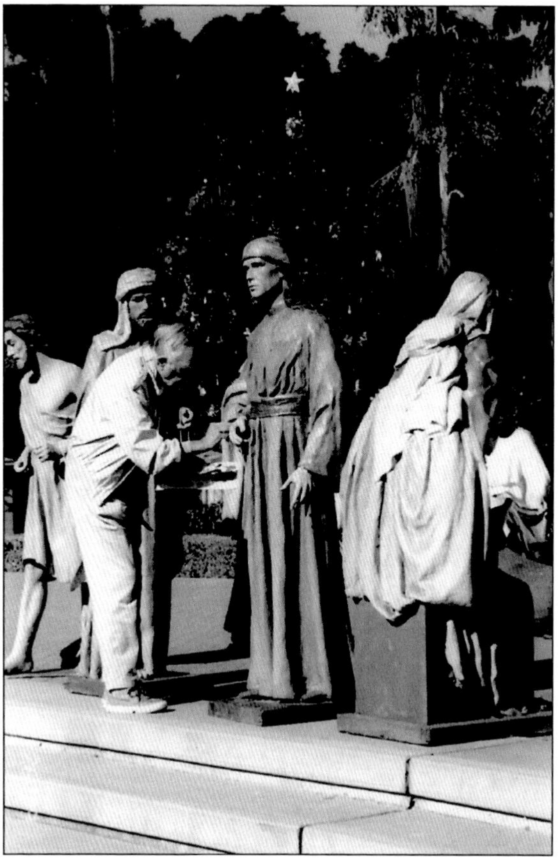

**The 1981 Community Christmas Center.** A brochure for the 1981 Community Christmas display highlighted the tree lighting ceremony. The low-key Nativity scene had been on display in Balboa Park for almost 30 years. At left, Al Gabbs checks one of the Nativity figures for chips and possible repair. The newly dedicated, live Community Christmas Tree and star can be seen in the background. (Courtesy of the Community Christmas Center.)

# Atheists Sue to Move Christmas Displays From Balboa Park

**Turmoil in the Late 1980s.** During the Christmas season of 1987, under pressure from the Jewish Community Relations Council, San Diego City Attorney John Witt announced that—in view of recent court rulings about separation of church and state—the Nativity scenes would no longer appear at the Organ Pavilion. A few days later, compromise was reached: A Jewish menorah lighting ceremony would be held in the park, and the Community Christmas Center Committee would assume responsibility for the storage of the Nativity scenes—which had previously been kept on city property. Days before Christmas, the San Diego chapter of American Atheists threatened to take the matter to court. A year later, on December 23, 1988, the atheist Society of Separationists sued the City of San Diego to remove the eight Nativity dioramas from Balboa Park. A federal judge would dismiss the lawsuit in November 1989. (Courtesy of *The Los Angeles Times*.)

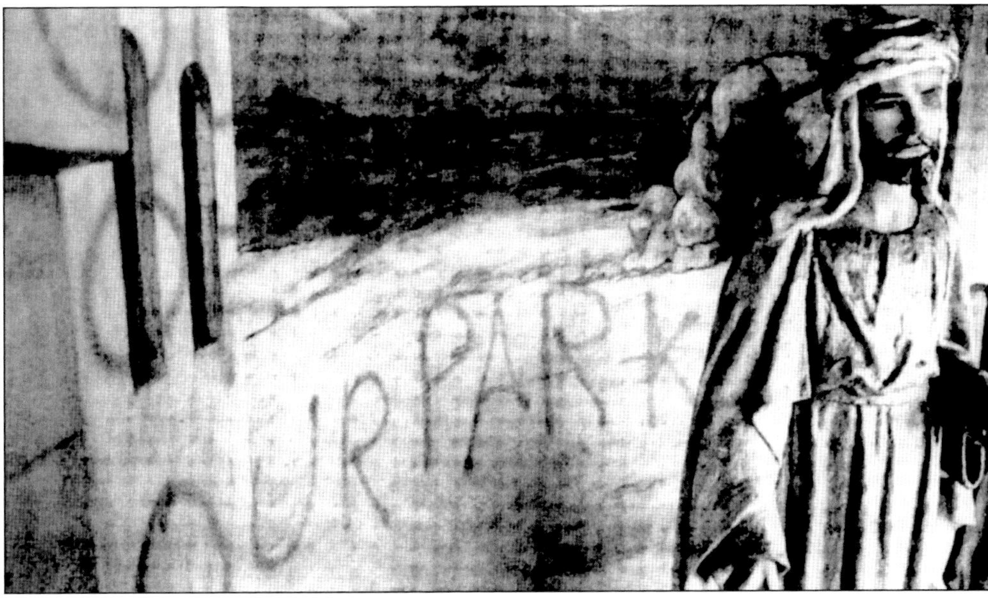


**NATIVITY SCENES DAMAGED BY VANDALS.** In December 1989, vandals defaced most of the Nativity figures and scripture passages in Balboa Park. Graffiti messages were sprayed on the background murals: "Out of Our Park," "Keep Religion Private," and "1st Amendment." The local chapter of American Atheists and the Jewish community publicly denounced these acts. Police investigated the incident as a hate crime, but arrests were never made. (Courtesy of the Community Christmas Center.)

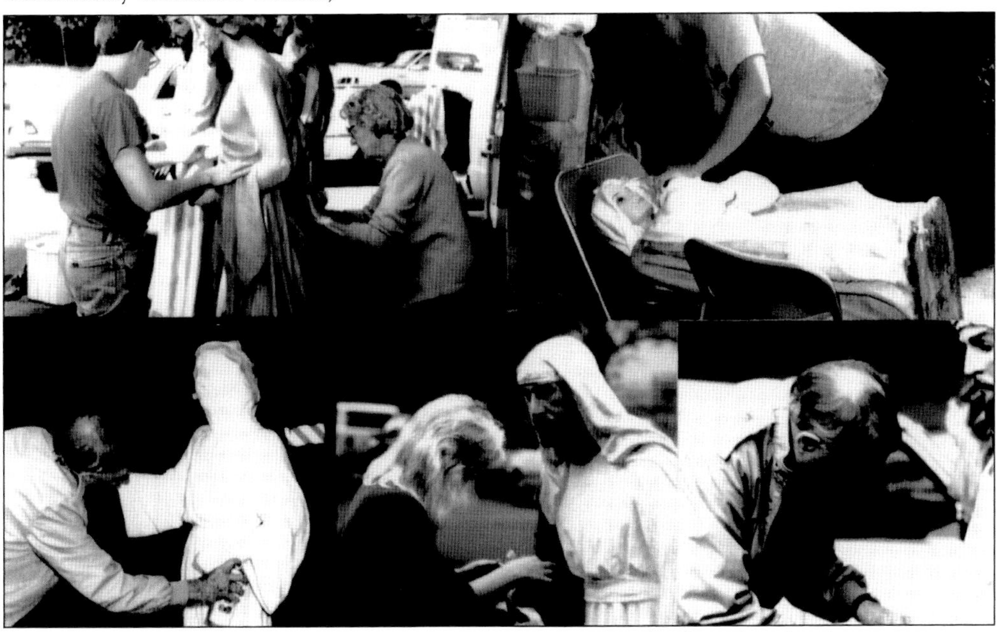

**VOLUNTEERS AND ARTISTS REPAIR VANDALIZED NATIVITY.** The day after the desecration, over 50 volunteers appeared with rags, toothbrushes, and Q-tips to help the Community Christmas Committee clean and repair damages to the Nativity dioramas. Volunteer artists repainted several figures and others volunteered to guard the scenes from further attack. (Courtesy of the Community Christmas Center.)

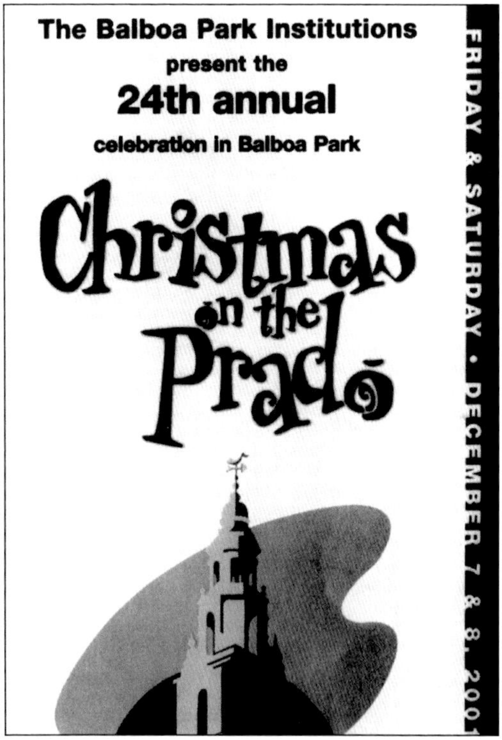


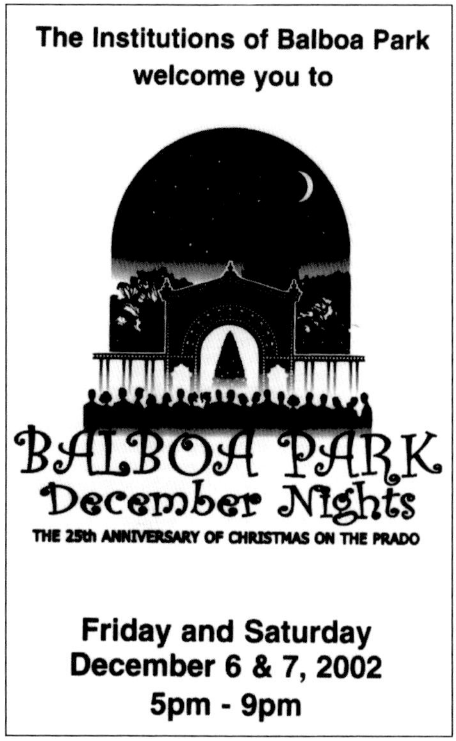


DECEMBER NIGHTS IN THE PARK. In 2002, for reasons of religious diversity and cultural inclusion, "Christmas on the Prado" was rebranded as "December Nights in the Park." A lack of funding almost cancelled the celebration in 2004, but the event was saved by donations from the private sector. December Nights in the Park has gradually become more commercial to offset rising costs, but the formula must be a success—attendance has swelled from 100,000 a year to a reported 350,000.

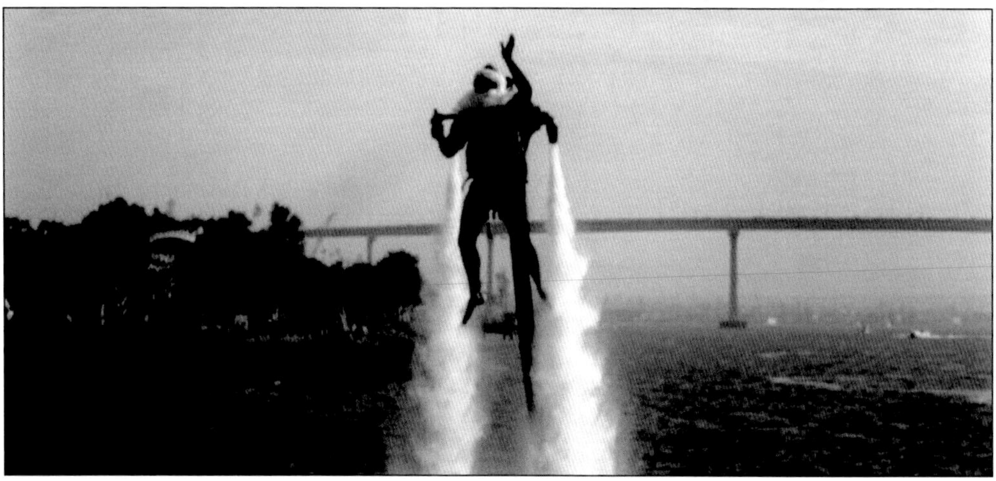

COOL SANTA FOR THE NEW MILLENNIUM. *USA Today* selected "Surfin' Santa" as one of the 10 best Santas in the United States, and BuzzFeed named him No. 1 "Most Badass Santa in the World." A San Diego original, he can be found with his red surfboard at Seaport Village, wearing his Hawaiian shirt, shorts, and flip-flops. The man makes a grand entrance, and it would be difficult to trump Surfin' Santa's 2013 arrival by water jetpack. He "hangs 10" on a scale of 10. (Courtesy of coolsandiegosights.com.)

# *Two*

# TRADITIONS

*Merry Christmas from Sunny San Diego*

*December 25, 1917 Temperature: 70 Degrees*

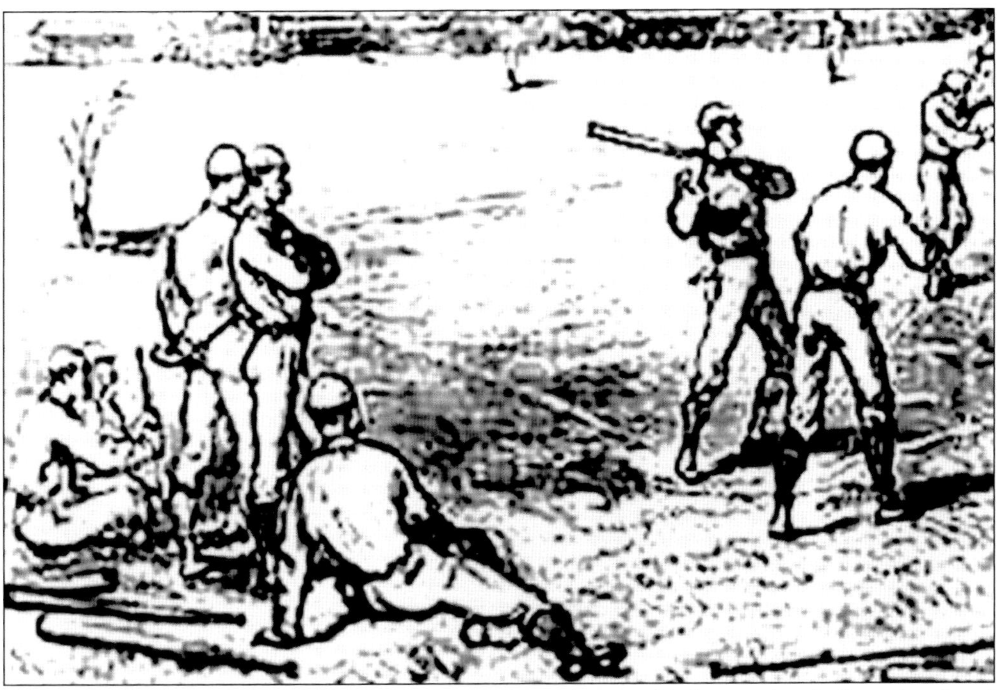

AN EARLY CHRISTMAS TRADITION. Because San Diego has a mild climate, baseball can be played throughout the year. During the final quarter of the 19th century, the "match game of the year" was annually contested on Christmas Day. "The biggest game of base ball that has ever been played in this end of the state" was scheduled between the Pacifics and the Eckfords on Christmas Day 1874. Two days later, the *Union* reported that the championship match was, "a close contest ending in favor of the Eckfords. We have not been favored with the score, but are satisfied the boys did their level best."

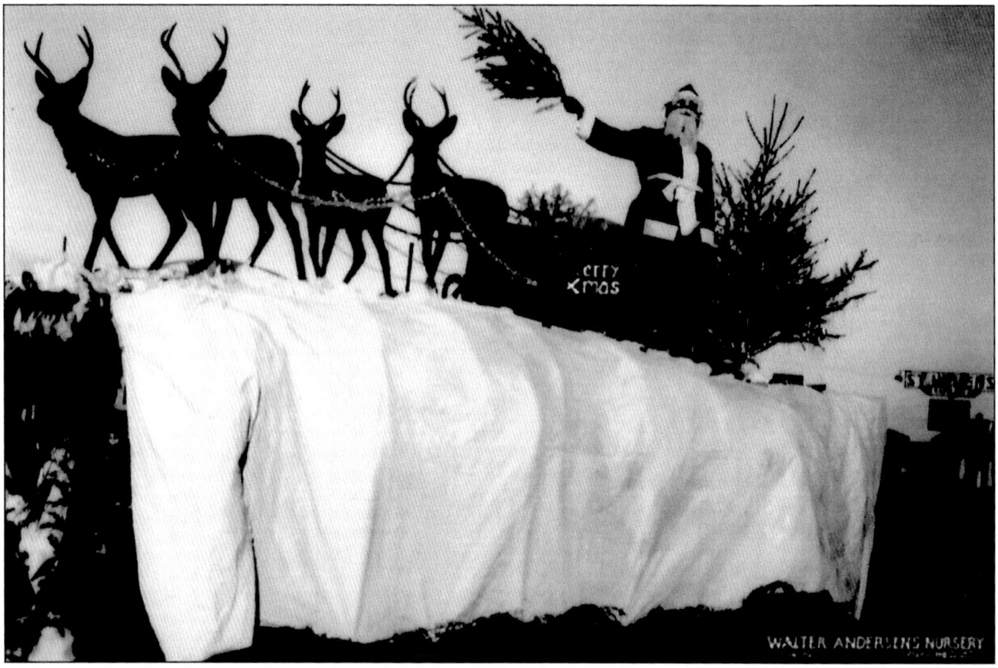



**Walter Andersen Float in the 1940s Christmas Parade.** The wreath on this Santa's sleigh reads "Merry Xmas"—an abbreviation that offended religious groups in the 1940s and 1950s. They made a concerted effort to "Put Christ back in Christmas," but their anger was misdirected. The "X" in "Xmas" represents the Greek letter "chi." Its usage dates back to the 16th century, when most people were illiterate but knew that "X" meant "Christ" and "Xmas" meant "Christmas." (Courtesy of Walter Andersen.)

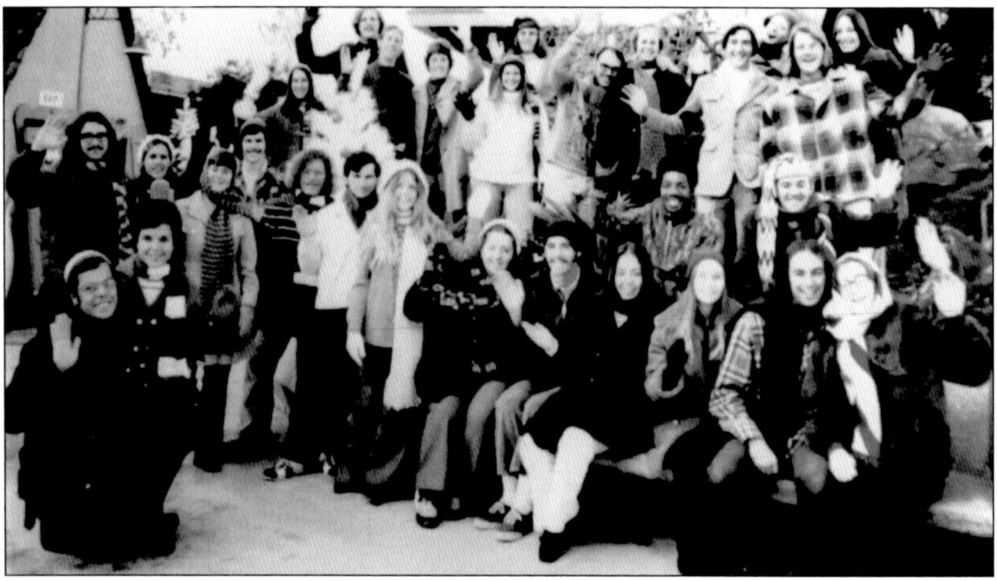

***Now Is the Caroling Season.*** In 1972, the Mesa College Olympic Singers cut a 33 RPM LP Christmas album titled *Now is the Caroling Season*, which featured a collection old French and English Christmas carols. Included is "The First Nowell," an Anglicized version of the French word "noel," for nativity. Historians speculated the melody could date back to 1200.

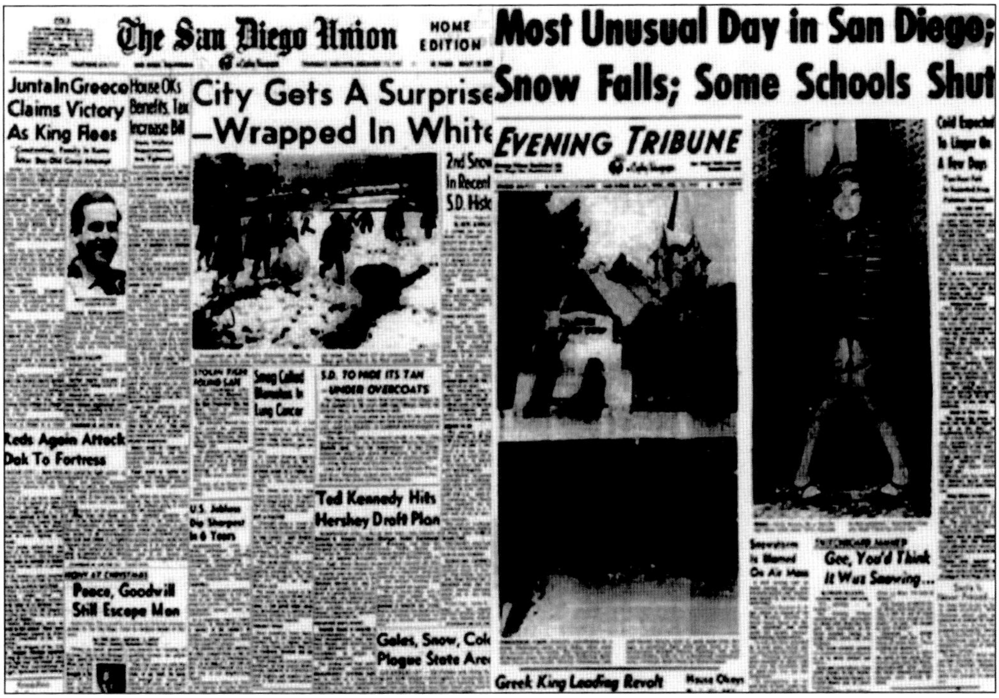

The San Diego Union HOME EDITION

Most Unusual Day in San Diego; Snow Falls; Some Schools Shut

Junta In Greece Claims Victory As King Flees

House OKs Benefits, Tax Increase Bill

City Gets A Surprise—Wrapped In White

2nd Snow In Recent S.D. Hist

EVENING TRIBUNE

S.D. TO HIDE ITS TAN UNDER OVERCOATS

Reds Again Attack Dak To Fortress

Ted Kennedy Hits Hershey Draft Plan

Peace, Goodwill Still Escape Man

Gales, Snow, Col Plague State Are

Greek King Leading Revolt

Gee, You'd Think It Was Snowing...

Cold Expected to Linger On A Few Days

WHITE CHRISTMAS. These are the front pages of the December 14, 1967, *San Diego Union* and *Evening Tribune*. Snowfall in San Diego is rare, with only traces in 1949 and flurries in 1987, but in 1967, it appeared that San Diego might get a white Christmas. In all, 50 inches of snow would blanket the Laguna Mountains that winter.

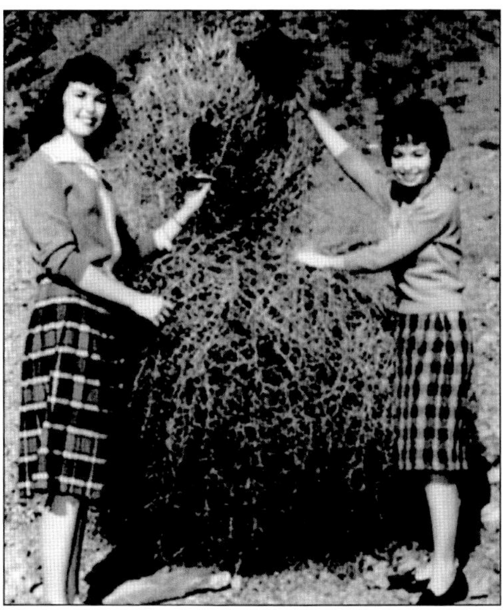

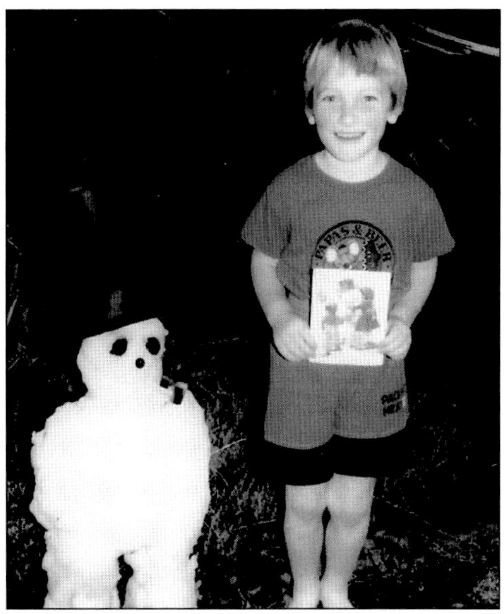


SAN DIEGO SNOWMEN. Tumbleweed snowmen were popular yard decorations in the 1950s. At left, high school girls from the days of patterned skirts and sweater tops are shown with a debonair San Diego snowman. "Tumbleweed Snowman" is also a forgotten Christmas song. The best way to make a snowman in San Diego is to drive to the Lagunas and return with snow in the back of your pickup. Build your Frosty fast, because he won't last long.

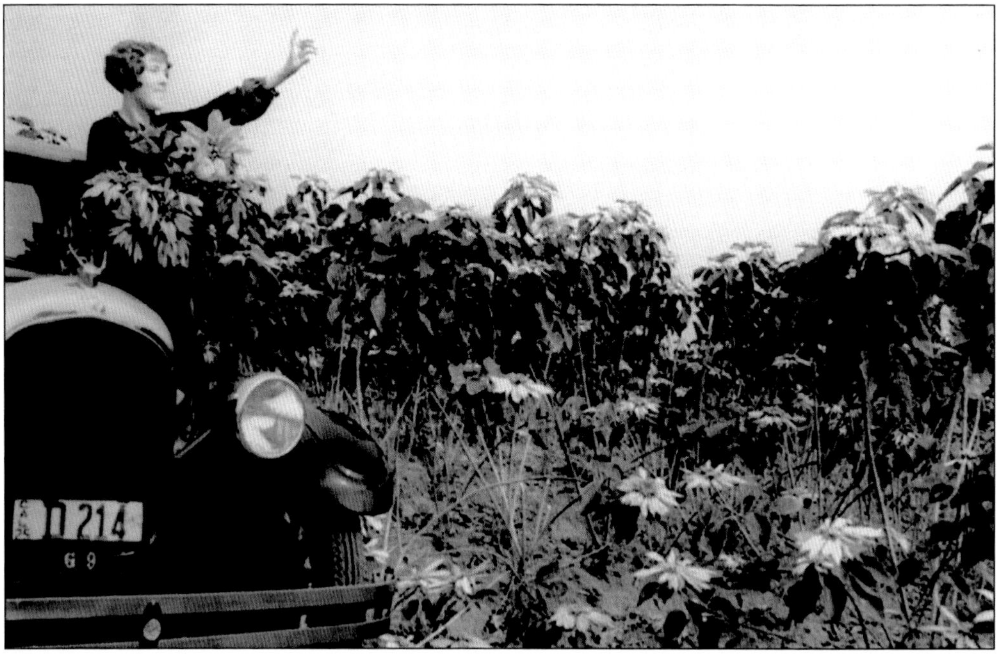

**FLOR DE NOCHE BUENA—THE FLOWER OF CHRISTMAS EVE.** The poinsettia is synonymous with Christmas and the city of Encinitas because of the Ecke family. Native to Mexico, the plant is known as "Flor de Noche Buena." In the early 20th century, Albert Ecke grew and sold poinsettias in the Los Angeles area. In 1923, his son, Paul Ecke Sr., moved the business to an Encinitas ranch. Here, Mrs. Ecke waves from the running board of a truck.

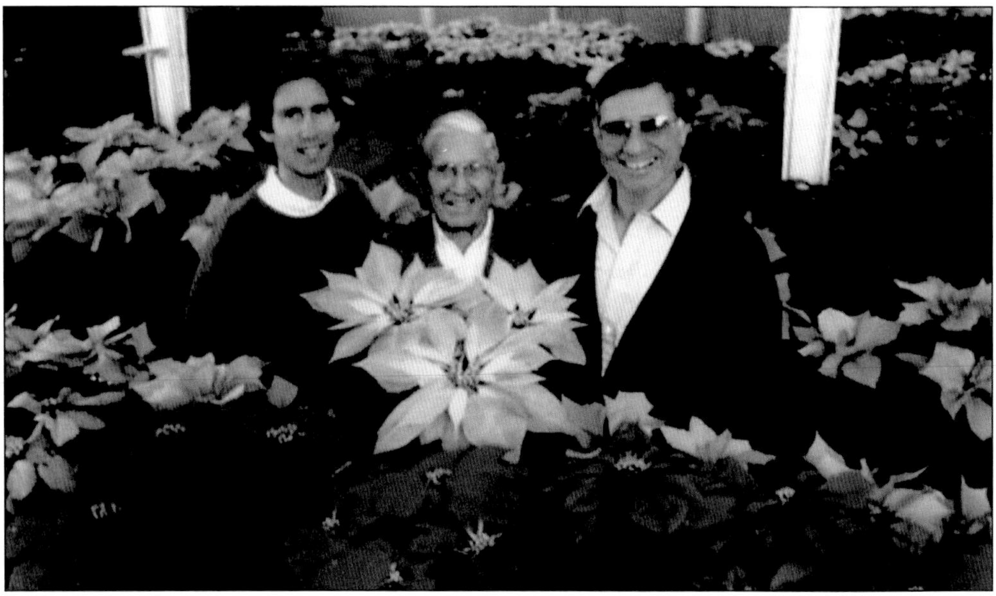

**THE POINSETTIA, SYMBOL OF CHRISTMAS.** Ecke developed an exclusive grafting process that produced tighter, bushier poinsettia plants. The family also marketed the vibrant red flowers, with their lush green foliage, as a symbol of Christmas. Paul Ecke III, Paul Ecke Sr., and Paul Jr. are shown from left to right, surrounded by their famous Encinitas poinsettias in "The Flower Capital of the World." (Courtesy of Paul Ecke III.)

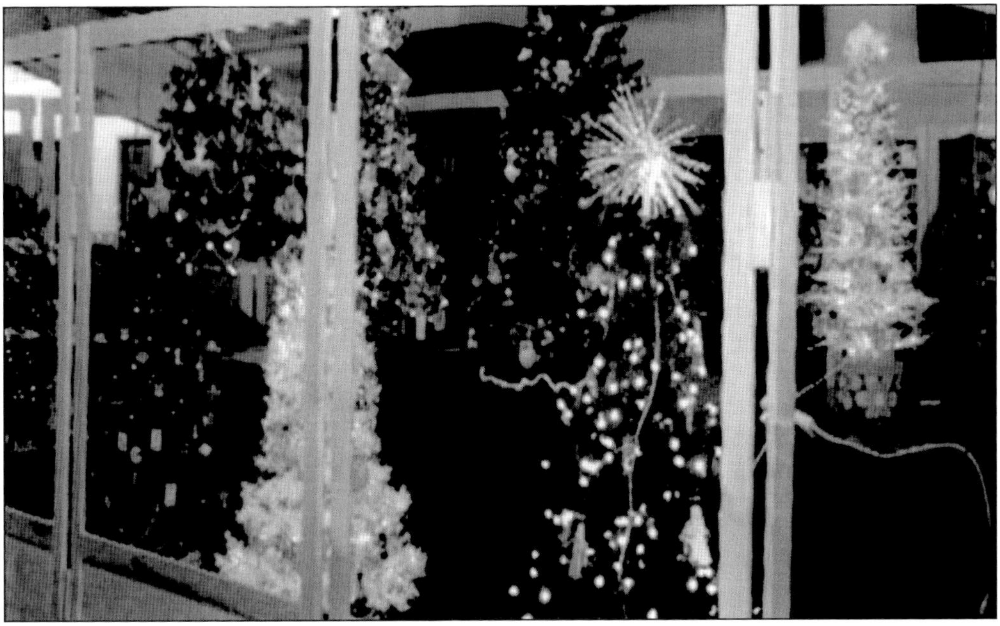

**San Diego County Fair, Home, and Hobby Show.** In 1880, local farmers gathered at the fair to determine who grew the best fruit, baked the best pie, and owned the fastest horse. The Home and Hobby Show continues to be a major attraction. Among the many prize categories are Christmas boot or stocking, Christmas characters, Christmas household accessory, Christmas quilt, Christmas tree ornaments, and Christmas trees. (Courtesy of San Diego County Fair.)

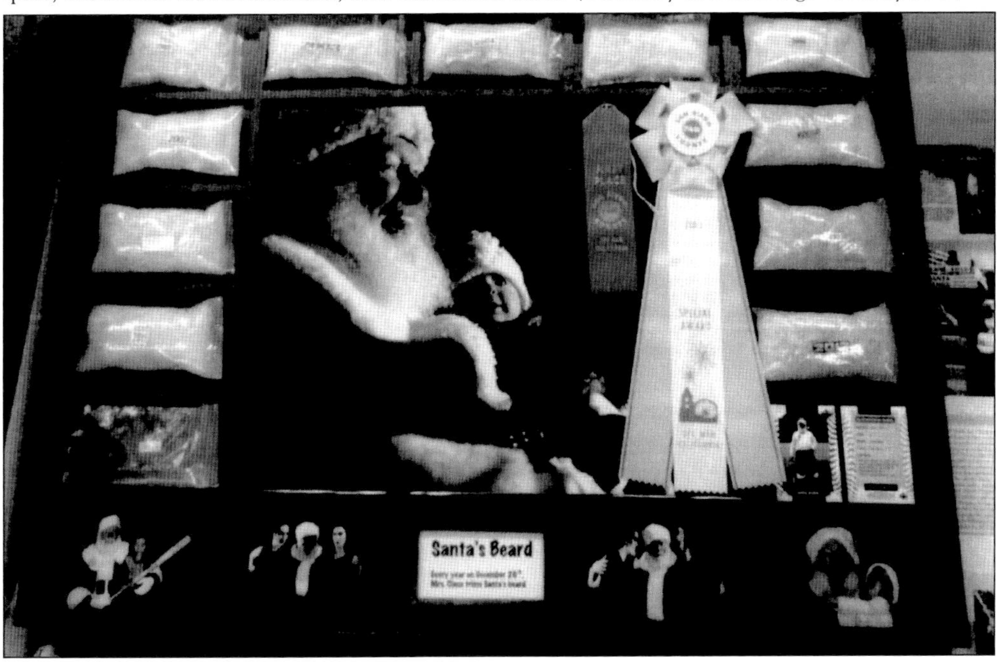


**A Most Unique Collection.** In 2013, the author entered 11 years of his Santa beard trimmings in the San Diego County Fair. Since there wasn't a specific classification for Santa's beard, the collection was placed in the "other than listed" category. It won the blue ribbon, plus a special award ribbon for "Most Unique" collection at the fair. (Courtesy of Robert Gigl.)

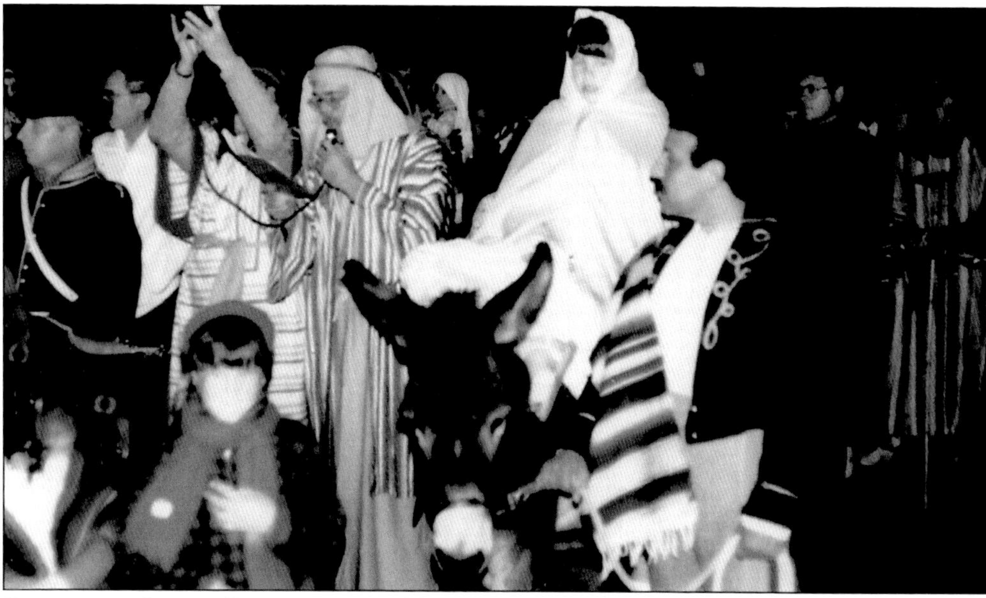

**One of the Oldest Posadas in the United States.** The oldest semi-continuous Christmas tradition in San Diego has been Las Posadas, in Old Town. Merchants staged a simple *posada-piñata* party at the Machado House in 1941, but Virginia Lucas and her fellow adult history students at the Fremont School organized what has become a continuous celebration of Las Posadas in 1955. The annual procession, shown here in 1986, remains faithful to its humble origin. As described by historian Richard Amero, "It cuts through commercialism and sophistication to the basic Christmas message."

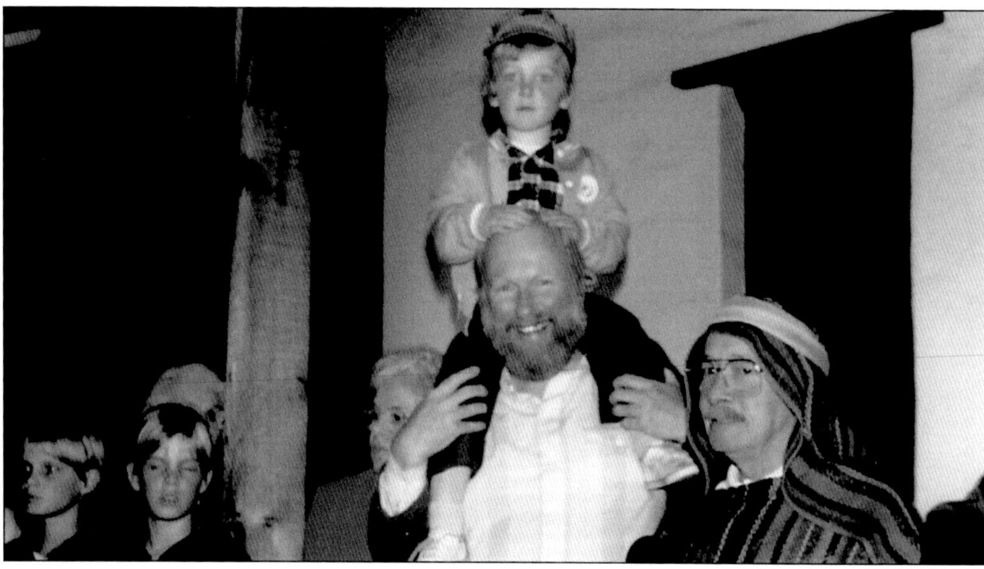

**"I Want to See Baby Jesus!"** The author's youngest son, Billy, had a Glo-Worm toy that he named "Baby Jesus" and gently carried around the house. In 1986, he was much more excited about the prospect of seeing Baby Jesus in Old Town than he was in visiting Santa Claus at the mall. Everything was fine until only Mary and Joseph were granted entry to Seeley Stable. It was embarrassing to carry a normally well-behaved little boy away as he screamed, "I want to see Baby Jesus! I want to see Baby Jesus!"

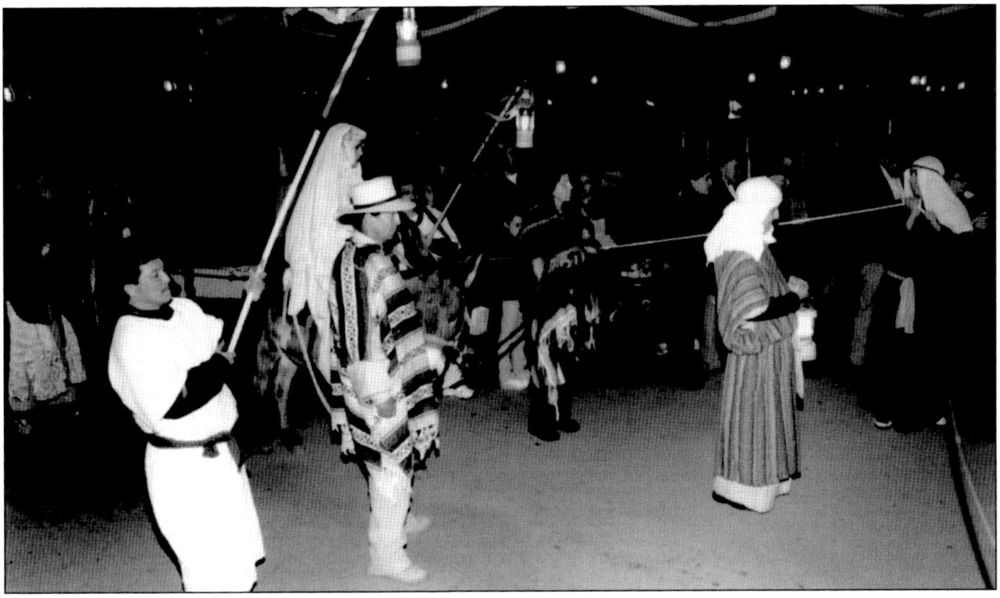

**"There Was No Room for Them in the Inn."** Las Posadas, which had been sponsored by the San Diego County Historic Days Association, was rescued by SOHO (Save Our Heritage Organization) in 2006. As with similar Christmas celebrations throughout the county, it is through the dedicated efforts of many groups and volunteers that these cherished traditions are perpetuated. Joseph and Mary are shown here in 2008, going door-to-door and asking for a place to stay. (Courtesy of the Merchant Marketing Committee.)

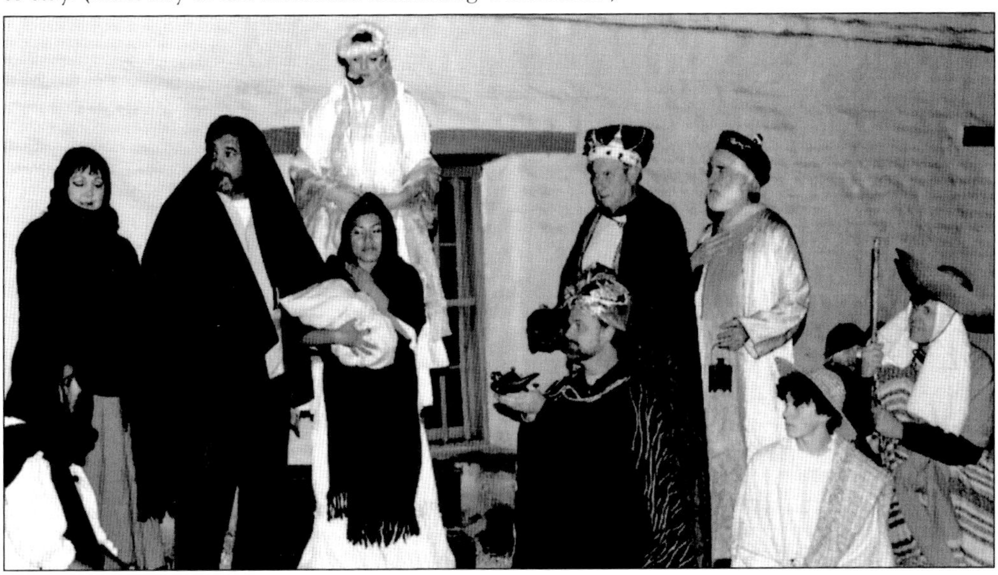

**"Wrapped Him in Swaddling Clothes and Laid Him in a Manger."** The Old Town San Diego State Historic Park Merchants Marketing and Events Committee has assumed responsibility for the continuation of Las Posadas since 2009. Joseph and Mary are shown here with Los Tres Reyes (the Three Wise Men) at Seeley Stable. A live infant was used as baby Jesus in 2009 and 2010. For several years, two generations of women from the historic Estudillo family have played the role of Mary. The 60th anniversary of the Old Town Las Posadas will be celebrated in 2015. (Courtesy of the Merchant Marketing Committee.)

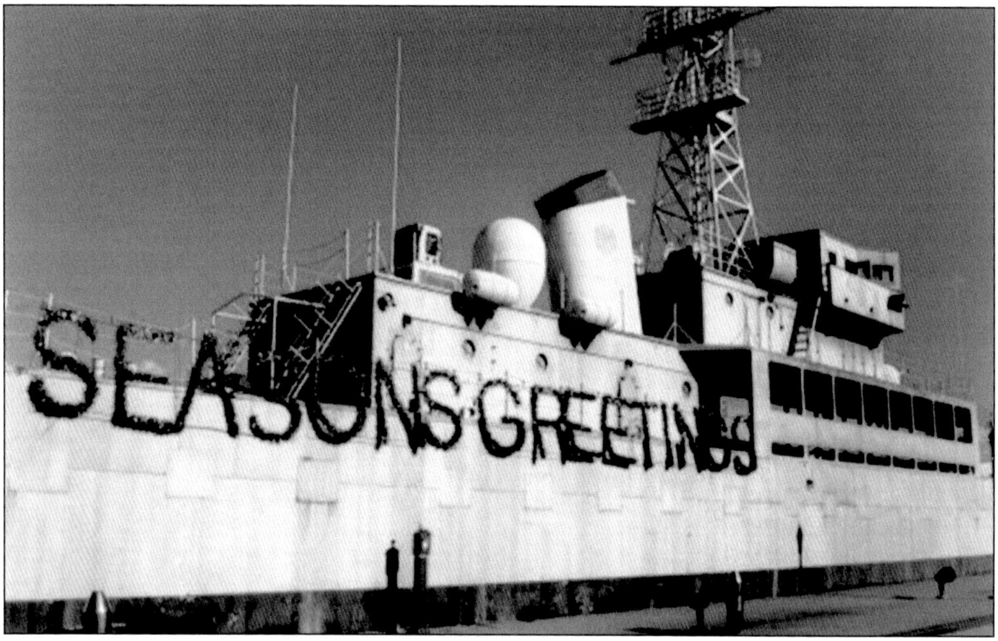


**"SEASONS GREETINGS" FROM TDE-1.** Naval Training Center San Diego opened in 1923, and many a young kid spent his first Christmas away from home while going through boot camp at NTC. The USS *Recruit* (TDE-1) has sailed in a sea of cement since it was commissioned in 1949. It served as a training facility for as many as 50,000 sailors a year, until the base closed in 1997. The *Recruit* is a registered California Landmark and remains the only landlocked ship in the US Navy. This festive photograph is from 2013. (Courtesy of coolsandiegosights.com.)

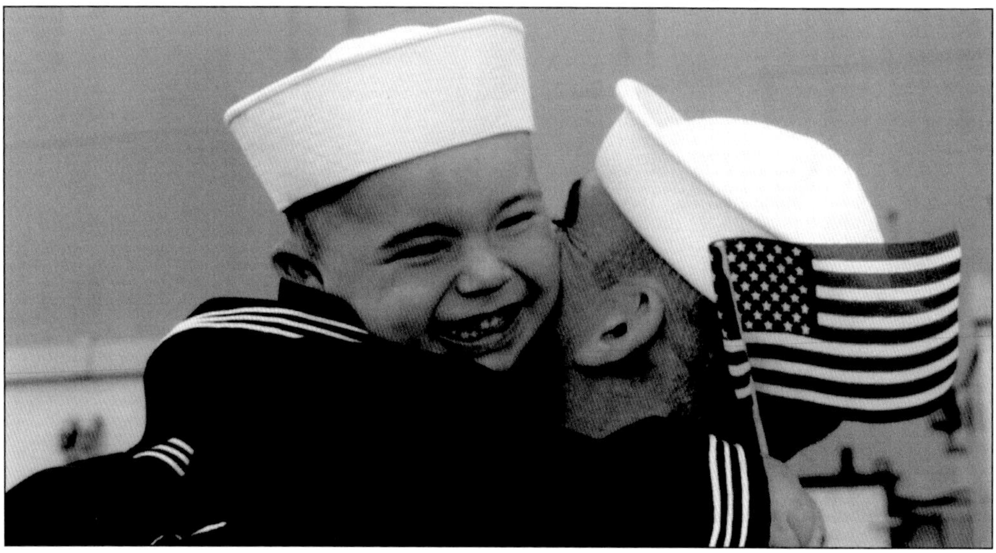

**CHRISTMAS EVE RETURN OF *PELELIU*.** San Diego has a long-standing tradition of welcoming Navy ships home for Christmas. This image captures all the joy on three-year-old sailor boy Brodin's face as he hugs his father, Joshua Labbe, on Christmas Eve 2014. The USS *Peleliu* had just returned from its final deployment, and many of the crew had not yet seen their newborn children. Dustin Sharbono won the lottery to be the first sailor to kiss his wife upon arrival in San Diego. (Courtesy of Chris Stone, TimesofSanDiego.com)

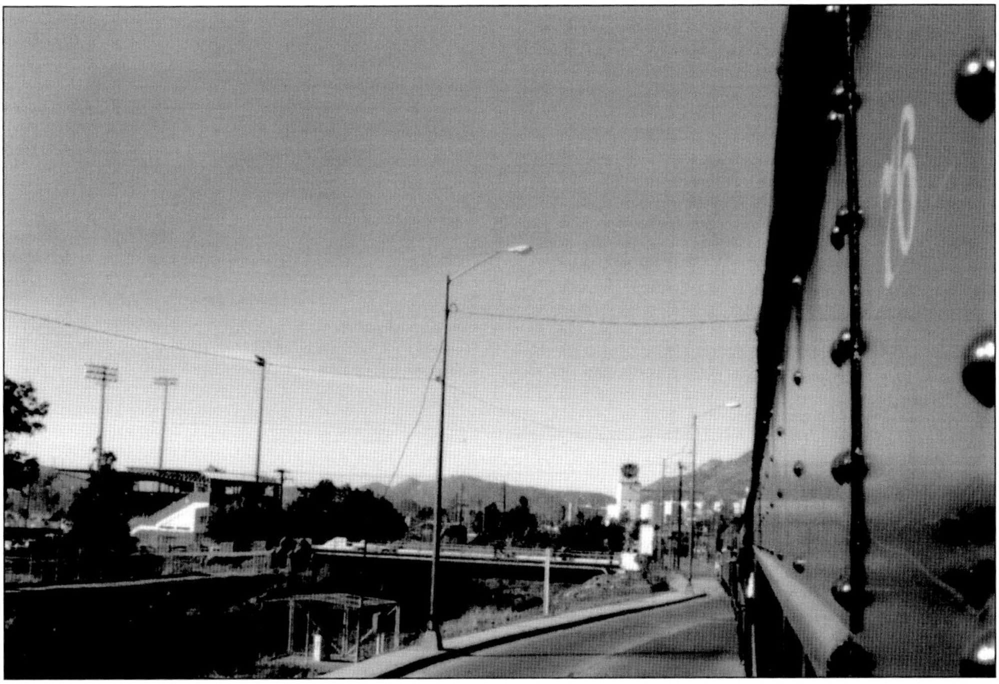

**TECATE CHRISTMAS TRAIN.** On "El Dia de los Tres Reyes Magos" (January 6th), the Christmas Train from Campo annually delivered over 5,000 gift bags—in memory of Bekki Stewart—to eager youngsters waiting at Tecate's municipal baseball stadium. What started as $20 worth of candy canes in 1996 became the most highly anticipated day of the year for poor boys and girls in the border town. Eventually, a 2009 railroad tunnel fire, and stringent custom restrictions including permits and payment to Mexican officials, stifled the gift-giving efforts.

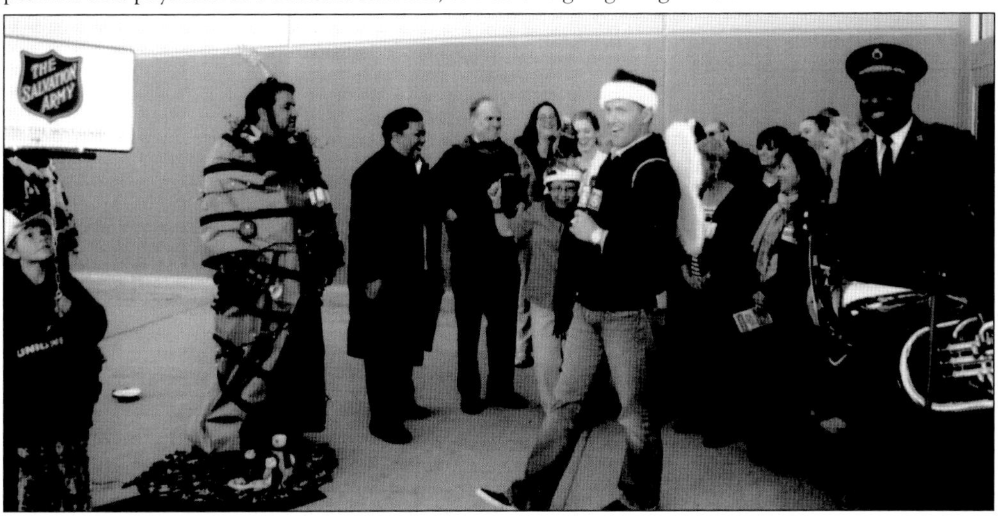


**SALVATION ARMY BELL RINGERS.** In 2011, San Diego Salvation Army captain Ken Perine (above) decorated himself as a Christmas tree and continuously rang his bell for over 38 hours. He was among the handful of bell ringers nationwide who broke the existing world record of 36 hours. In 2014, in commemoration of the Salvation Army's 150th anniversary, Maj. Marcelino "Butch" Soriano, formerly with SA San Diego, set an unbreakable record with 150 straight hours of bell ringing. (Courtesy of the San Diego Salvation Army.)

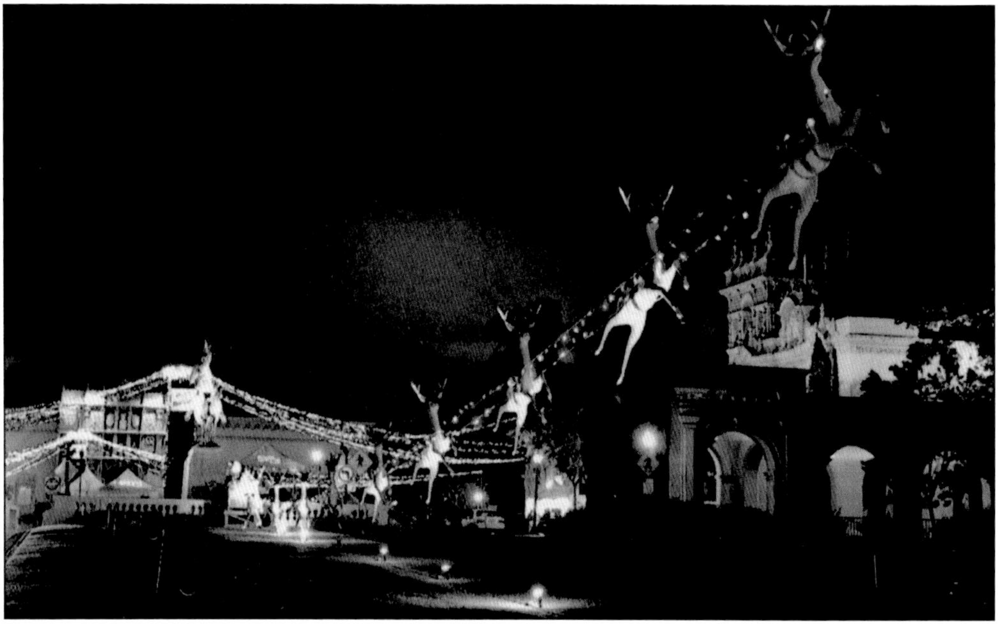

**SANTA AND HIS FLYING REINDEER.** Every year since the 1950s, the Community Christmas Center Committee assembles Santa, his sleigh, and his team of flying reindeer in the center of the park. The iconic reindeer are strung above the Esplanade. In 1979, Santa's team was replaced with fiberglass replicas made from the original plaster castings, and a flashing, red-nosed Rudolph was added at that time. The flying reindeer have become the symbol of Christmas in Balboa Park. (Courtesy of the Balboa Park Conservancy and Richard Benton.)

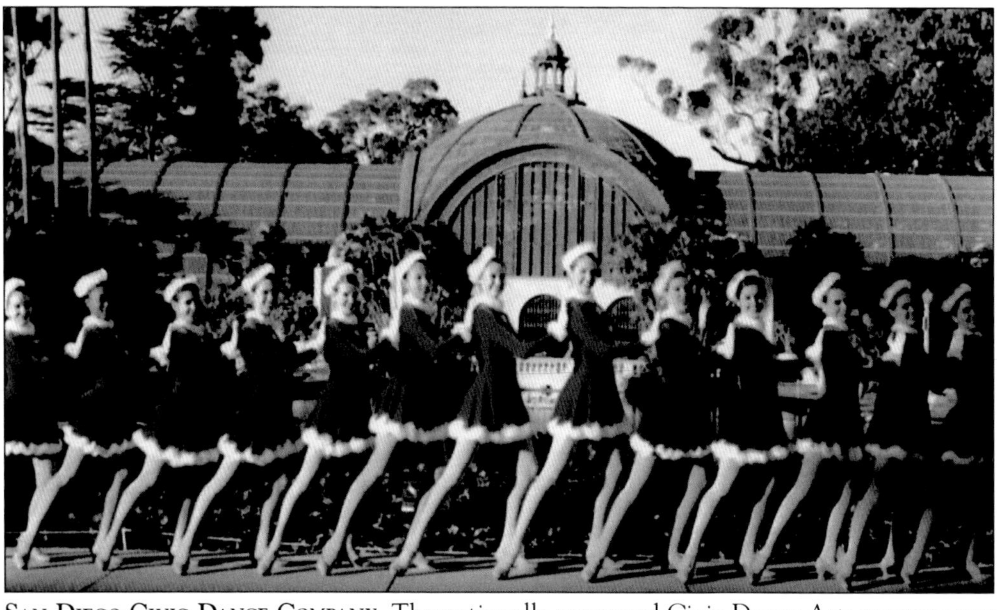

**SAN DIEGO CIVIC DANCE COMPANY.** The nationally renowned Civic Dance Arts program was founded by the San Diego Park and Recreation Department in 1942. Volunteers donate over 20,000 hours each year, supporting dance programs for 3,000 students. Among their many performances, December Nights in the Park is the showcase for their "signature holiday 'Rockette-style' routine." (Courtesy of Lola Thomas.)

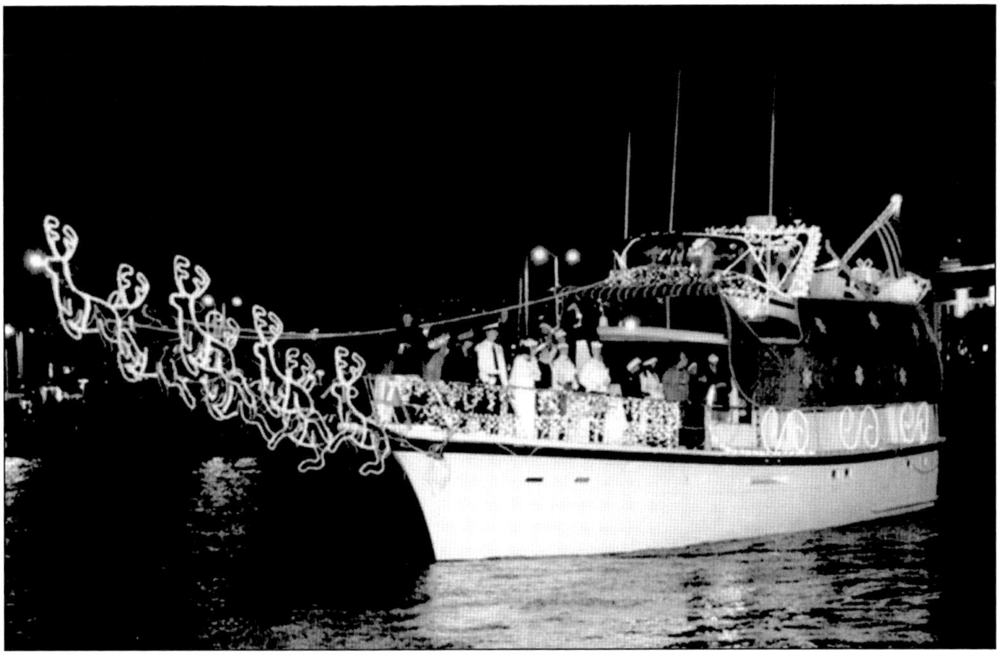

**San Diego Bay Parade of Lights.** The Parade of Lights has been a tradition on San Diego Bay since 1971. Boat owners decorate their vessels with lights to create an armada of holiday cheer, which navigates from Shelter Island, past Harbor Island, to the Embarcadero and Seaport Village, and to the Coronado Ferry Landing. An estimated 80,000 spectators watch the parade every year. The Mission Bay Christmas Boat Parade of Lights and the Oceanside Harbor Parade of Lights are smaller scale versions of the big bay parade. (Courtesy of the San Diego Yacht Club.)

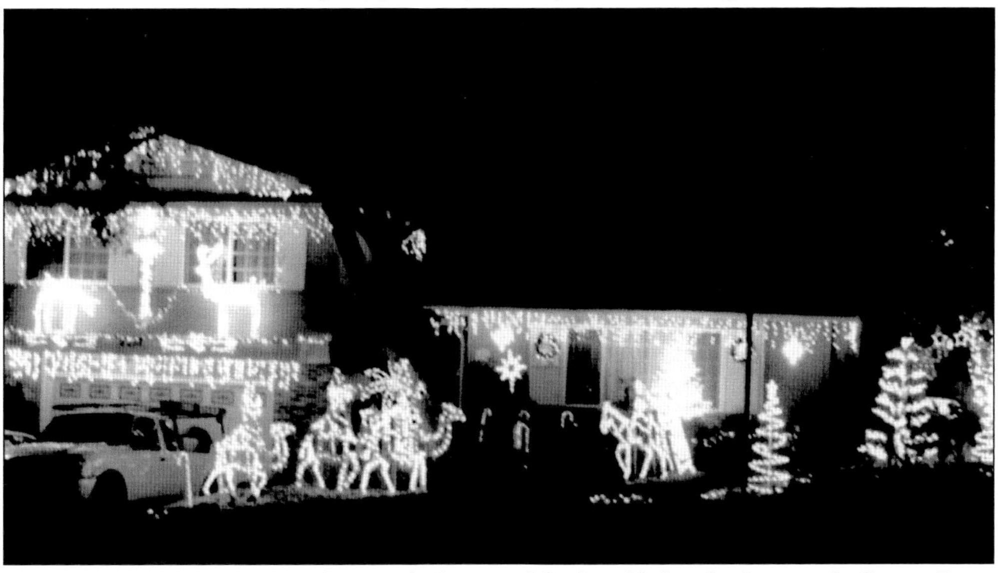

**Christmas Lights Displays.** Among the best neighborhood lights displays are the Pepper Drive Lights in El Cajon (pictured), Lana & Jamar Streets (Clairemont), Christmas on Knob Hill (San Marcos), Christmas Card Lane (Rancho Penasquitos), Holiday Magic at Fairway Village (Carmel Mountain Ranch), Christmas Circle (Chula Vista), Starlight Circle (Santee), Candy Cane Lane (Poway) and Garrison Street in Point Loma. (Courtesy of Suzanne Sannwald.)

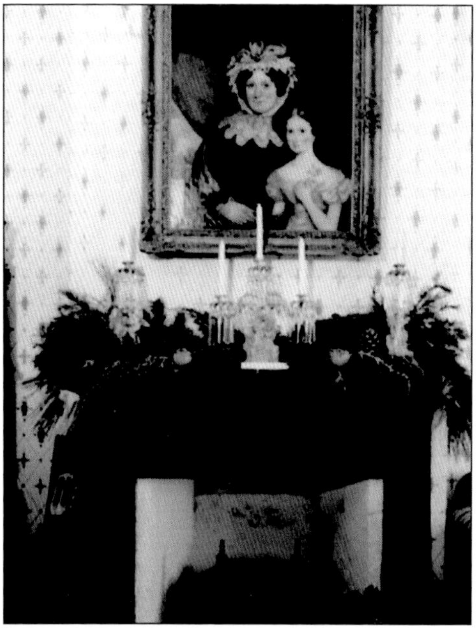
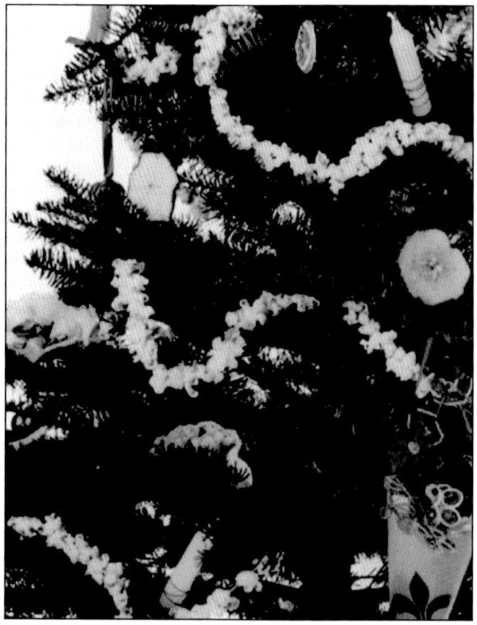

**Christmas at the Whaley House.** What better venue for the ghosts of *A Christmas Carol* than the haunted Whaley House in Old Town? The Charles Dickens Christmas classic was performed on the museum's intimate stage in 2011. A 2014 *A Christmas Carol* exhibit featured Scrooge's four-poster bed and assorted apparitions. The Whaley House fireplace mantle, and a pine tree with stringed popcorn, candles, dried fruit, and cornucopias are shown here, dressed for a Victorian Christmas. (Courtesy of Sandé Lollis, SOHO.)

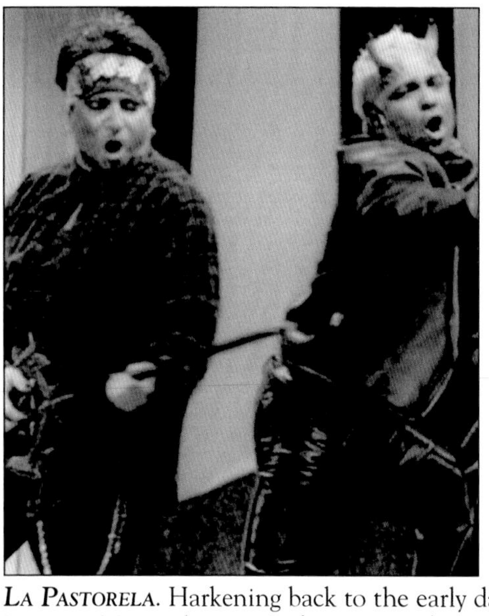
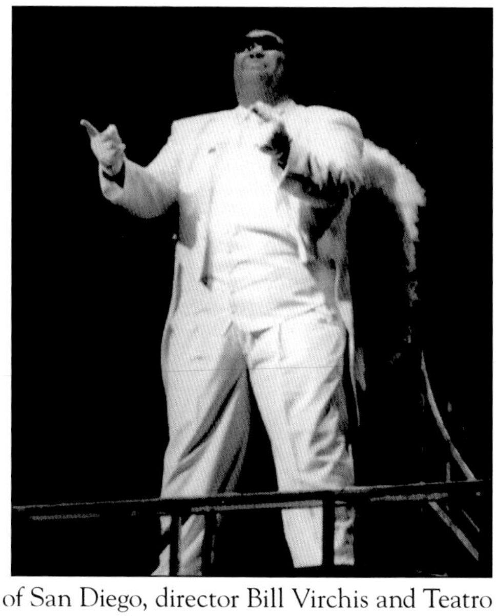

**La Pastorela.** Harkening back to the early days of San Diego, director Bill Virchis and Teatro Máscara Mágica have staged outrageously contemporary and politically charged versions of *La Pastorela* (*The Shepherd's Tale*) since 1989. On his journey to Bethlehem, a shepherd encounters the Three Stooges of the Underworld: Lucifer, Satan, and Moloch. The Archangel Michael, and his sidekick Gabriel, come to the aid of the young shepherd and the slapstick begins. The angels are elegant in white, but the rascals in red deliver the good lines. (Bill Virchis)

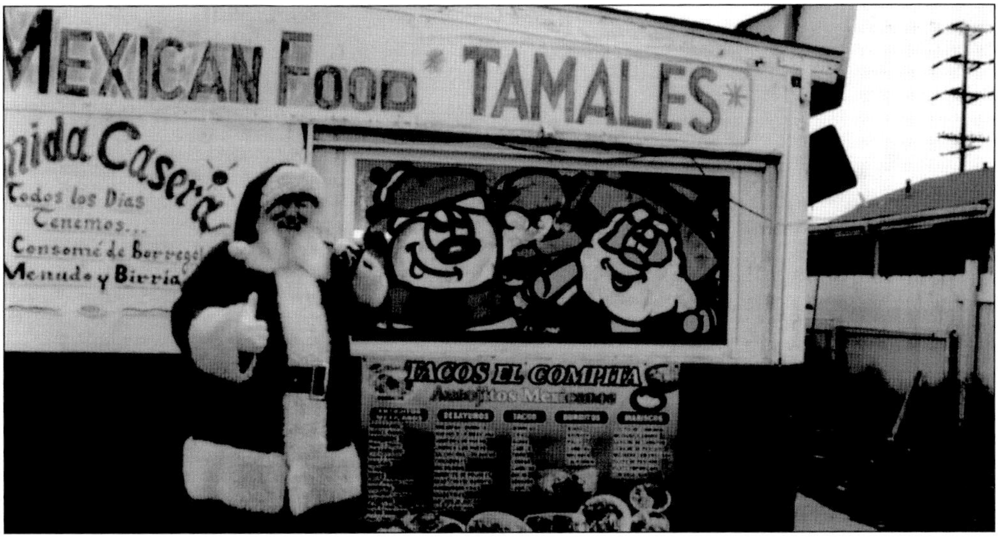


CHRISTMAS TAMALES. Tamales are a staple of holiday and festive meals throughout Mexico, and they are particularly popular at Christmas time. El Indio restaurant began selling tortilla masa for tamales in the early 1940s. According to owner Ralph Pesqueira, they sold 8,000 pounds (four tons) of masa this past Christmas. Several small eateries in Logan Heights (shown) specialize in tamales, and Santa Claus likes them all.

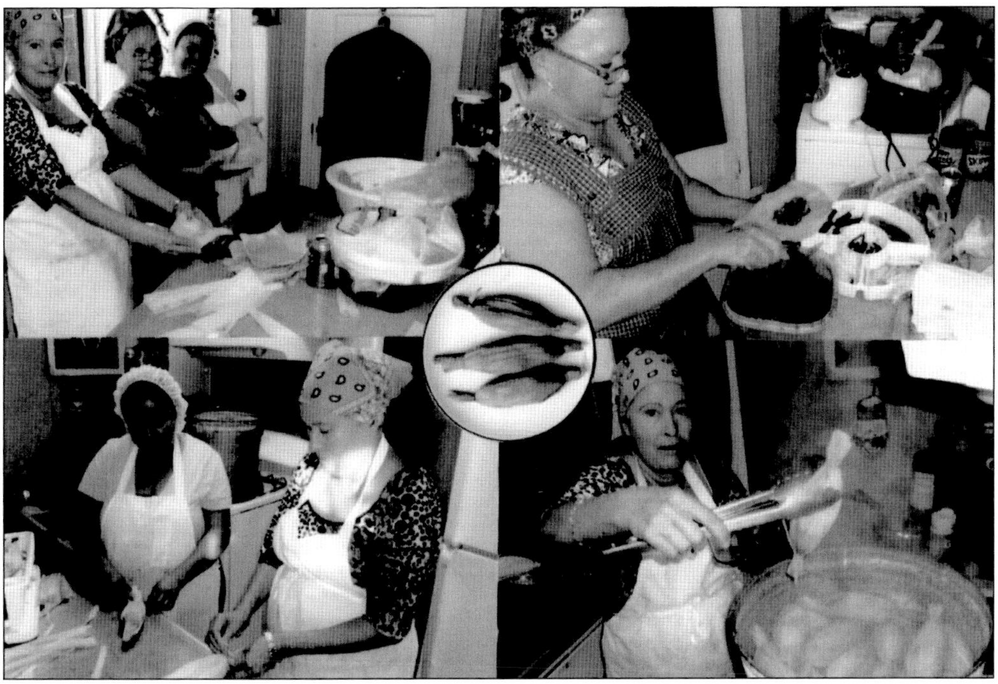

HOMEMADE TAMALES. Some of the best Christmas tamales in San Diego are sold through word of mouth. Friends know friends who know women who make great tamales in their own homes. The process is usually a family effort, known as a *tamalada*. Petra Maes, her sister Marcelina Peraza, and her daughter Fabiola Camacho are shown making Christmas tamales in the kitchen of Petra's City Heights home. Pictured in the upper left of this photograph from left to right are Marcelina Peraza, Petra Maes, and Fabiola Camacho.

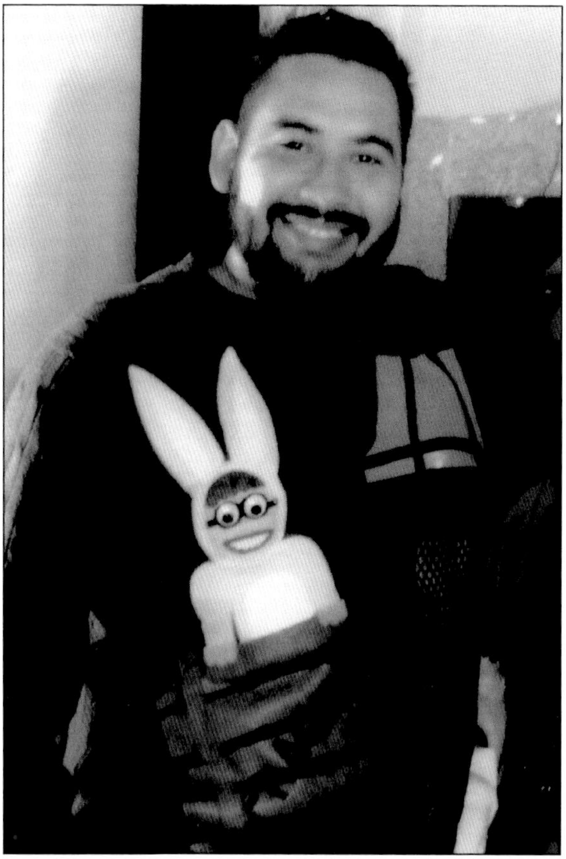

**Christmas Story Sweater.** Every year, jokes are made about fruitcakes, Charlie Brown trees, and ugly Christmas sweaters. This man—pictured sitting on the author's knee—made his own *A Christmas Story* sweater, complete with Ralphie and a light-up version of the Old Man's fishnet stocking lamp. It's a work of art. Every year, fathers ask for a BB gun, and I get to tell them, "You'll shoot your eye out, kid."

**Put My Brother on the Naughty List.** This young man and his mother have visited the author for several years. Mom's great enthusiasm for Christmas has been passed on to her son. He always wears a funny sweater, and this one reads, "Dear Santa, for Christmas, i want a dog a bike and put my brother on the naughty list." The kid doesn't even have a brother—Mom just thought the sweater was funny, and Santa agrees.

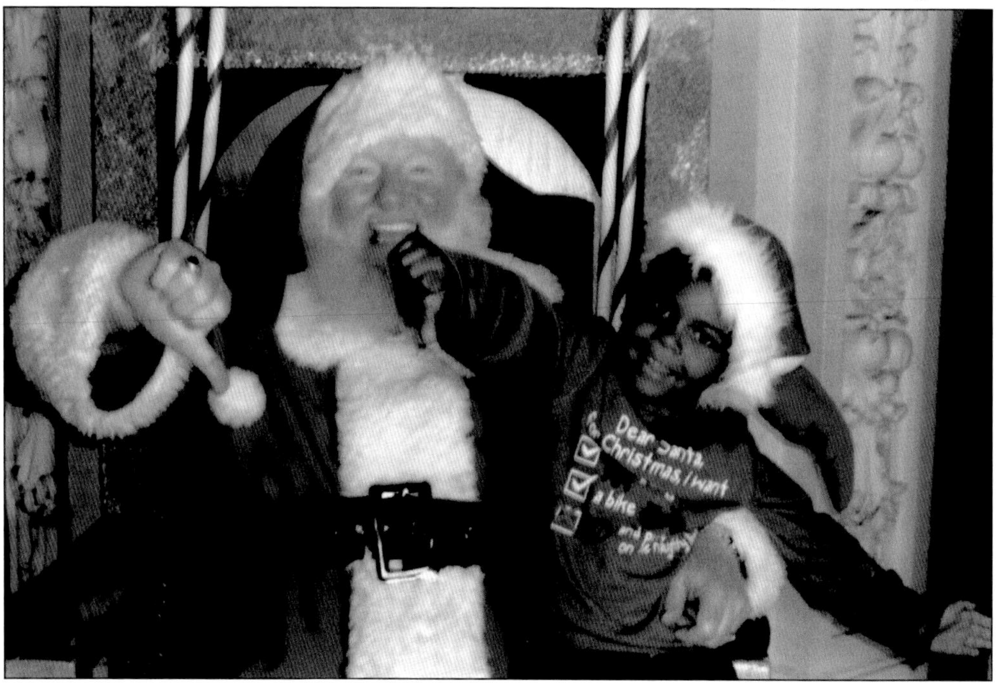

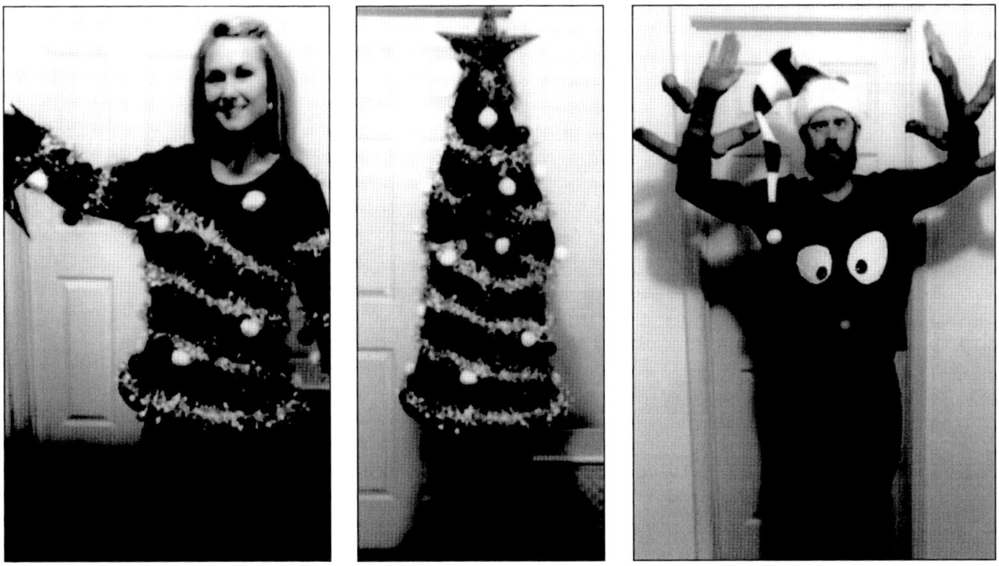

**Christmas Tree Sweaters.** Southern California designers Joe Hodnicki and his "wildly creative and beautiful girlfriend" Heather Laslo share many connections with San Diego County, including the San Diego Surf Film Festival, the rock band Switchfoot, and the Mother Earth Brewing Company in Vista. Be assured that Joe and Heather don't stand around with heir arms above their heads for very long. (Courtesy of Joe Hodnicki.)

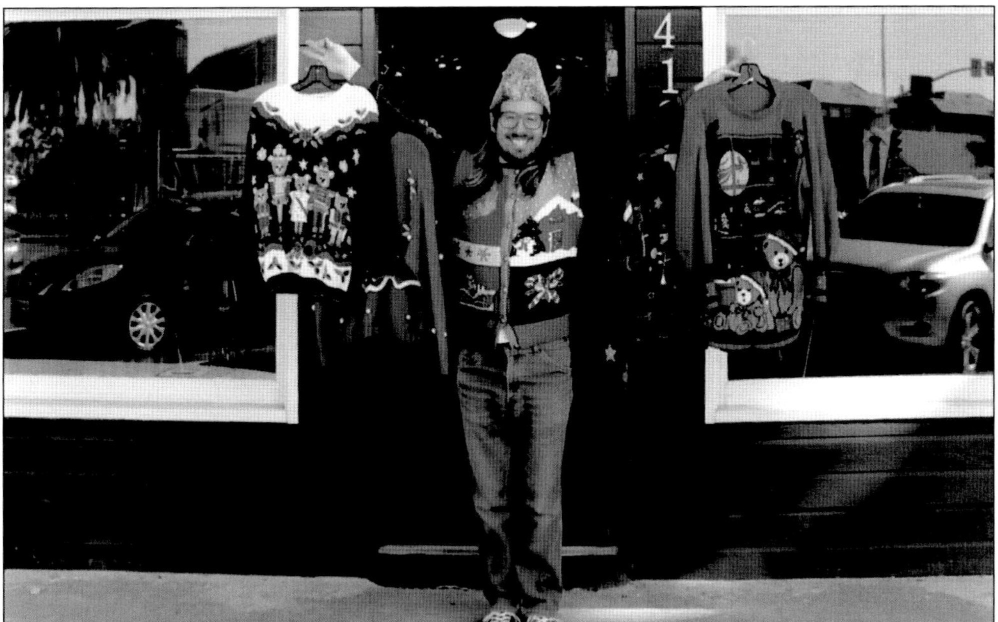


**Ugly Christmas Sweaters Headquarters.** Channel 8's Larry Himmel loved the Frock You Vintage Boutique on Park Boulevard. In a story about businesses with funny names, he closed with a picture of the Frock You storefront. At the time, he didn't think the name could be mentioned on the air. Employee Kenny King is shown holding a selection of sweaters. Owners Kristin Tinderholt and Curt Benedetto take great pride in their wide selection of the ugliest Christmas sweaters in San Diego. (Courtesy of SDUptownNews.com.)

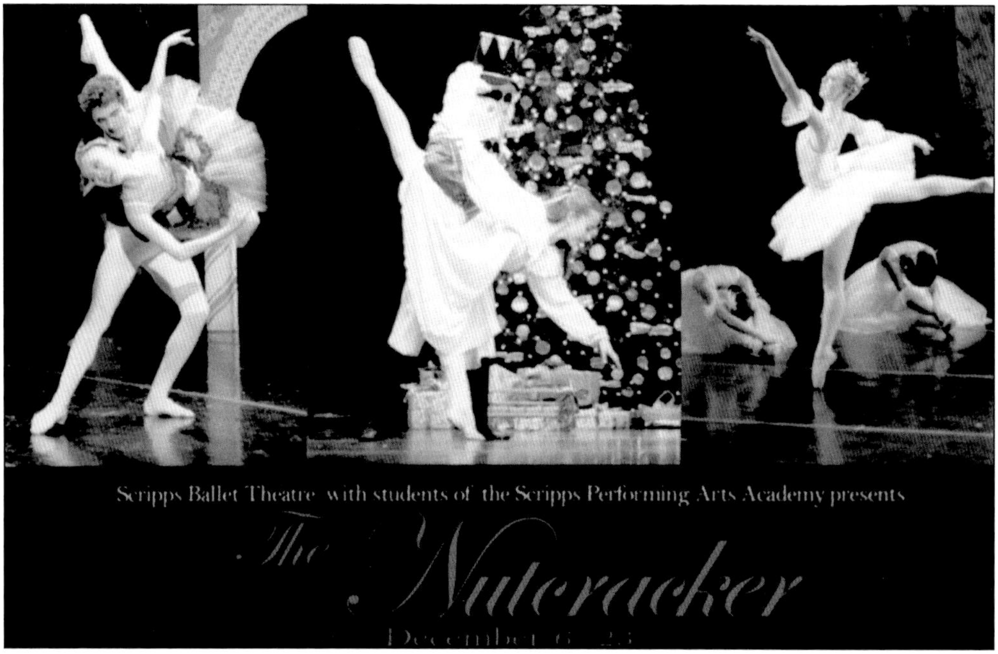


**THE *NUTCRACKER* BALLET.** San Diego loves *The Nutcracker.* Balletomanes can attend productions by the California Ballet, CAST Academy of Dance, City Ballet, Civic Youth Ballet, Encinitas Ballet Academy, Moscow Ballet, North County Academy of Dance, San Diego Ballet, Scripps Performing Arts Academy, Southern California Ballet and West Coast Ballet. Pictured is the beautiful 2014 playbill for the Scripps Performing Arts Academy's production of the show. (Courtesy of Miah Nwosu.)

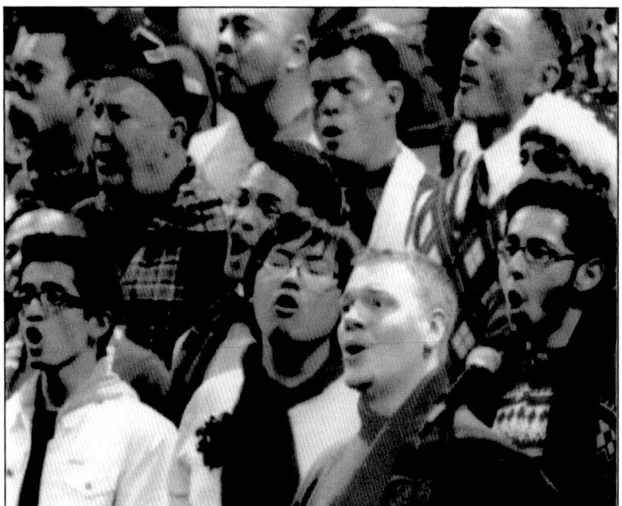

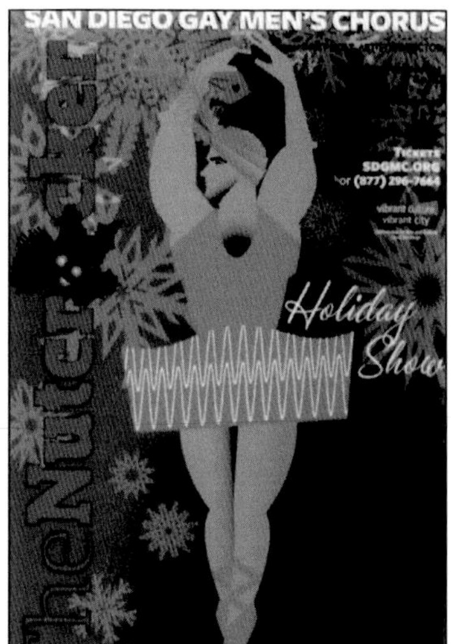


**THE *NUTCRACKER* (MEN IN TIGHTS).** Chorus president Bob Lehman reports, "The San Diego Gay Men's Chorus's holiday show is one of San Diego's favorite holiday traditions. 200 singers, dancers and production people have entertained San Diego audiences at the Balboa Theater for nearly 30 years." Their mission is to engage audiences, build community support, and provide a dynamic force for social change. The hit of their *Nutcracker* is a large man in a small costume: The Sugar Plum Fairy. (Courtesy of Bob Lehman.)

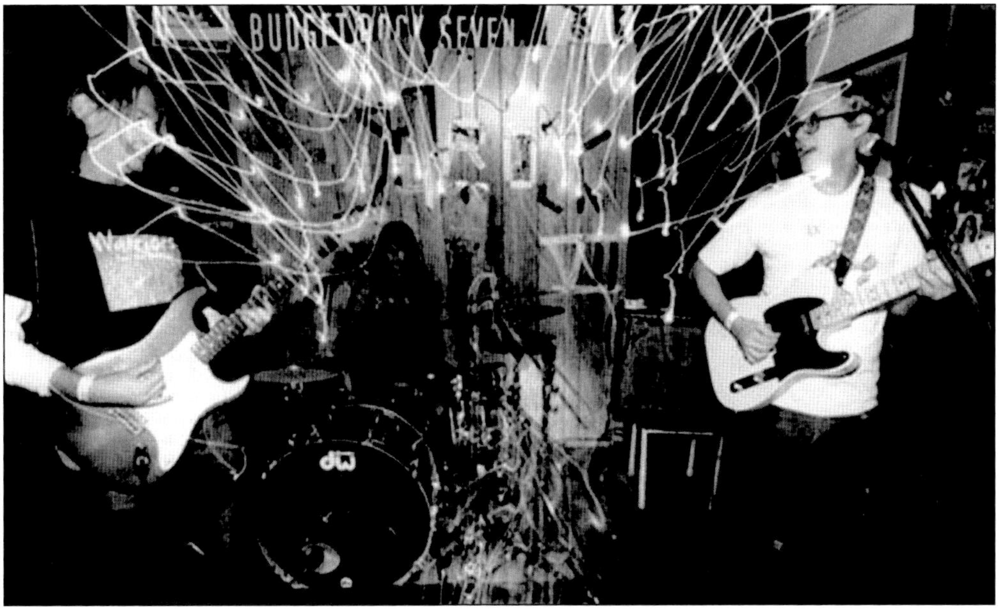

**CHRISTMAS ISLAND.** According to the music recommendation service Last.fm, San Diego musical act Christmas Island's "music is happy and poppy on the surface, yet there is a dark undercurrent to their brand of lo-fi punk pop. Simultaneously joyous and almost twee while secretly depressed and deeply disturbed." Christmas carols and Handel's "Messiah" are not part of the band's repertoire. "We don't play holiday music," explains guitarist Brian Island. (Courtesy of Christmas Island.)

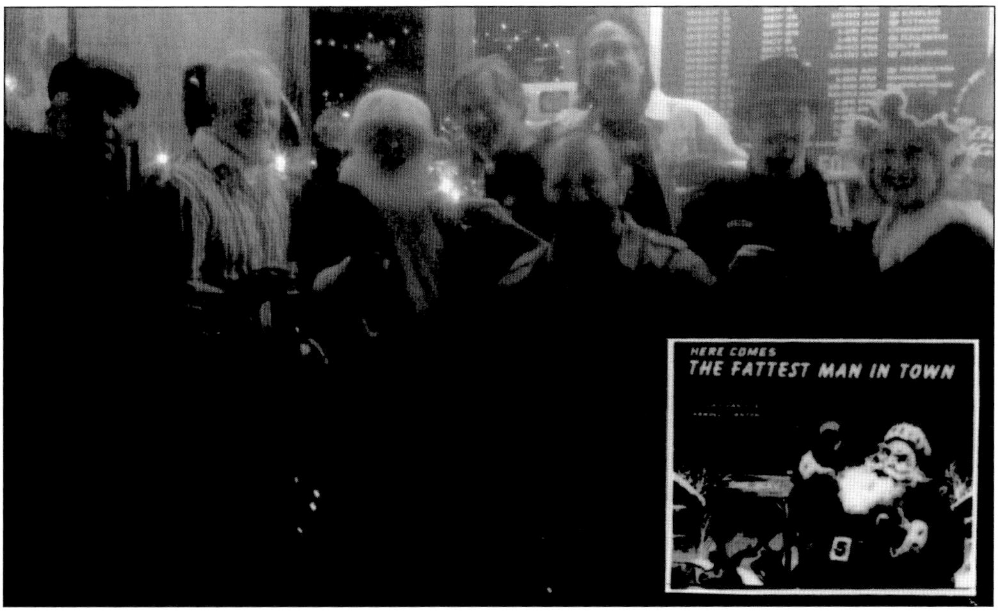


**TAKILLYA ENJOYS A SHOT WITH SANTA.** Takillya is a classic San Diego rock band. They are shown here with Santa and Mrs. Claus, at the Chico Club in La Mesa. Santa (Larry Fox) owns the bar. Takillya's Christmas playlist contained the song "Here Comes the Fattest Man in Town"—a 1944 carol that never quite caught on. Guitarist Jerry Fogel is blunt about it, saying, "We tried to work it into our holiday concert, but it might be the worst Christmas song ever written." (Courtesy of Jerry Fogel.)

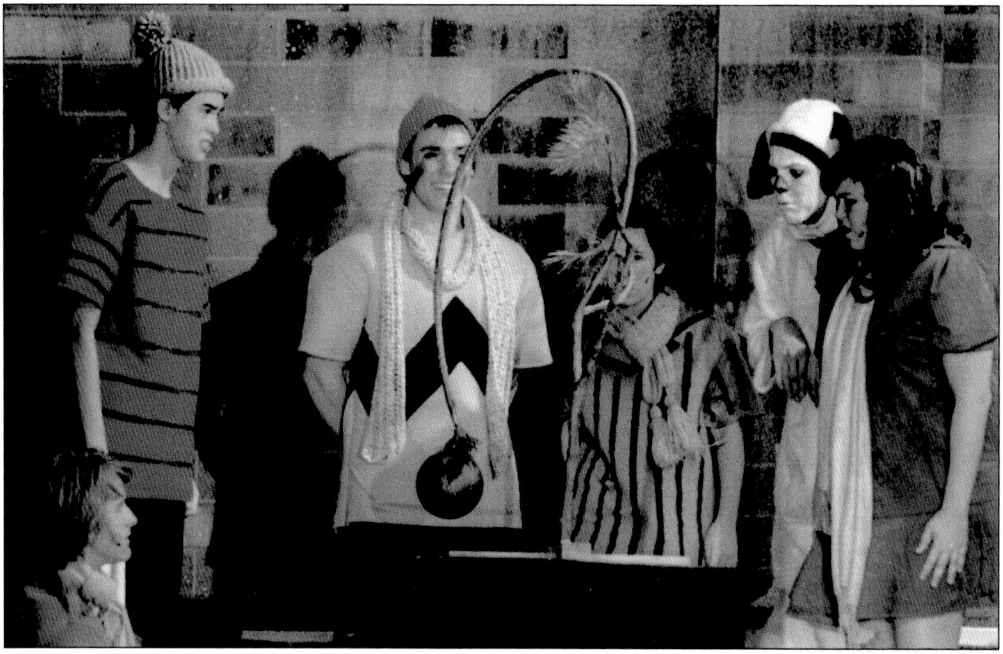

**Holiday Plays at Clairemont High School.** Stacey Allen is the theater arts director at Clairemont High School. In 2011, his students performed *A Christmas Carol* before the winter break of the school year. It was a success, so the drama department followed with *A Charlie Brown Holiday Special* in 2013 and *Madame Scrooge* in 2014. Allen said, "I enjoy them because they bring the families out to share in a celebration of the holidays." (Courtesy of Stacey Allen.)

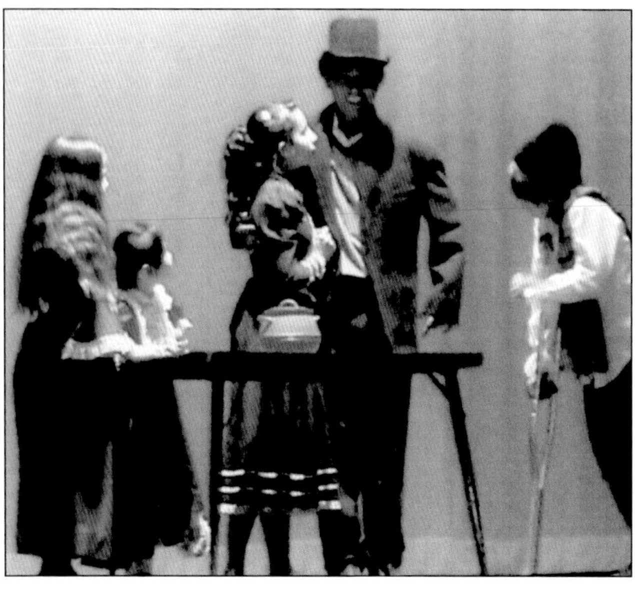

***A Christmas Carol* at Olympian High School.** Drama teacher Jennifer Schaeffer loves *A Christmas Carol*. She explains, "People don't realize that Charles Dickens both saved and created Christmas in England and, by extension, in the United States. We can thank him for the Christmas feast with family and friends, but, more importantly, Dickens taught us to be generous to others less fortunate. We did the play in 2008. It was a learning experience for the kids and the audience." (Courtesy of Jennifer Schaeffer.)

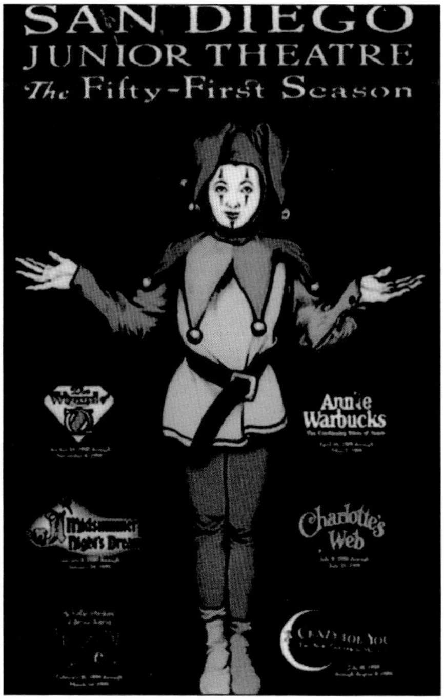

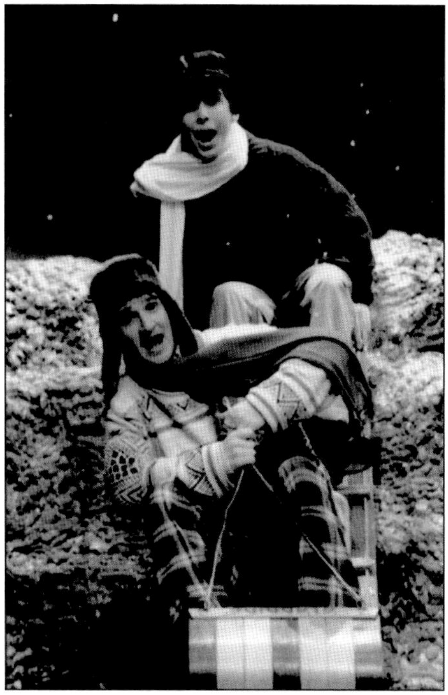

**A CHRISTMAS STORY.** The San Diego Junior Theatre began in 1948. Alumni include Annette Bening, Victor Buono, Dennis Hopper, and Raquel Welch. In 2009, the company presented *A Christmas Story*, a nostalgic visit to Christmas in the 1940s and protagonist Ralphie's obsession with a Red Ryder BB gun. (Courtesy of the San Diego Junior Theater and Ken Jacques Photography.)

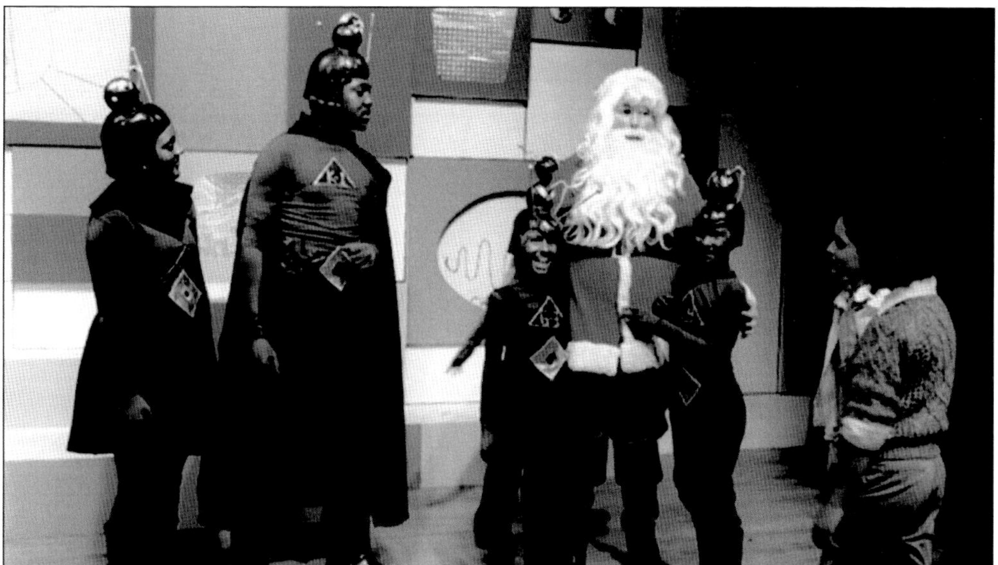

**SANTA VS. THE MARTIANS.** *Santa Claus Conquers the Martians* (1964) is widely recognized as one of the worst movies ever made and has attained cult status. There is even a campy stage play called *Santa vs. the Martians.* The San Diego Junior Theatre proudly produced the West Coast premiere in 2011. The comedy was "a hit with the casts and audiences alike." (Courtesy of the San Diego Junior Theatre and Ken Jacques Photography.)

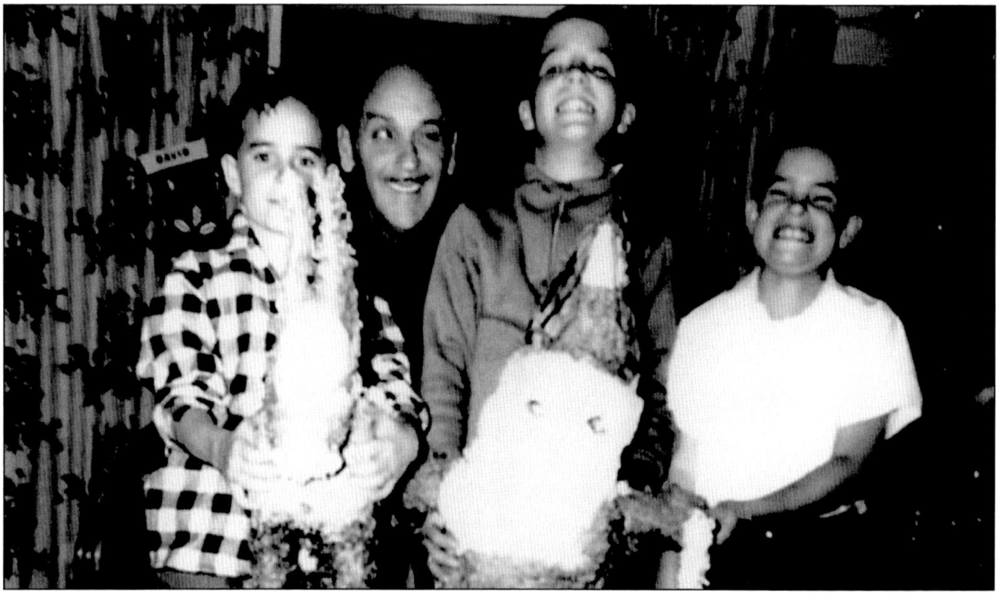

**Christmas Is a Time to Be Goofy.** Dan Bessie hams it up with his twin sons, Pat (left) and Mike (right), and nephew Mike Randolph (holding the Santa Claus piñata from Tijuana). When the boys cracked Santa open with a baseball bat, bubble gum cigars, Necco wafers, wax lips, Boston Baked Beans, Walnettos, Mike & Ikes, BB Bats, Atomic Fireballs, candy cigarettes, Big Hunks, Chuckles, root beer barrels, Lik-Em-Aids, jawbreakers, and Jujubes poured to the ground. (Courtesy of Dan Bessie.)

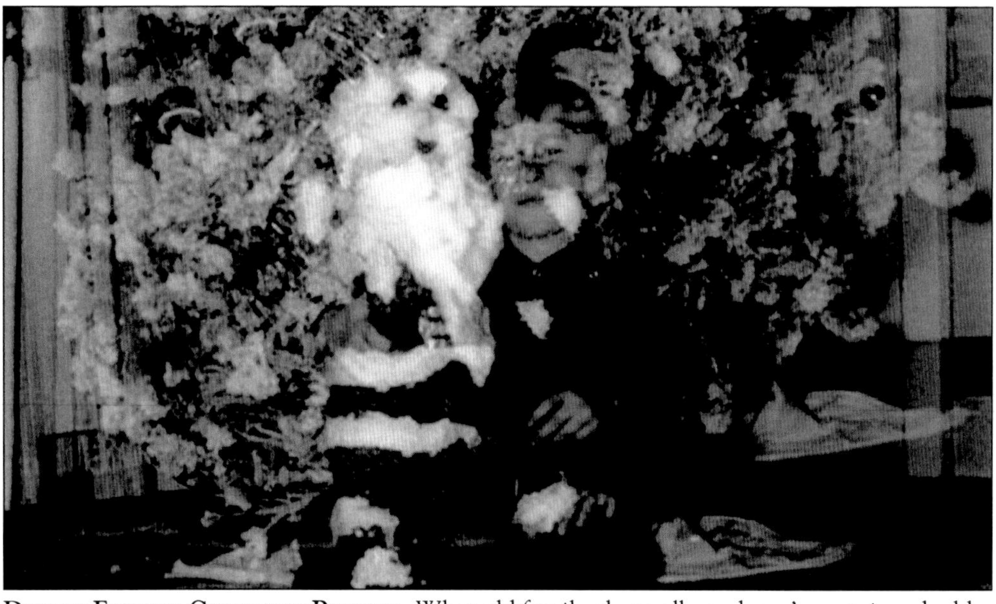

**Double-Exposed Christmas Picture.** What old family photo album doesn't contain a double-exposed Christmas picture or two? These boys took turns having their traditional portrait taken with a Santa piñata in front of the tree on Christmas Day, but something went wrong inside the family Brownie. Flocked Christmas Trees were popular in San Diego during the 1950s and 1960s. The snow reminded new residents of the white Christmases they left behind in the Midwest and East.

# *Three*

# COMMUNITIES

*Merry Christmas from Sunny San Diego*

*December 25, 1934   Temperature: 70 Degrees*

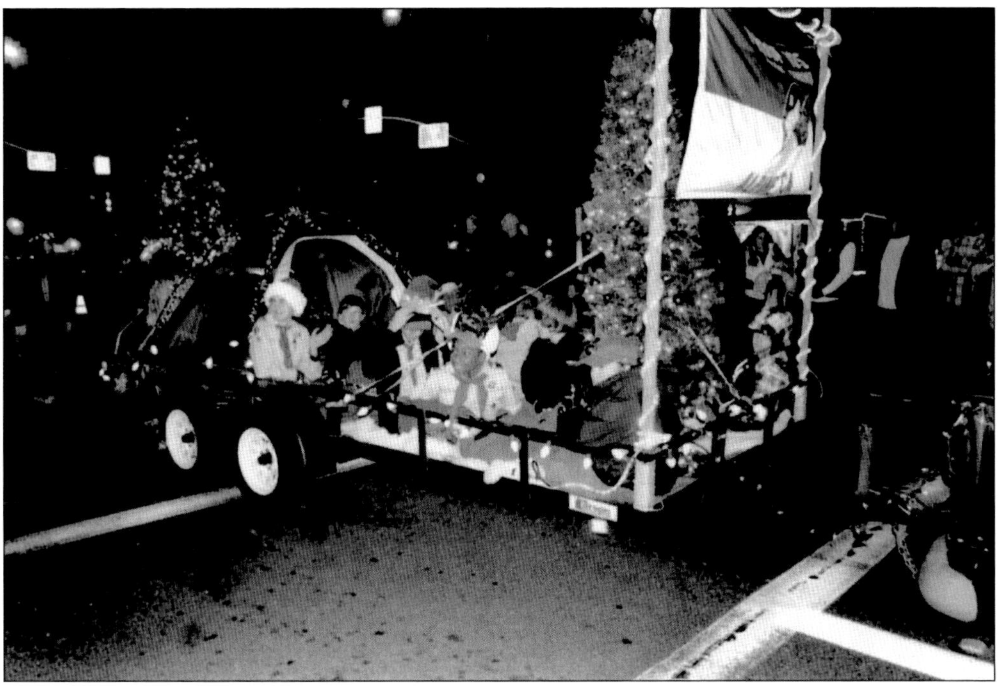

ALPINE VILLAGE CHRISTMAS PARADE OF LIGHTS & SNOW FESTIVAL. If it has wheels and can be decorated for Christmas (floats, cars, trucks, lawnmowers, baby carriages, bicycles, skateboards), enter it in the Alpine Mountain Empire Chamber of Commerce Christmas Parade. Manufactured snow provides sledding for the young and young at heart. The festival is 20 years old, but Alpine families and churches have held major gatherings and programs since the early 1900s. (Courtesy of *The Alpine Sun*.)

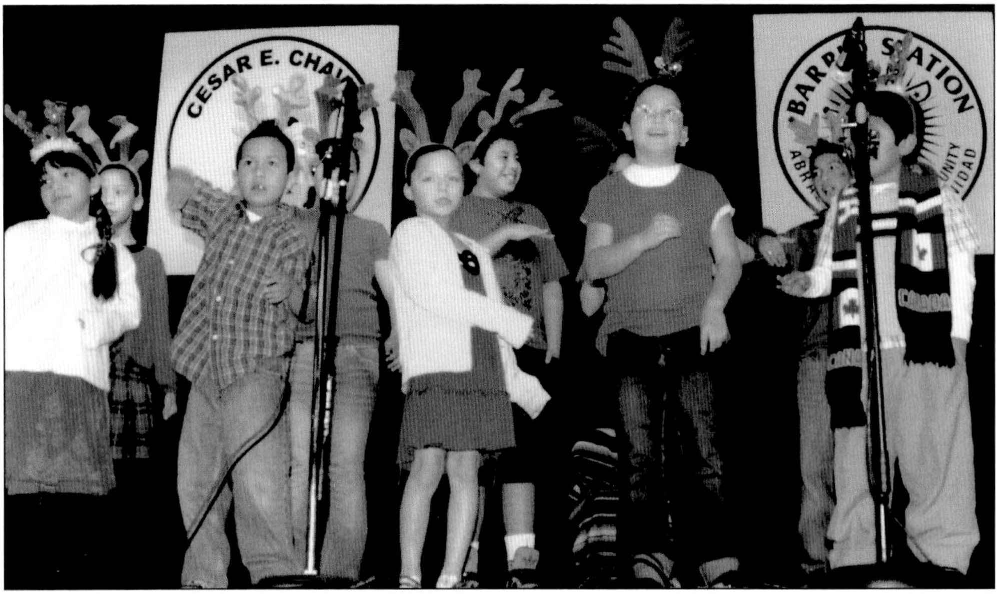


THE 44TH ANNUAL BARRIO (LOGAN) CHILDREN'S HOLIDAY. The Barrio Station opened to serve the youth of Barrio Logan in 1970. They celebrated their 44th Annual Barrio Children's Holiday in 2014, where Santa Claus handed out 500 gifts to children from the community. The children's reindeer choir is shown above, performing a Christmas song. Barrio Station also matches sponsors with needy families during the holiday season. (Courtesy of Rachael Ortiz.)

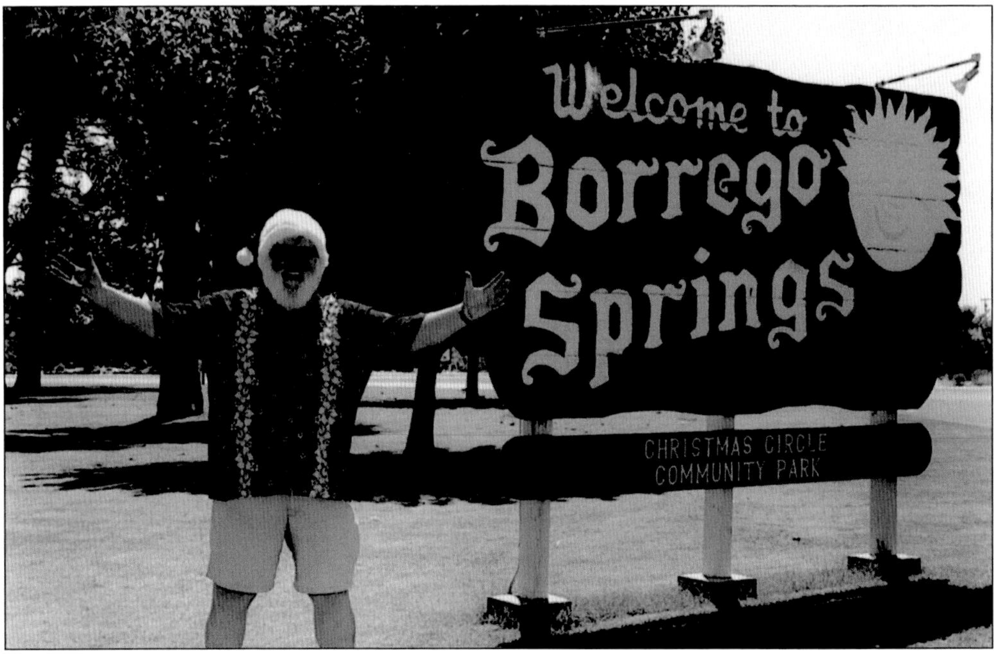


CHRISTMAS CIRCLE IN BORREGO SPRINGS. Christmas Circle, the verdant hub of Borrego Springs, is surrounded by over 900 square miles of sand and the Anza Borrego Desert State Park. Few tourists realize the historic significance of this grassy green oasis. Created when the town was laid out in 1946, Christmas Circle is a tribute to Salvador Ignacio Linares, the "Christmas Babe" of 1775. (Courtesy of Mei Chan Ng.)

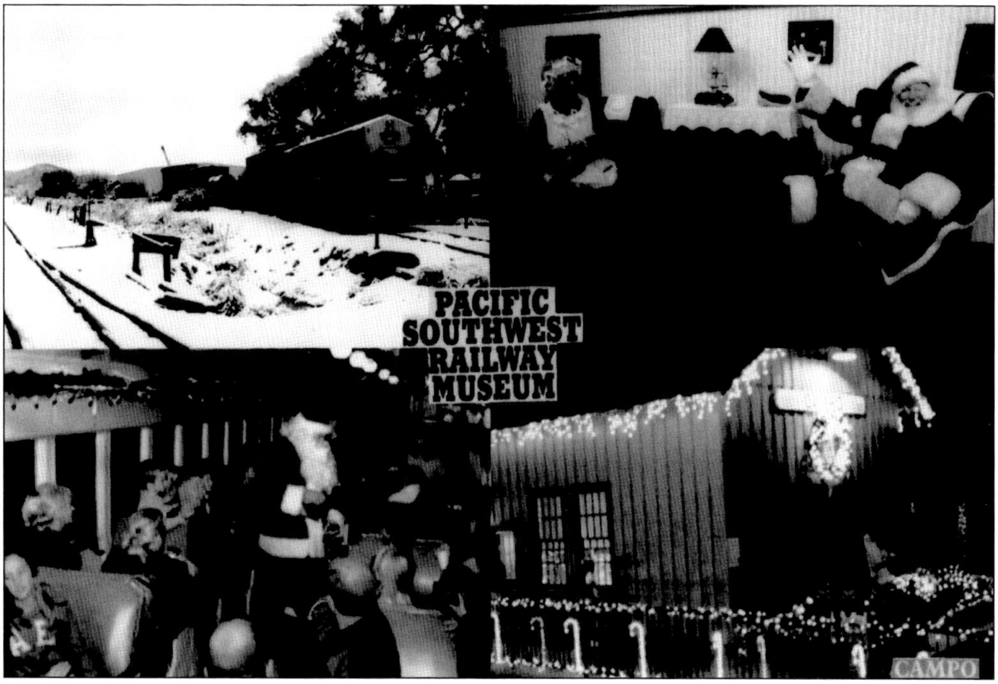


**North Pole Express Rolls out of Campo.** The Pacific Southwest Railway Museum in Campo operates Santa's North Pole Express during the Christmas season. The elves suggest that kids should dress warm and wear flannel pajamas for their pictures with Santa. The train travels to the North Pole, where Mr. and Mrs. Claus board for the ride back to Campo. (Courtesy of the Pacific Southwest Railway Museum.)

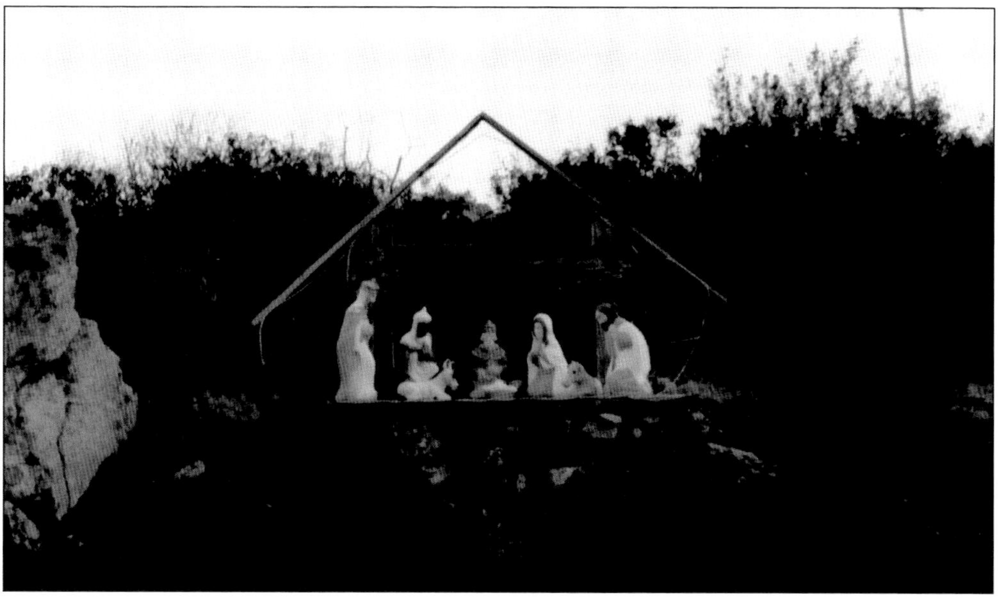

**Christmas in Canyon City.** Canyon City is located 50 miles east of San Diego, on state highway 94. This town has no post office, no school, no church, no store, no gas station, and no McDonald's, but Canyon City does have a nativity scene. It stands beneath a barely legible sign on the south side of the road.

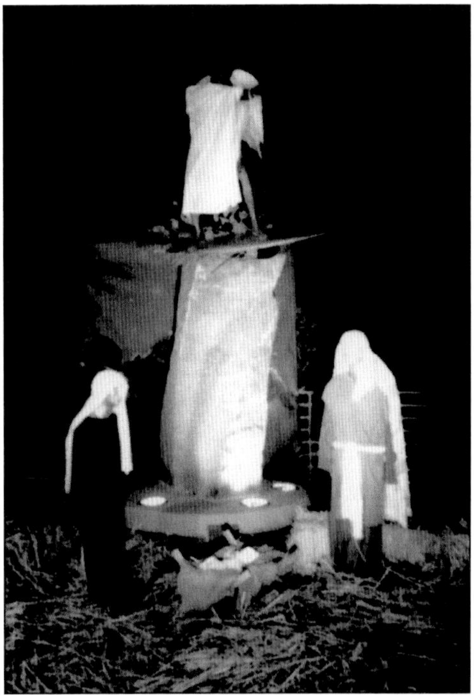

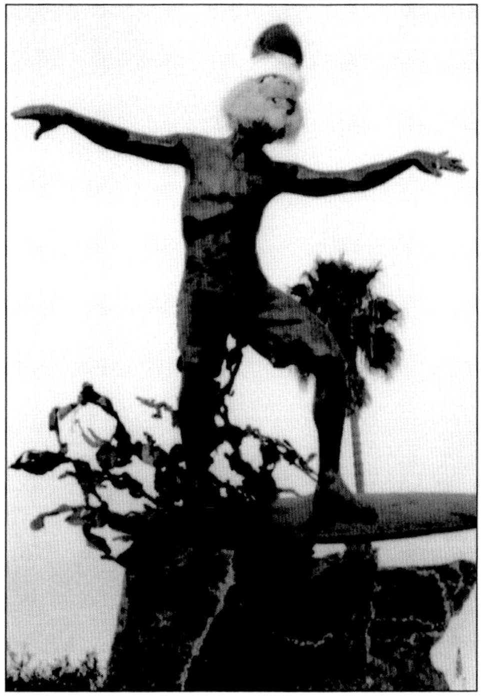

**The Cardiff Kook.** A 16-foot bronze statue of a novice surfer—which stands beside the San Elijo State Beach campground—is known as the "Cardiff Kook," and creative vandalism has made this figure into a tourist attraction. On Christmas Eve 2013, the Kook was an angel above the Nativity, but he turned into the Grinch on Christmas Day. The *Encinitas Undercover* blog wryly noted, "In an apparent reference to the city workers who purged Sweet Baby Jesus with great haste on Christmas Eve, the kook bears a Grinch mask today." (Courtesy of *Encinitas Undercover.*)

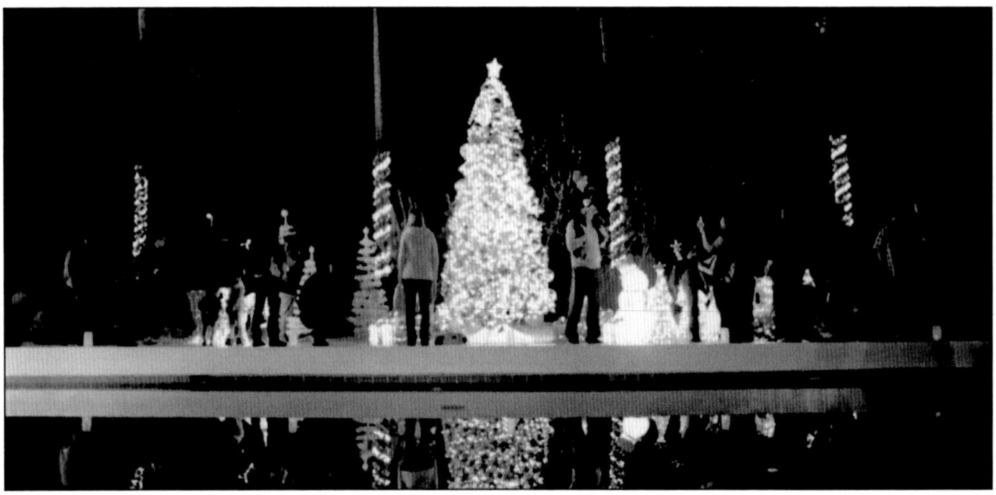

**Holiday at the Leo Carillo Ranch (Carlsbad).** Leo Carillo was famous for playing Pancho in the popular 1950s television series *The Cisco Kid.* Carillo purchased and began development of his historic Carlsbad rancho in 1937. A preservationist and conservationist, he served 18 years on the California Beaches and Parks Commission and became California's official "Ambassador of Good Will." Shown is the annual tree lighting ceremony by the pool and cabana area of his beloved *hacienda.* (Courtesy of Cassie Lee.)

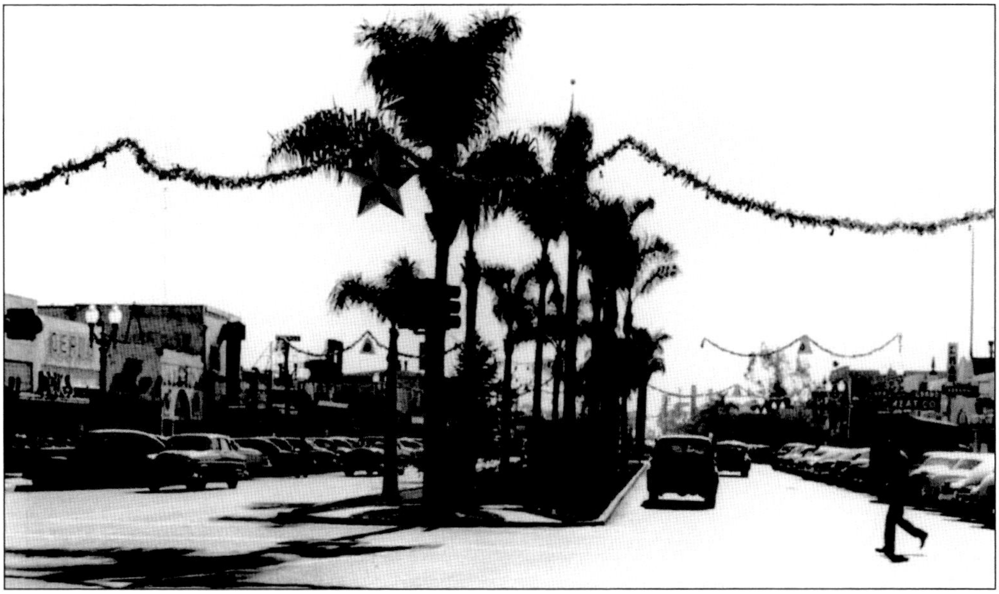

**Chula Vista Christmas Parades.** Chula Vista began decorating Third Avenue with Christmas ornaments and lights in 1939. During World War II, Santa cruised the main drag in a jeep. In 1964, he rode an elephant down Broadway. The Starlight Yule Parade started in 1965 and lasted through 2011. Its stated purpose was for families to see their own kids in a hometown parade. The picture above shows Third Avenue, decorated for Christmas in 1954. (Courtesy of the South Bay Historical Society.)

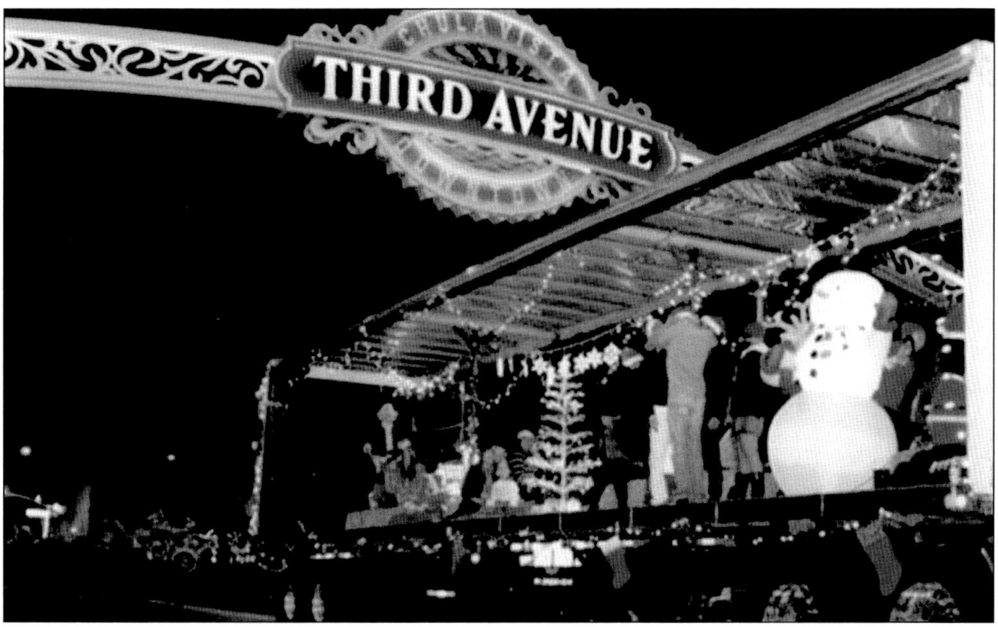


**Chula Vista Starlight Parade.** After two years without a holiday parade, the Third Avenue Village Association of Chula Vista revived the Starlight Parade in 2014. The county's largest nighttime parade is held in conjunction with TAVA's Holiday in the Village festival. The mayor lit the Christmas tree in nearby Memorial Park, and kids played in the snow on SDG&E's "Frosty Hill." (Courtesy of Steve Wood, *Star-News*.)

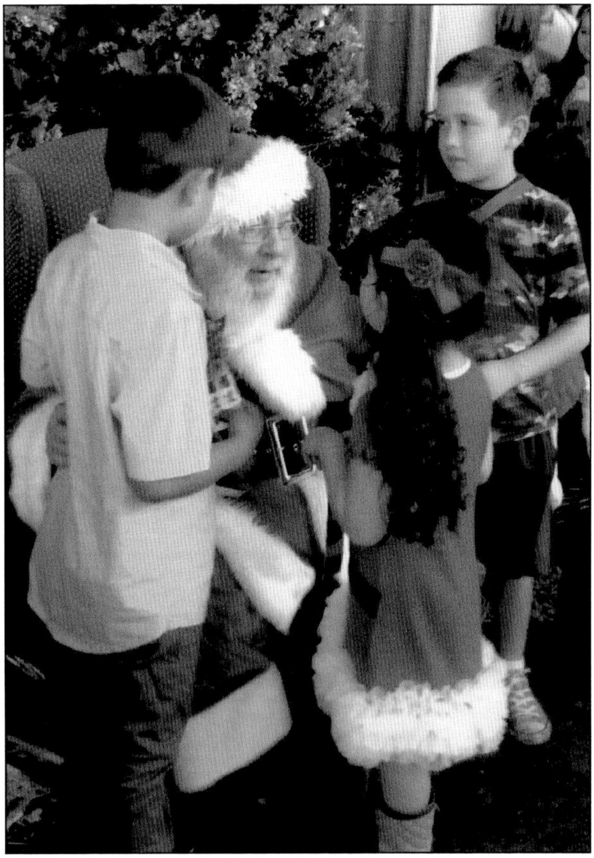

**SANTA AT THE CLAIREMONT SQUARE.** Gabe Bradford has been Santa Claus at the Clairemont Square since 1978. Although beards were popular in the 1970s, real bearded Santas were rare. It's possible that Gabe is San Diego's original real bearded Santa. He is such a tradition in Clairemont that people who once sat on his knee now bring their own children to visit with him. The line is always long, because this Santa takes time to talk with the kids.

**HIGH-FLYING SANTA IN DULZURA.** The Santa Claus Grand Prix has been a fixture at Dulzura's famed Vogt Ranch since 2008. This high-flying Santa is Scott "Burner" Burnworth—described by *Motorcycle USA* as "the undisputed veteran King of American mini bike racing lore." Burnworth was motivated to organize the Santa GP as a "fun holiday race" for other off-road riders. (Courtesy of Scott Burnworth.)

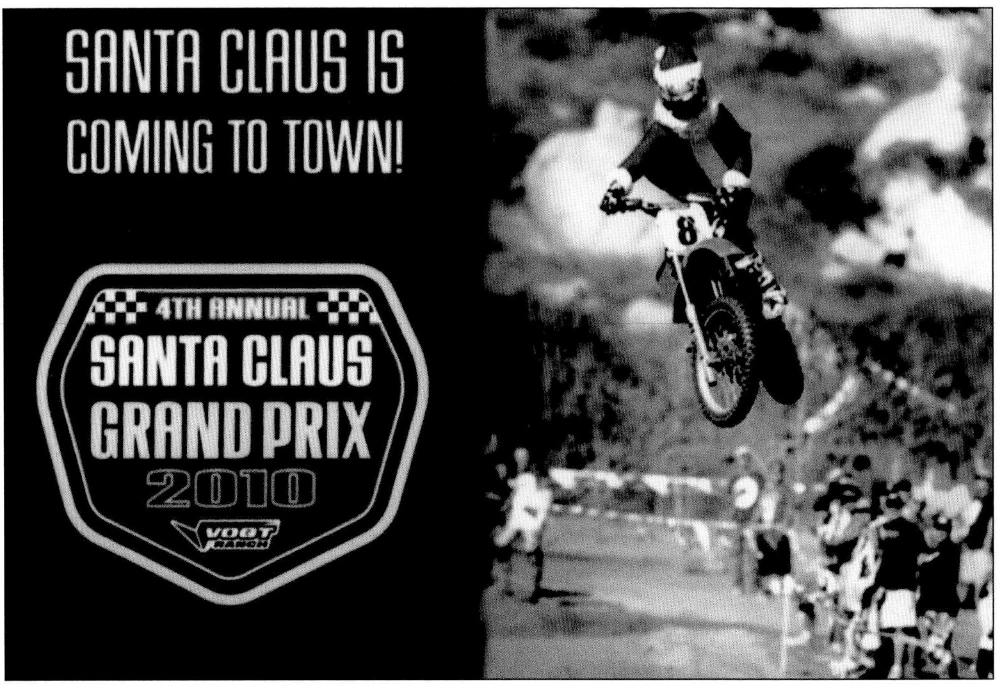

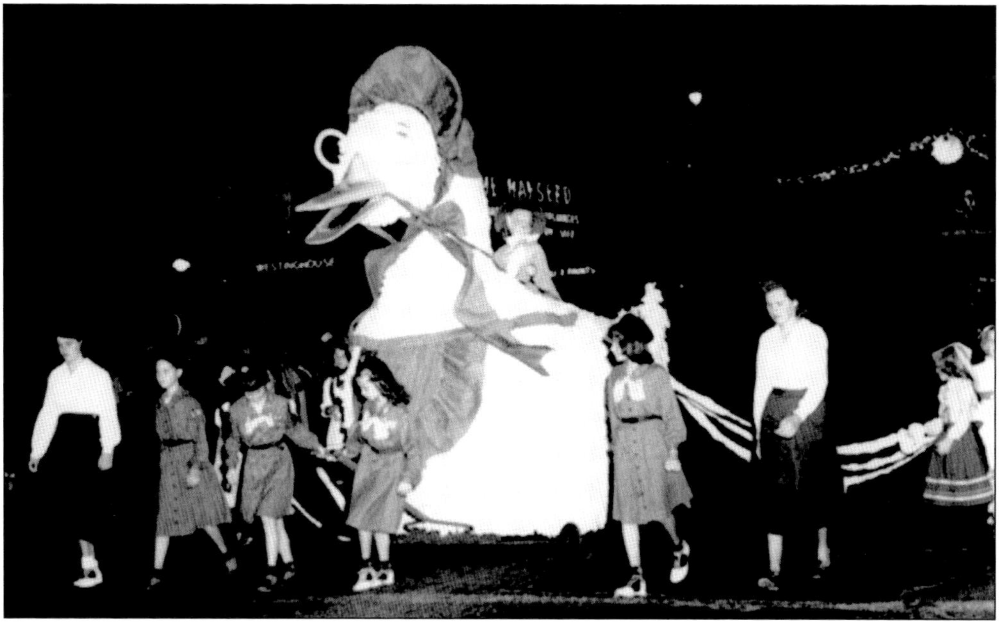

**First Mother Goose Parade.** In 1947, the Girls Scouts pulled a Mother Goose float in El Cajon's first Mother Goose Parade, which grew to become one of the largest holiday parades in the Western United States. California governor Goodwin Knight was the grand marshal of the parade from 1951 to 1957, while Mickey Mouse himself filled the role in 1973, 1976, 1985, 1997, and 2004. Over 400,000 people watched Mickey and Minnie wave to the crowd in the 1973 parade.

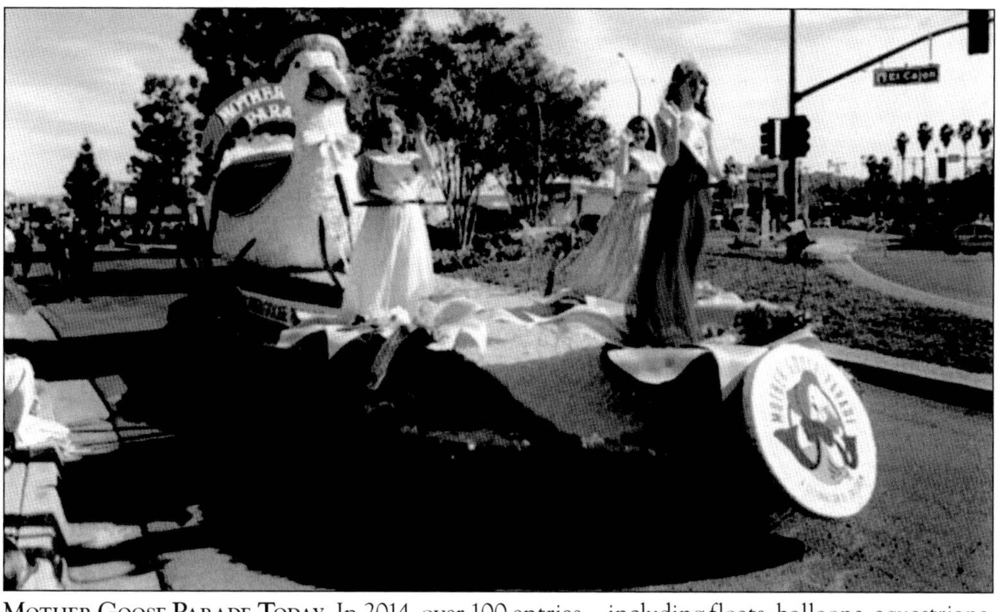

**Mother Goose Parade Today.** In 2014, over 100 entries—including floats, balloons, equestrians, bands, drill teams, clowns and honorees—travelled the two-mile parade route. In 1990, Bart Simpson was a hit with the kids, though parents objected to his "bad boy image." Now unable to afford high-priced celebrities, the parade has downsized in recent years. Using local celebrities, it still draws over 200,000 people. The Mother Goose Parade is traditionally held the Sunday before Thanksgiving. (Courtesy of *East County Magazine*.)

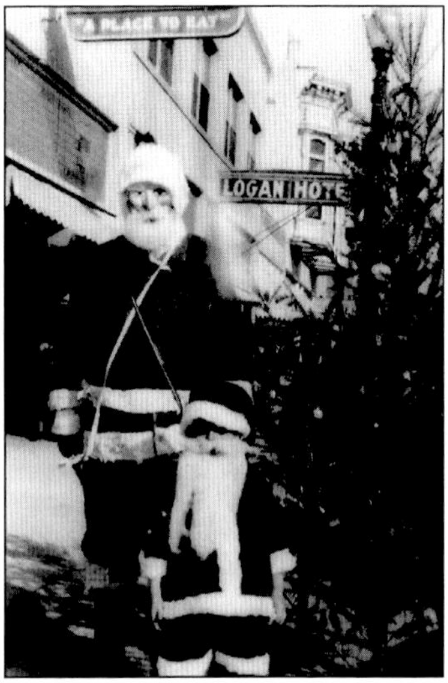


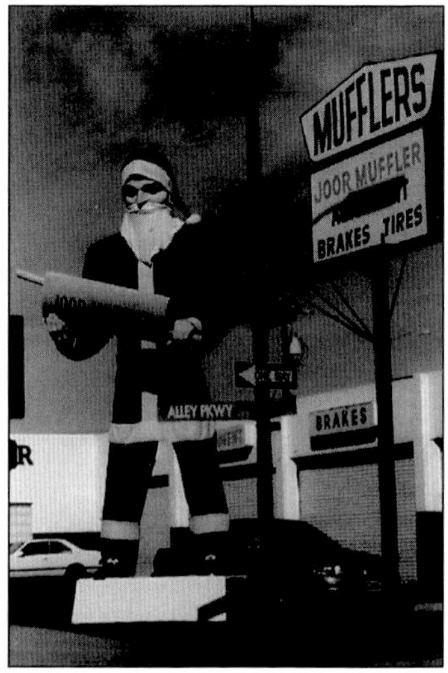


**Escondido Santas.** Escondido Santas come in all shapes and sizes—such as the cute little boy and the man in the creepy mask in the 1928 photograph at left, which was taken in the 100 block of Grand Avenue. At right is the Joor Muffler Man, which has been a landmark at the corner of Juniper and Valley Parkway in Escondido since 1967. He began wearing a Santa suit in the 1980s and is shown in 2006. The muffler shop couldn't afford a new suit after 2008. (Courtesy of the Escondido Historical Society.)

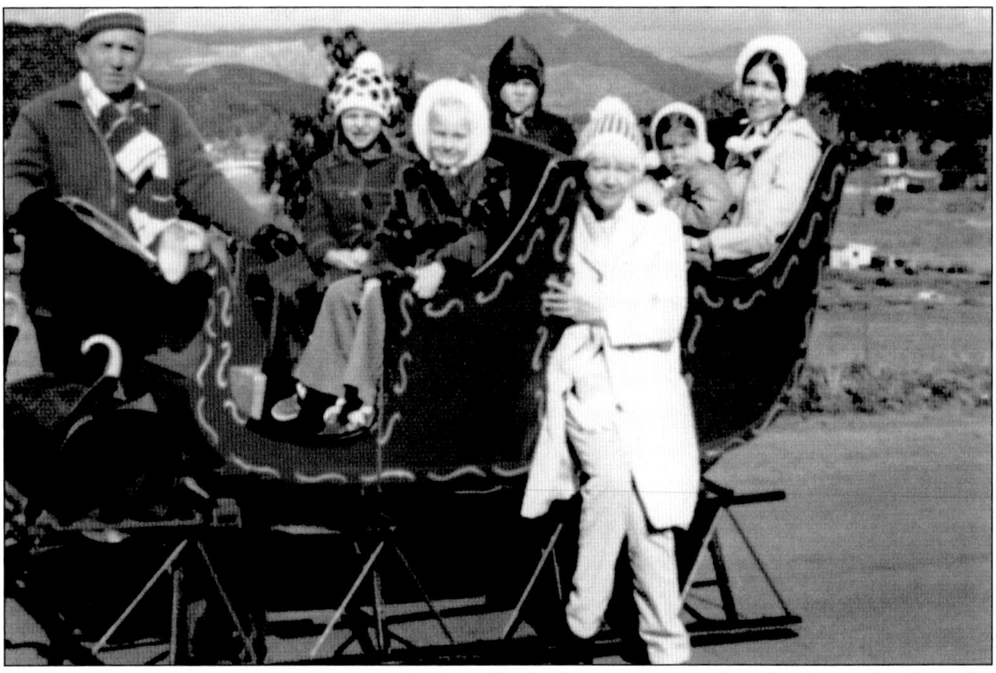

**In a Two Horse Open Sleigh.** Leonard Schroeder built an open, wooden sleigh on wheels in the 1960s. On Christmas morning, he and his neighbor, Earl Gimple (who dressed as Santa), would hitch up two horses and give kids rides through the eastside streets of Escondido. Shown here, from left to right, are Leonard, Nancy Huebner, Martha Phillips, Jeffrey Eitel, Martha Eitel, Meri Eitel, and Kathie Eitel. The Junior Chamber of Commerce has sponsored the official Escondido Christmas Parade since 1951. (Courtesy of the Escondido Historical Society.)

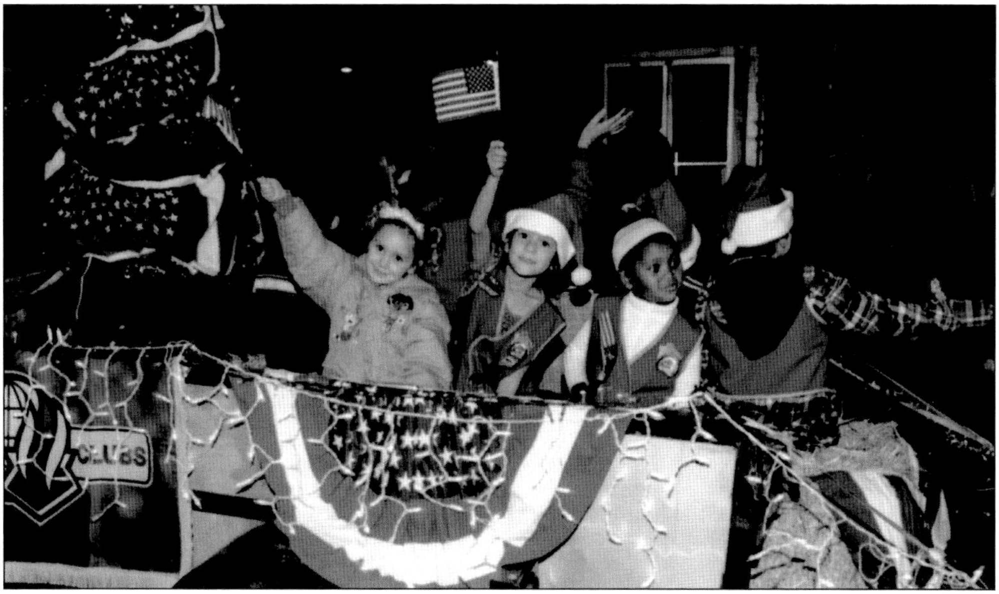


ANNUAL FALLBROOK CHRISTMAS PARADE. The first Fallbrook Christmas Parade consisted of flashing lights on sheriff and fire department vehicles, the Warriors high school band, flag unit, and cheerleaders, and a Santa aboard a flatbed trailer. Now in its 33rd year, the parade averages 120 entries and 30,000 viewers, and the route has grown to over a mile. The Fallbrook Chamber of Commerce enjoys receiving this recurring comment: "Reminds us of home; just like I remember as a kid." (Courtesy of Fred Young.)

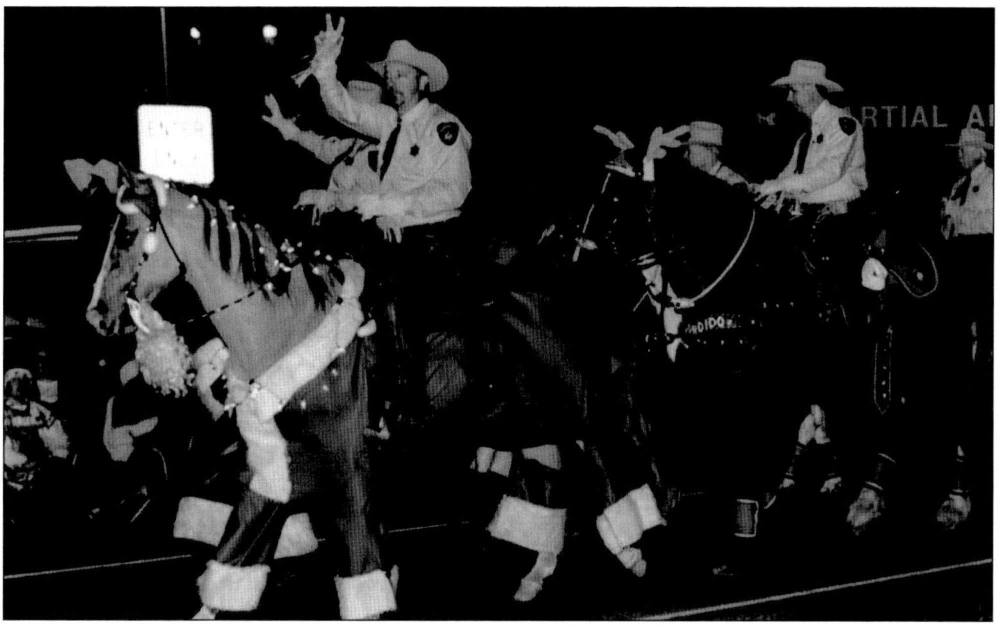

SANTA HORSE. The Escondido Mounted Posse was formed in 1948 to patrol parks and assist the San Diego Sheriff in search and rescue operations. No longer a law enforcement unit, the posse now represents Escondido in parades. Storm, the quarter horse in the Santa suit, is a popular participant in the Fallbrook Christmas Parade. The mounted posse also rides in the Vista and Escondido Christmas Parades. (Courtesy of Fred Young.)

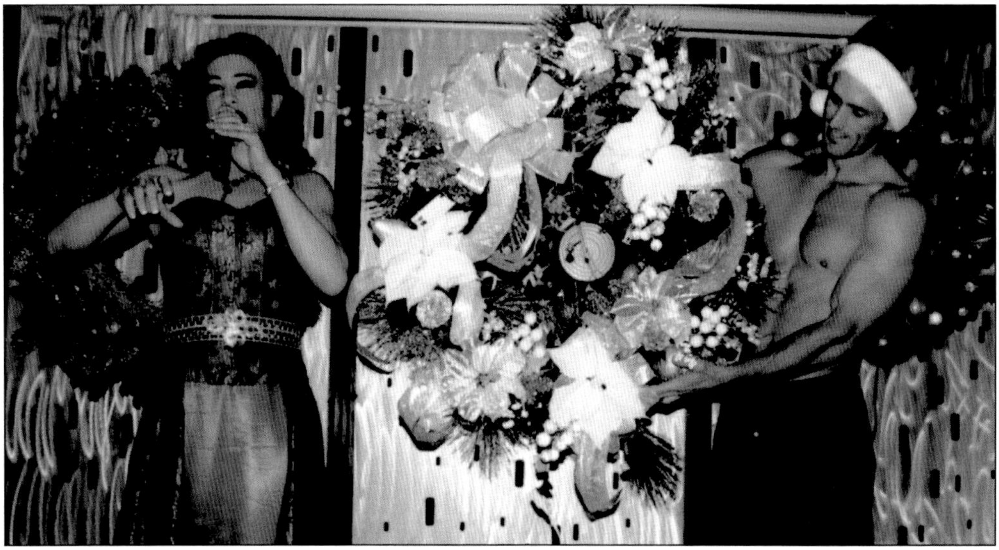

**Christmas Wreath Auction in Hillcrest.** Martinis Above Fourth and the San Diego LGBT Community Center have sponsored the highly successful Charity Wreath Auction since 2004. Last year, $32,000 was raised to benefit the Queen Eddie Youth Fund and the Sunburst Youth Housing Project. The money is used to help homeless LGBT youth who have been shunned by their families. Auctioneer Lady Ajax is shown with one of the wreath boys. (Courtesy of gay-sd.com.)

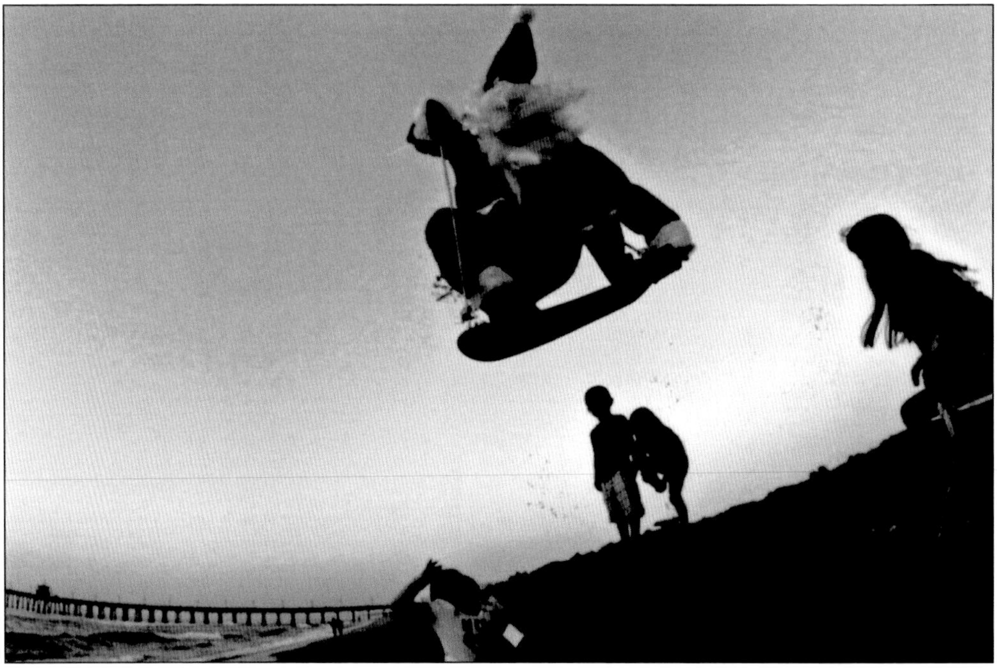

**Spooner Board Santa in Imperial Beach.** Here, Reuben Guymer, marketing director of Spooner Board, wears a Santa suit and performs some tricks for Ebony Street kids—with the Imperial Beach Pier in the background. The Spooner Board was created by accident when Randy Putland was cutting up a plastic dog igloo in the back of his San Diego surf shop. Reuben's acrobatics aboard the Spooner Board are uniquely San Diego and have never been attempted at the North Pole. (Courtesy of Reuben Guymer.)

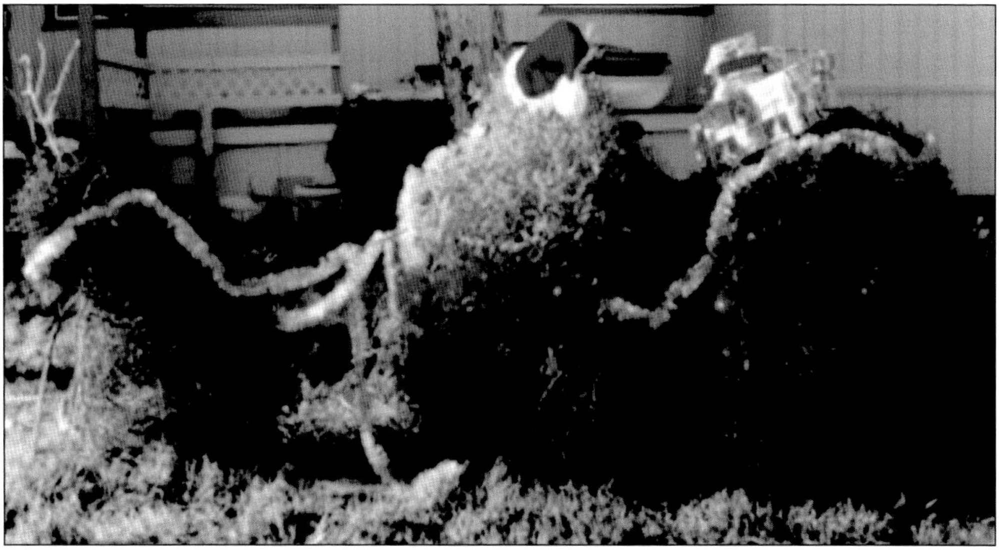

**¡Feliz Navidad! in Jacumba.** On December 6, 2014, the East County town of Jacumba closed its centennial celebration with the ¡Feliz Navidad! event. Mariachi Garibaldi, from Southwestern College, performed and sang carols in English and Spanish, and Santa's cap was placed atop Ricardo Breceda's 15-foot-tall rattlesnake statue in the middle of town. Jacumba Middle School seventh grader Ryan Luongo also won first prize for the pictured Santa & Sleigh entry in the Christmas tumbleweed contest. (Courtesy of Danielle Thomas.)

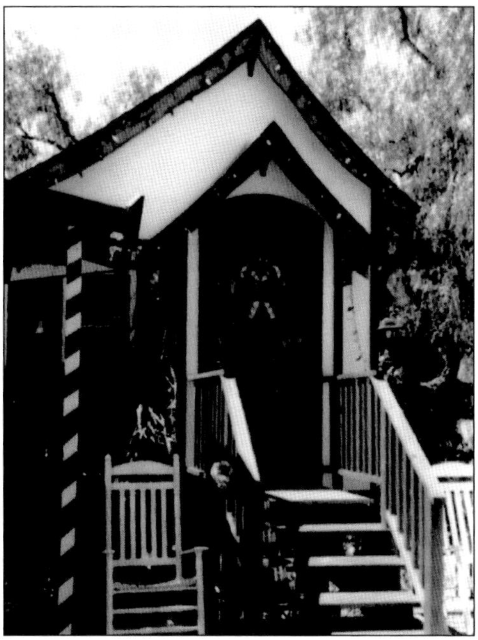

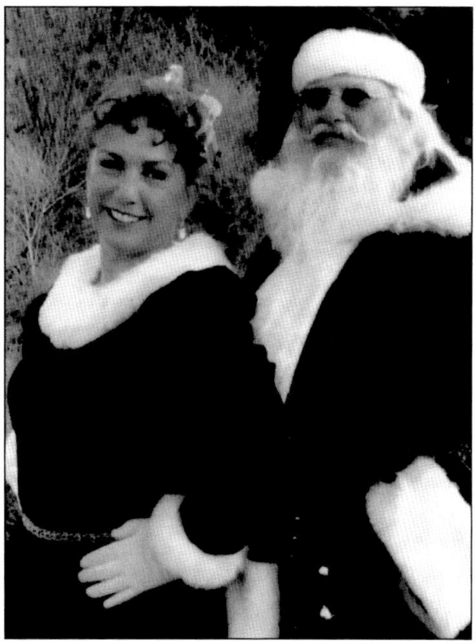

**As Seen on TV.** Santa's Treehouse in Jamul was featured on the Animal Planet television series *Treehouse Masters* as part of their 2013 Christmas special. It belongs to Tom and Kathie Wellington, who both dress in red for the season. The couple belongs to the San Diego chapter of the Fraternal Order of Real Bearded Santas. Tom has been a Santa for over 15 years, taking up the suit when a family member outgrew it. Tom has loved Santa since he was a little boy. (Courtesy of Santa's Treehouse.)

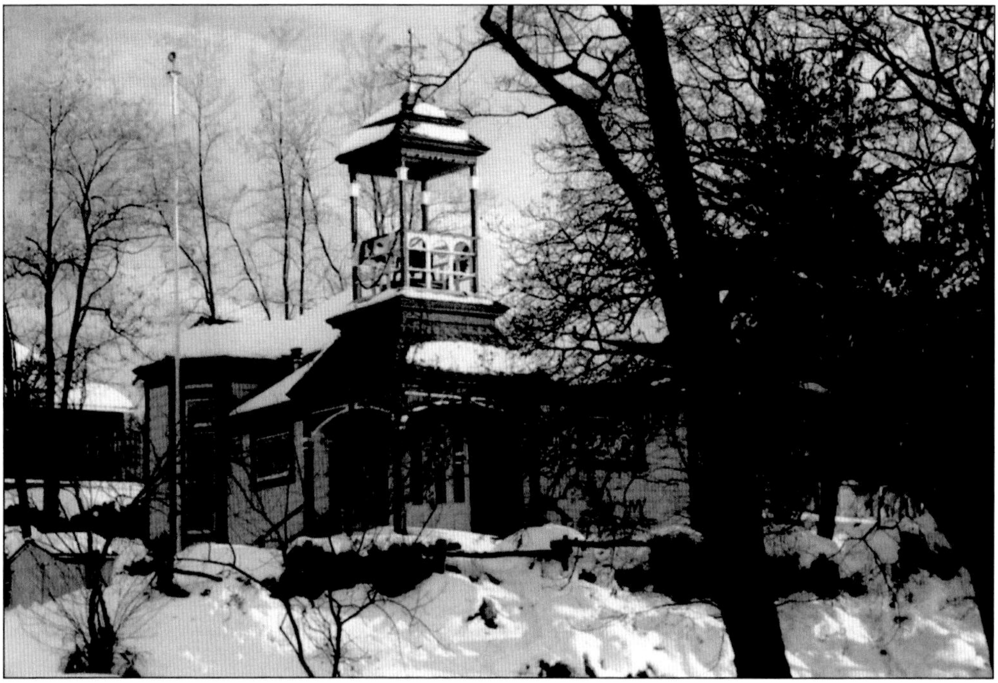

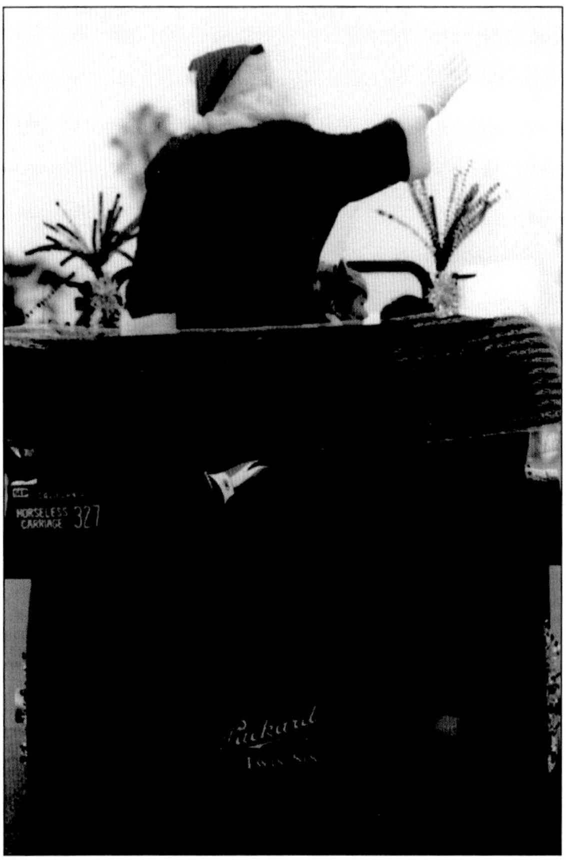


**CHRISTMAS IN JULIAN.** Julian historian David Lewis has spent years searching for an elusive picture of the Julian Christmas tree that stood in the middle of the intersection of Main and Washington Streets. Currently, the town's enormous living Christmas tree is lit in Julian Pioneer Park. Seen here under a blanket of snow is the quaint headquarters of the Julian Historical Society. The building is the former one-room Witch Creek school house, which was moved to Julian in 1974. (Courtesy of *East County Magazine*.)

**SANTA IN THE LA JOLLA CHRISTMAS PARADE.** The La Jolla Christmas Parade is a colorful and eclectic mix of camels, surfers, classic Thunderbirds, the Weinermobile, the Eiffel Tower, the Grinch, the Goodwill Industries synchronized Christmas Shopping Cart Team, a marching guitar band, a flying saucer, a biplane squadron flyover, and Santa. He is shown in a 1915 Packard known as "The Old Black Goose." (Courtesy of David Max.)

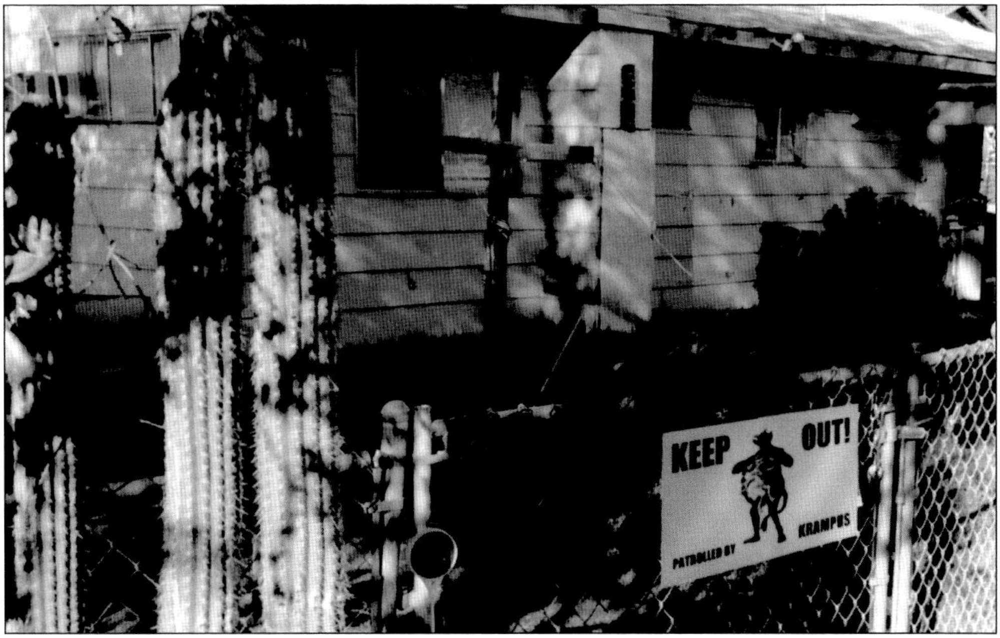


**Lake Morena Village Signage.** Over the years, there have been numerous sightings of paranormal activity at Lake Morena. Reports of a "ghostly young woman in a long white dress," and "a walking man whose feet don't touch the ground" are part of the area's backcountry lore. A local property owner posted this sign, reading "Keep Out. Patrolled by Krampus," to discourage interlopers from trespassing during the holiday season. Krampus is a medieval Germanic beast who grabbed naughty children at Christmas and hauled them off to his lair. (Courtesy of Patrick Mulroy.)

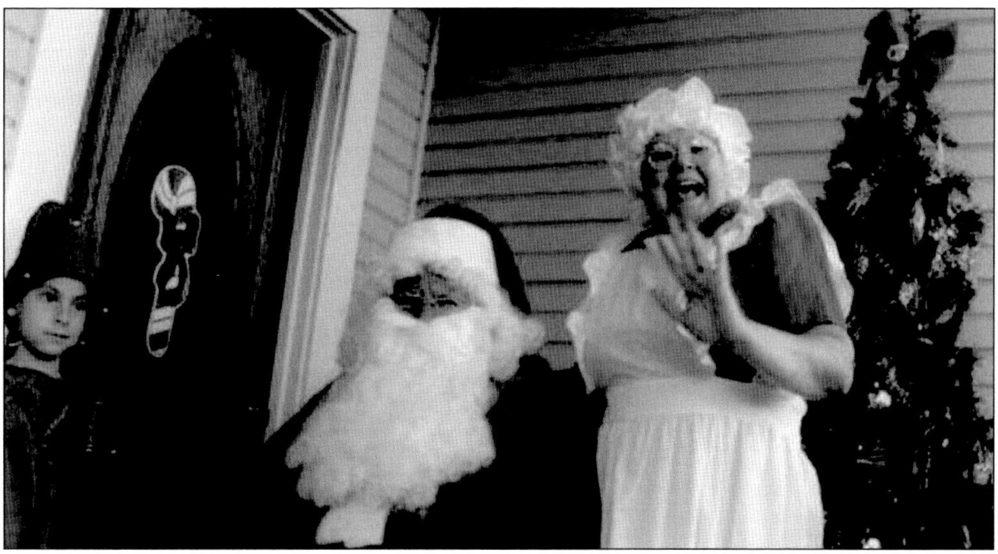

**Lakeside's "Spirit of Christmas."** The Lakeside Chamber of Commerce sponsors the annual Spirit of Christmas celebration along Maine Avenue. Entertainment includes a visit with Santa, games and activities, a "jumpy jump," food and drink, performances by local schools, and a tree lighting. Kids are encouraged to ride the train down Maine Avenue and drop letters to Santa in a special North Pole mailbox, along with an envelope for a personal reply from the man himself. (Courtesy of *East County Magazine*.)

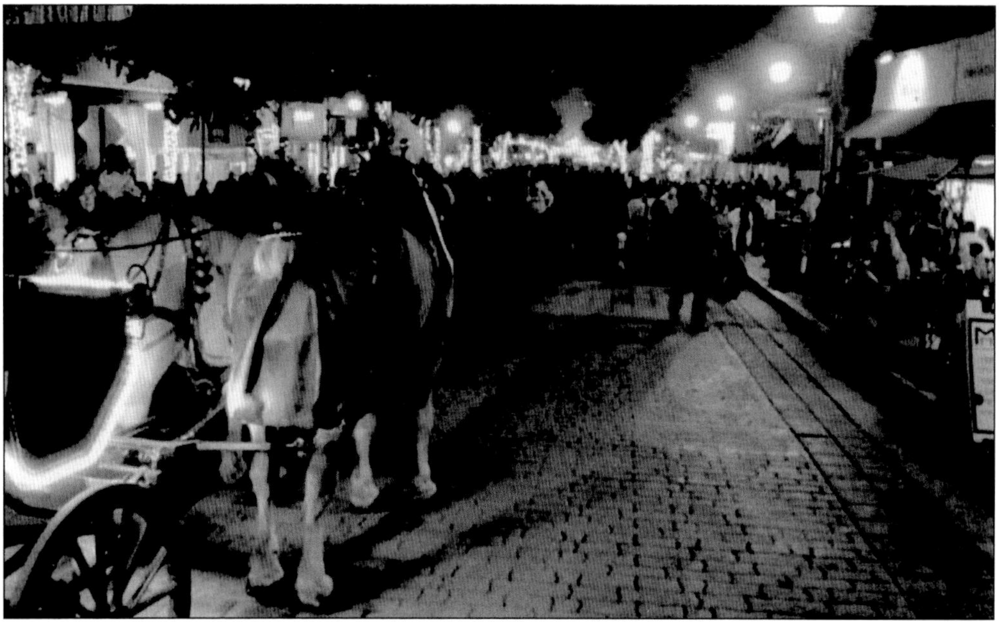

**La Mesa Christmas.** "Light up the Village" is the goal of the La Mesa Village Merchant's Association during their annual Victorian Village Wonderland. Along with a holiday parade, there are strolling minstrels, carolers, street entertainers, bonfires, carnival rides, puppet shows, ponies, Santa, and a toy drive. The storefronts along La Mesa Boulevard are lit up for an old-fashioned Christmas. (Courtesy of Gina Garcia, *La Mesa Today*.)

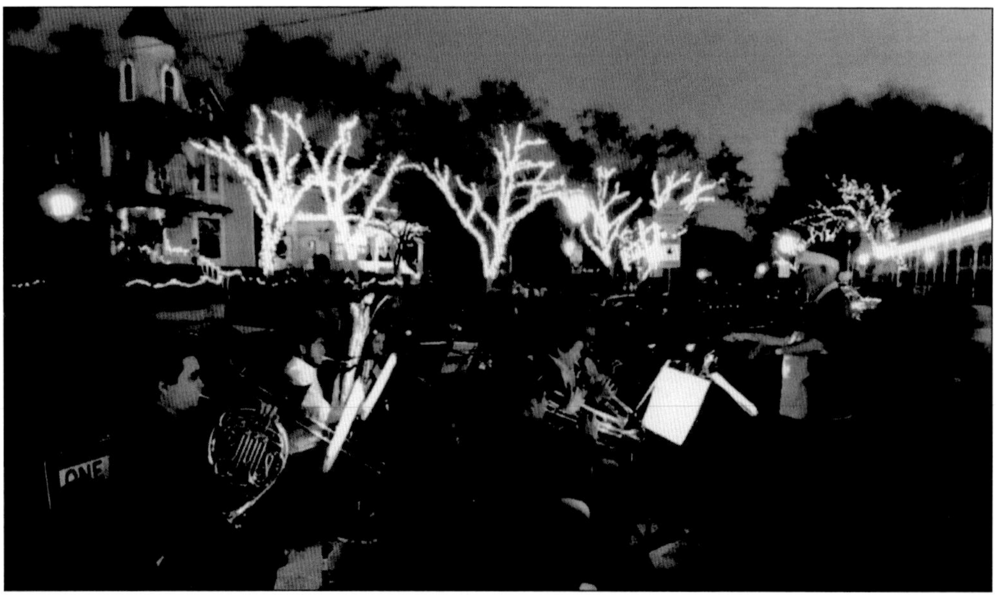

**National City.** In 1875, Frank Kimball hosted one of National City's earliest Christmas celebrations. As was the custom, gifts, cookies, and candy were hung on a pine tree he cut from the yard. The National City Community Concert Band played Christmas music at the 2013 Tree Lighting Celebration on Heritage Square, as seen here. In the background are the historic Elizur Steele and Frank Kimball houses on the left, and Brick Row on the right. (Courtesy of the South Bay Historical Society.)

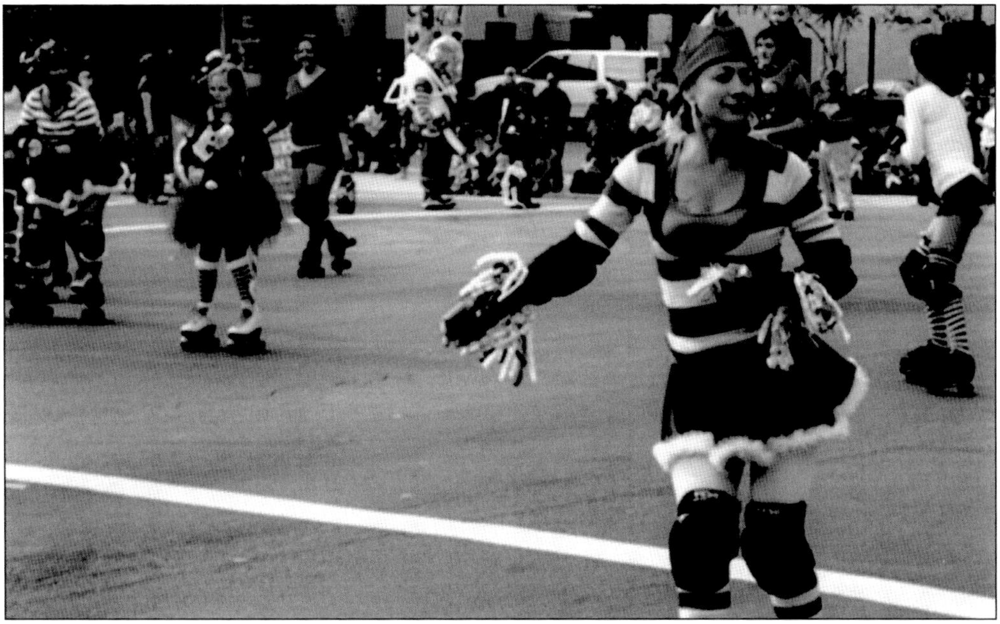

**North Park Toyland Parade.** The North Park Toyland Parade began in 1936. Joe Schloss, who opened A&B Sporting Goods in 1946, remembers that his father, Dave Schloss, was Santa in the parade for over 25 years. The parade disappeared in the 1960s, when shoppers headed to the malls, but made a successful return under the auspices of North Park Main Street in the late 1980s. Victorian House Corporation, which began as a women's shelter, assumed responsibility for the Toyland Parade in 2012. (Courtesy of M.L. Bey.)

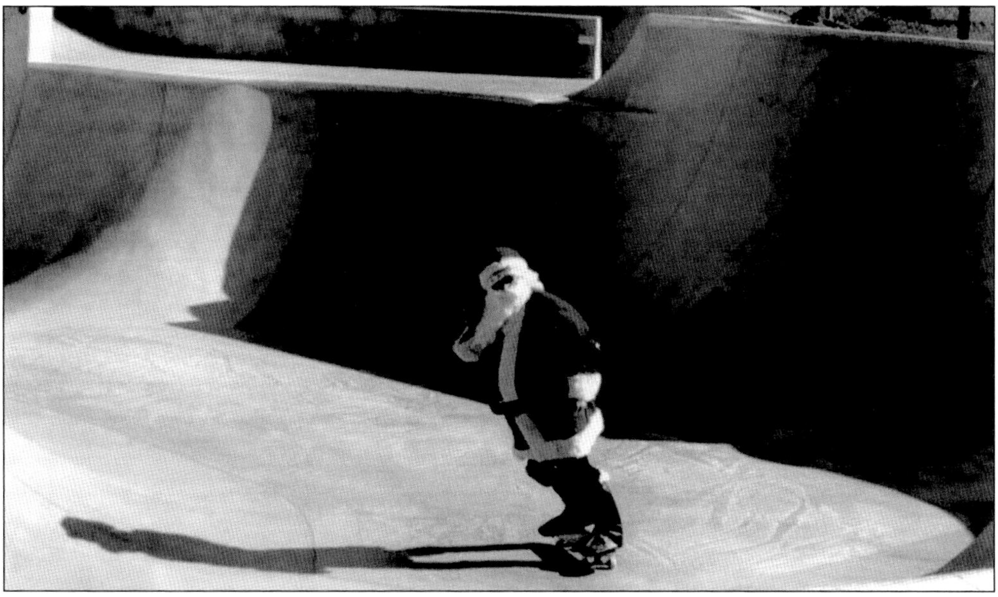

**Skateboard Santa in Oceanside.** Wearing the red suit, professional skateboarder Andy Macdonald shows his stuff at the Oceanside Martin Luther King Skate Park in December 2013. Macdonald, an eight-time World Cup Skateboarding champion, holds the X Games record for most medals won in "vert skateboard." Where else can you watch Santa perform a backside noseslide to nollie heelflip 180? (Courtesy of Eileen Lohner-Turk.)

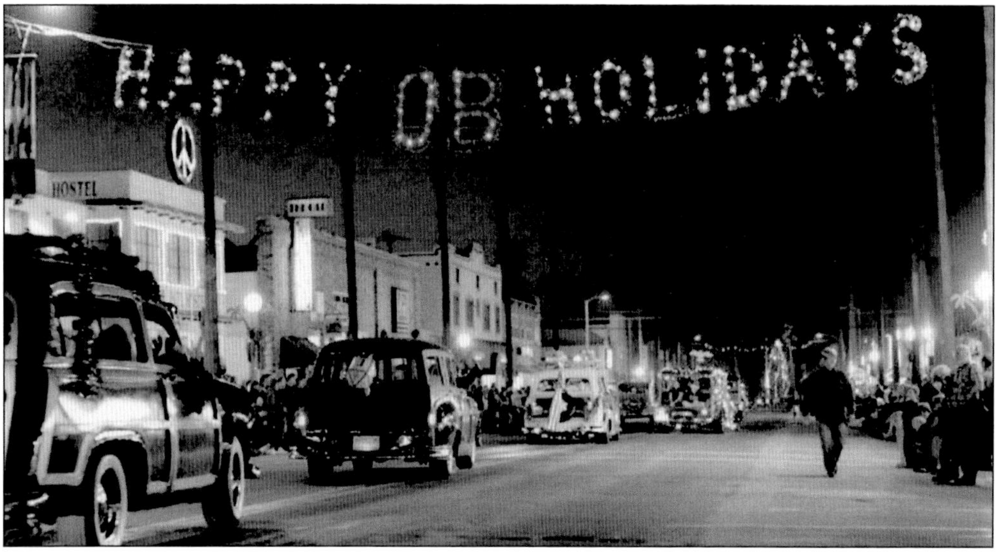


**Happy OB Holidays.** Classic wagons from the San Diego Woodie Club cruise Newport Avenue during the Ocean Beach Christmas Parade. Joining the cavalcade of wheels are decorated VW vans, Beetles, hot rods, vintage sports cars, Chopper the Biker Dog, OB's Finest Blue Streak Racer, the SDPD paddy wagon, and perennial mayoral candidate Loch David Crane aboard his Star Trike. (Courtesy of Joe Ewing.)

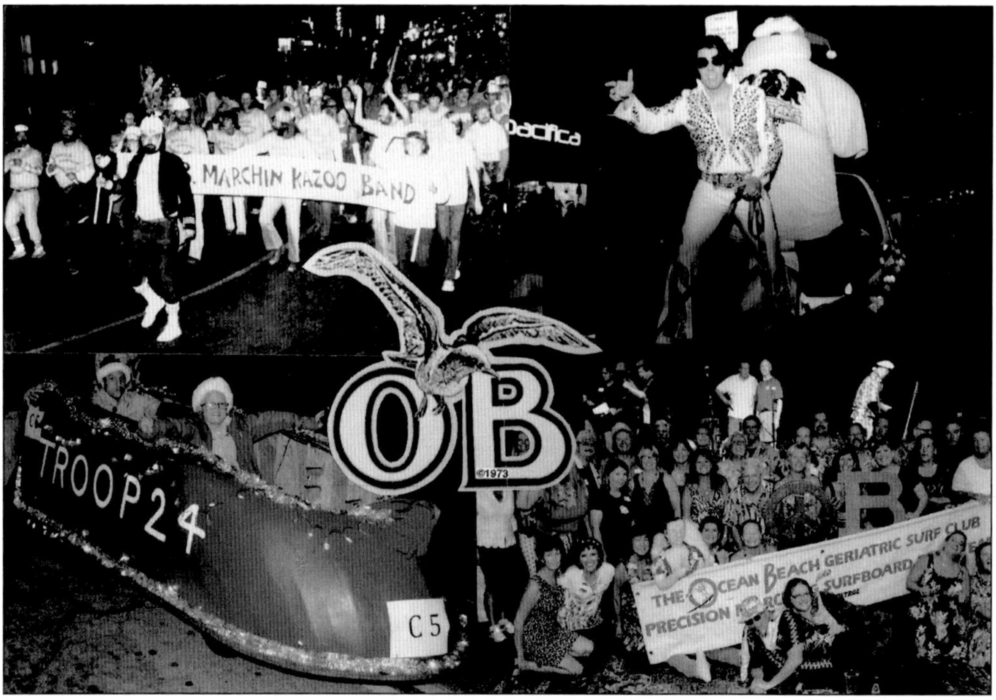


**OB Christmas Parade.** The Ocean Beach Christmas Parade didn't begin until the 1970s, but laidback OB remains a 1960s time capsule. Over the years, this eclectic spectacle has featured diverse elements such as the Geriatric Marching Surfboard Drill Team and Gidget Patrol, the San Diego Dolls roller derby team, Elvis, Boy Scout Troop 24's Red Hot Weinermobile, Godzilla, and, of course, the original OB Marchin' Kazoo Band. (Courtesy of Joe Ewing.)

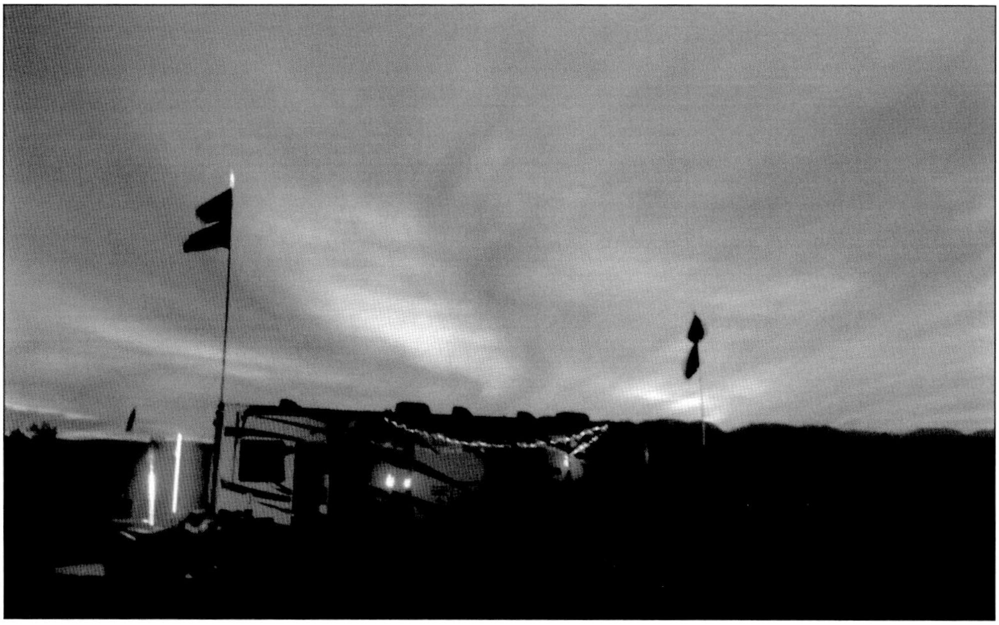

**Christmas Lights in Ocotillo Wells.** Tom and Tami Glander enjoy camping in the desert. They have a favorite site in Ocotillo Wells and, with a portable generator, all the comforts of home—including a string of Christmas lights. Tom described this trip as "extraordinarily uneventful." Looking west from the Imperial County line, the December sun has set behind the Laguna Mountains and the desert sky is a swirl of color. (Courtesy of Tom Glander.)

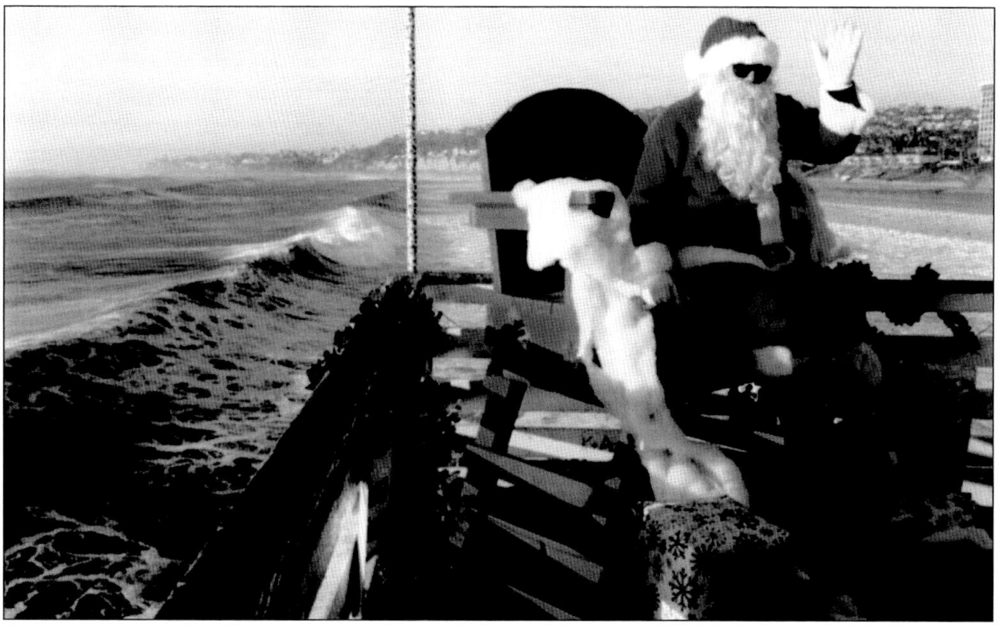

**Santa Claus Presides over the Pacific Ocean.** Santa holds court in his red lifeguard chair, on Crystal Pier, as the surf breaks beneath him. At sunset, the lights of the Christmas Tree glow over the Pacific Ocean. The Pacific Beach Community Advisory Committee also sponsors the PB Holiday Parade and the Bikes, Boards, and Brews winter festival. (Courtesy of the *Beach & Bay Press.*)

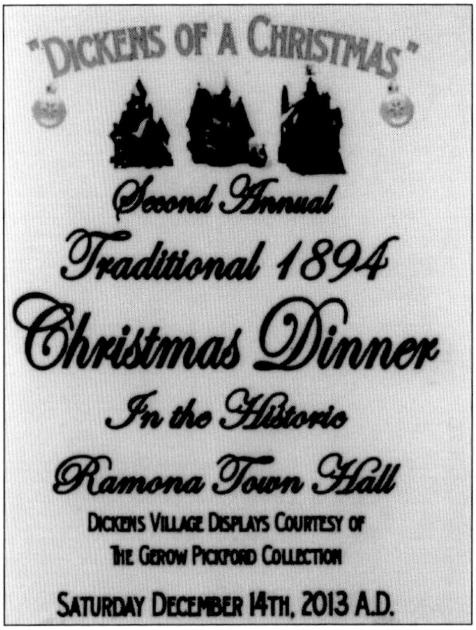


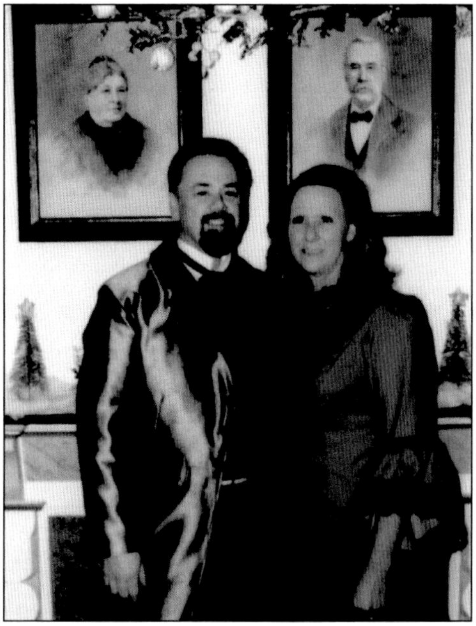

**Dickens of a Christmas Dinner.** Ramona was known as the Turkey Capital of the World in the 1930s, so appropriately, guests at the Dickens Christmas Dinner feast on roast turkey with all the trimmings. The historic Ramona Town Hall, is one of the largest and oldest adobe structures in the Southwest United States. The "Dickens of a Christmas Dinner" commemorates the first Christmas dinner held at the hall, in 1894. (Courtesy of the Ramona Town Hall.)

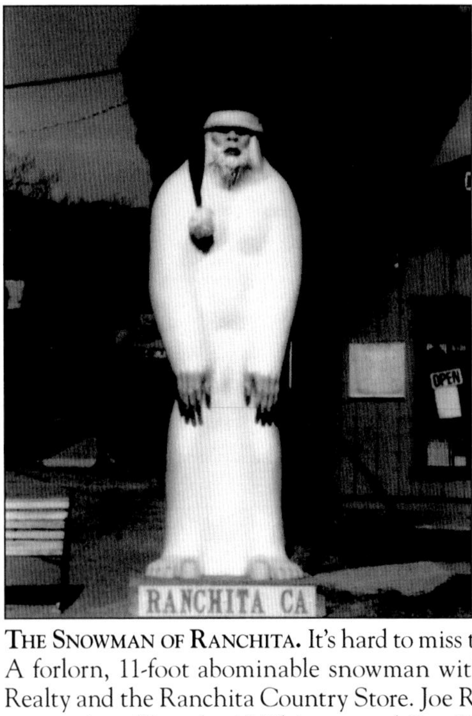


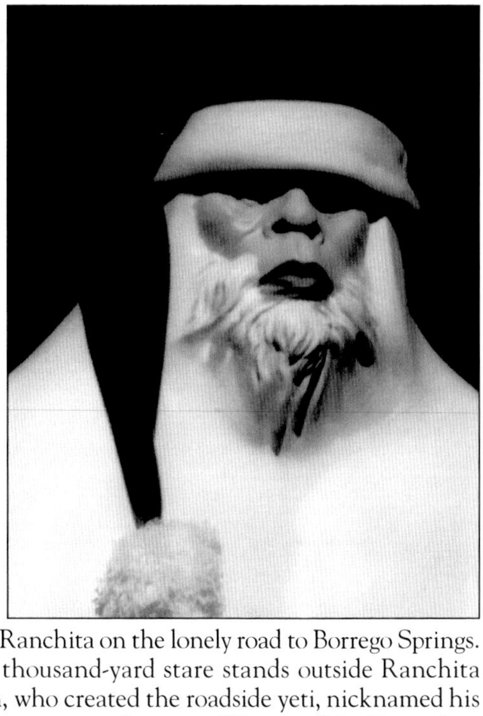

**The Snowman of Ranchita.** It's hard to miss tiny Ranchita on the lonely road to Borrego Springs. A forlorn, 11-foot abominable snowman with a thousand-yard stare stands outside Ranchita Realty and the Ranchita Country Store. Joe Rauh, who created the roadside yeti, nicknamed his masterpiece "Rancheti." This unusual San Diego snowman becomes "Santaeti" in December, when Rauh places a red chapeau over the head of the dour beast. (Courtesy of Joe Rauh.)

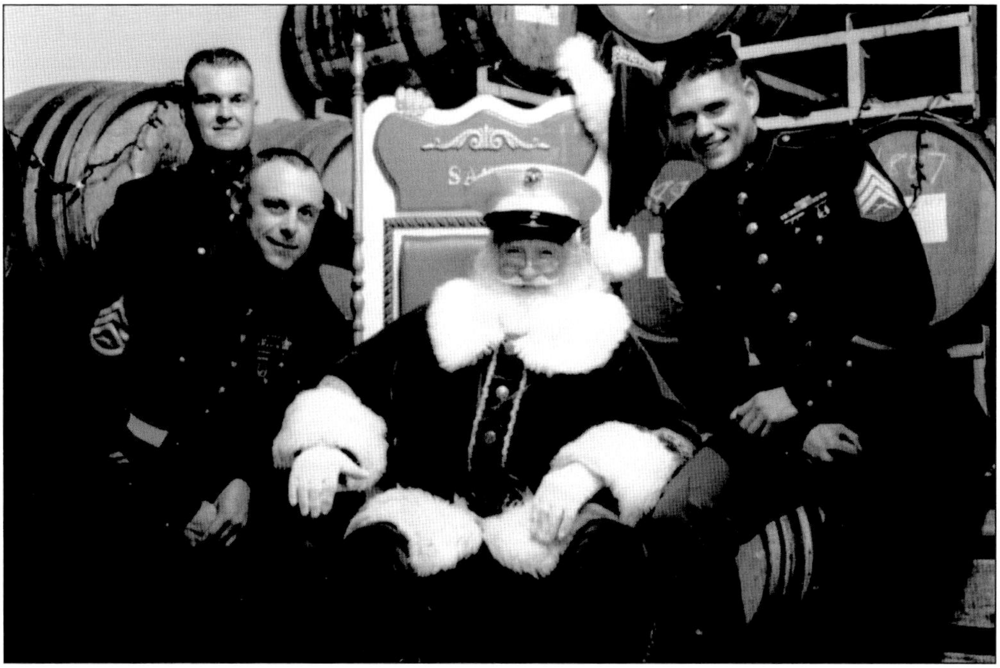

**CHRISTMAS IN JULY.** The Port Brewing Company hosts an annual Christmas in July party at the Lost Abbey Tasting Room in San Marcos. A full lineup of Port and Lost Abbey beverages is on tap, including the ever-popular Santa's Little Helper, "a robust beer with tones of sweet malt, dark cocoa and notes of deep bourbon . . . the perfect accompaniment to fruit cake during a California Christmas in July." Here, Marines and barrels of Santa's Little Helper surround G/Sgt. Christmas. (Courtesy of the Port Brewing Company.)

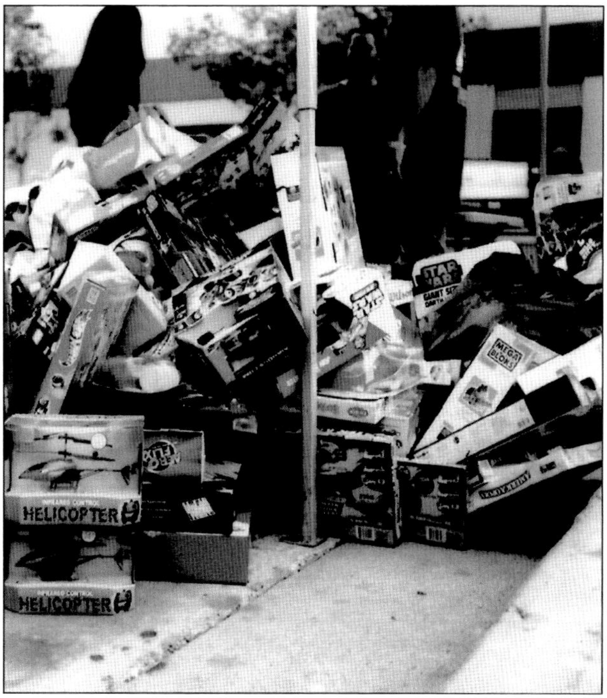


**TOYS FOR TOTS.** Party guests must bring a toy valued at $15 or more for the Marine Corps Toys for Tots campaign. Toys for Tots started in 1947, in Los Angeles, and was quickly adopted nationwide by the Marine Corps Reserve. During the past 67 years, the Marines have distributed over half-a-billion toys to boys and girls. *Reader's Digest* named the Marine Toys for Tots Foundation as America's Best Children's Charity in 2003. Some of the toys donated at Lost Abbey's 2014 Christmas in July party are shown here. (Courtesy of the Port Brewing Company.)

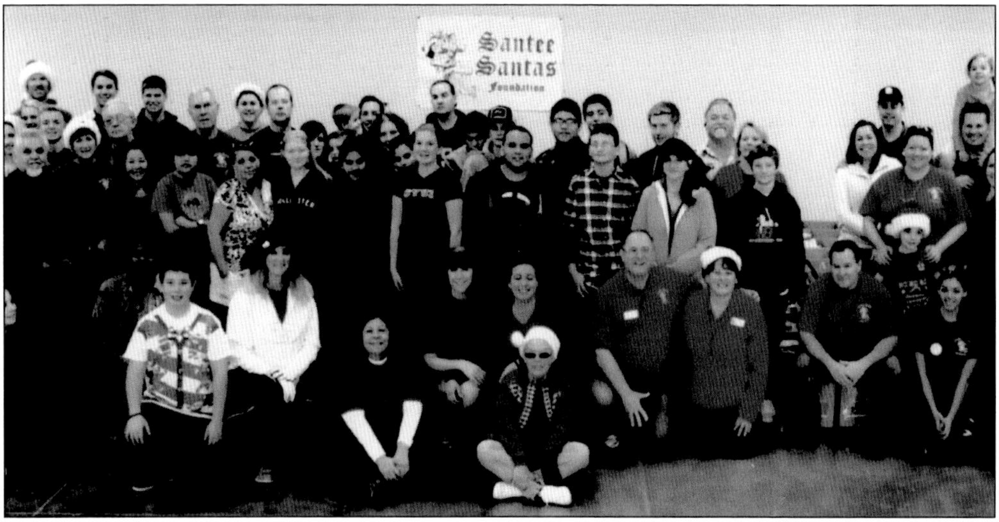


**SANTEE SANTAS.** In 1953, Santee only had one school. The Santee Santas were formed that year to help a few needy families at Christmas. Today, over 50,000 people live in Santee and over 200 volunteer Santas continue the legacy. In 2013, Santee Santas served 222 families—which included 406 children. A great name for a great organization! (Courtesy of Sam Modica.)

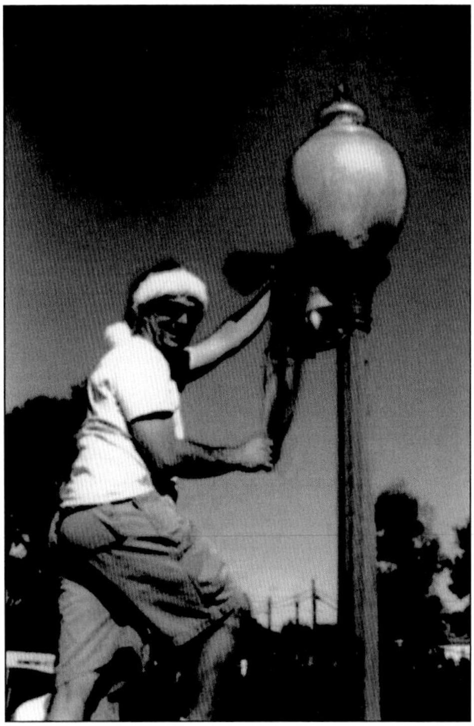

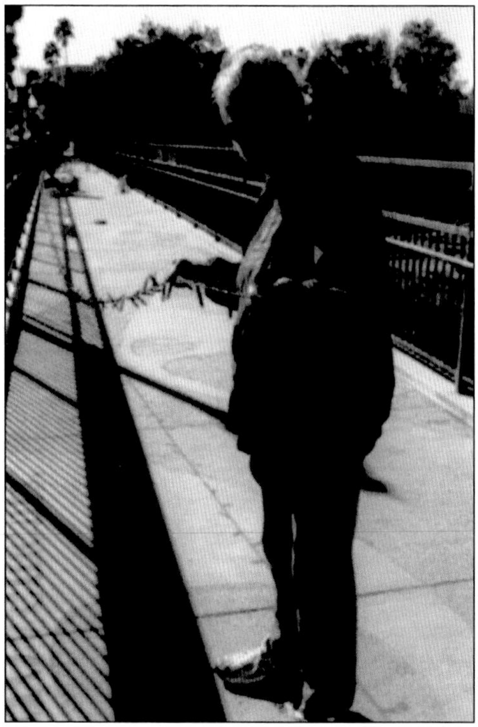

**THE VERMONT STREET BRIDGE.** The original, 1916, wooden trestle Vermont Street Bridge—spanning Washington Street—connected University Heights and Hillcrest. It was replaced in 1994 with a modern, 420-foot-long steel bridge. Every year, volunteers from the University Heights Community Association decorate the structure with lights, ribbons, and bells. UHCA also sponsors community caroling and the Light Up the Heights competition. (Courtesy of the University Heights Community Association.)

# *Four*

# Trees

*Merry Christmas from Sunny San Diego*

*December 25, 1957 Temperature: 70 Degrees*

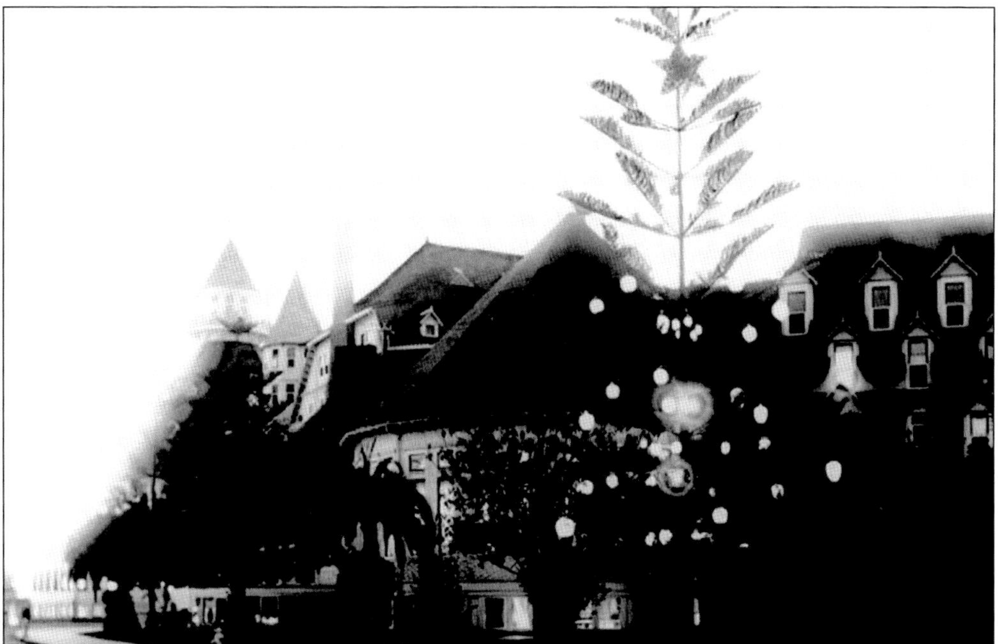

**First Electrically Lighted Outdoor Christmas Tree.** On Christmas Eve, 1904, there were 250 colored lights—strung on a 55-foot Norfolk Island pine outside the Hotel del Coronado—illuminated the world's first electrically lighted outdoor Christmas tree. The tree inside the hotel remained traditionally lit by candles, with buckets of sand and water close at hand.

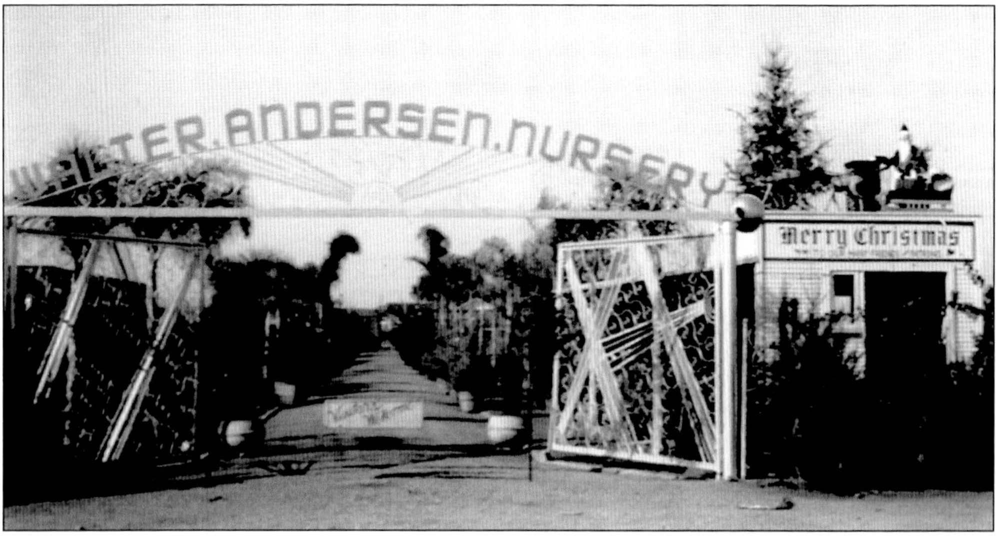


**Walter Andersen Nursery.** Since 1928, when the nursery opened in Old Town and later moved to Rosecrans (shown), Christmas has always been important to the Walter Andersen family. The senior Mr. Andersen began the tradition of offering customers a wide selection of quality Christmas trees and poinsettias. The nursery has been at its present location on Enterprise Street since 1969 and continues to be a popular destination for Christmas trees, poinsettia, and pictures with Santa Claus. (Courtesy of Walter Andersen.)

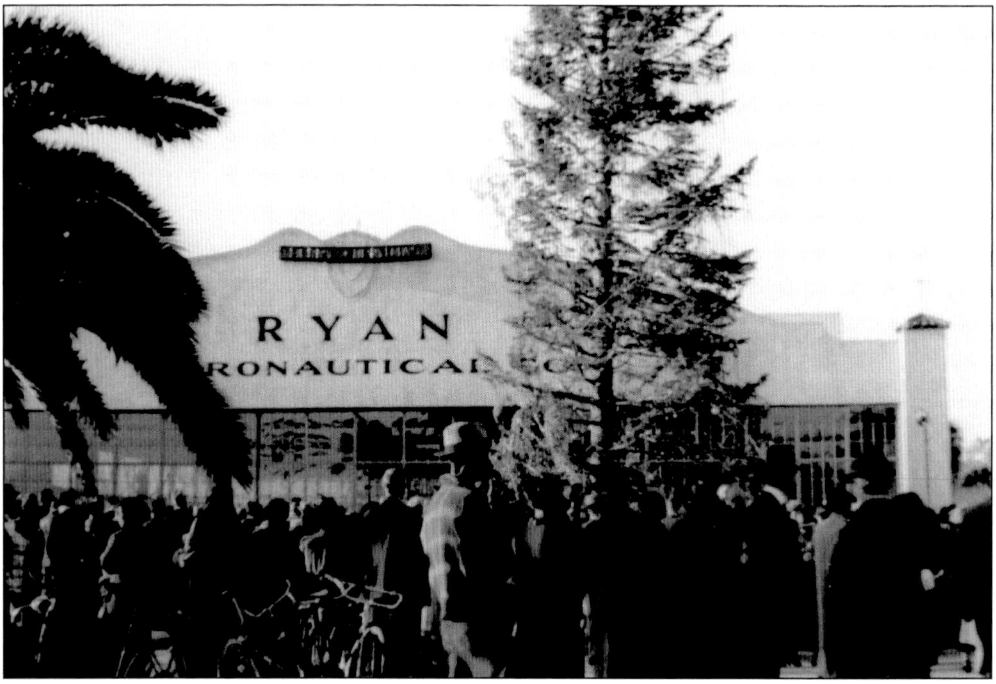


**Ryan Aeronautical Christmas Tree.** This picture was taken in the mid-1930s, when Ryan Aeronautical began full-scale production of the Army's first monoplane trainer—the PT-22 Recruit. The sign on the building reads "Merry Christmas." It was the middle of the Great Depression, and a crowd gathered to apply for employment. Those lucky enough to get jobs were probably much merrier that year.

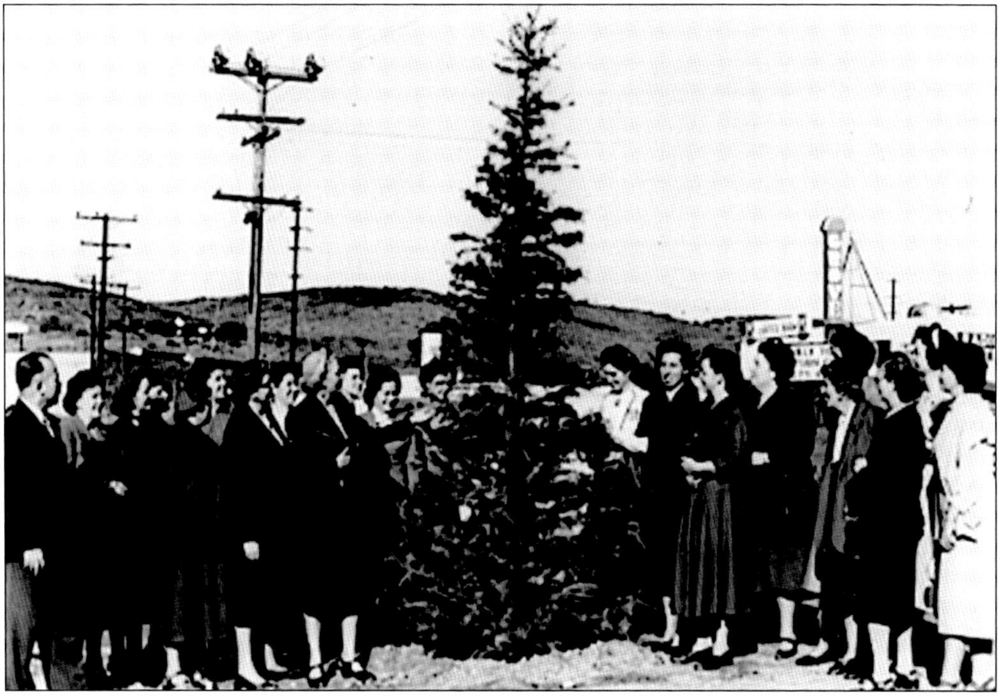

**Lemon Grove Christmas Tree.** In 1952, the Lemon Grove Business Women's League planted a beautiful Deodar Cedar Christmas tree at Broadway and Imperial Avenue. According to Lemon Grove Historical Society president Helen Ofield, "The tree, along with a nativity scene, remained for more than a decade until road-widening and disputes over civic-sanctioned Christmas decorations eliminated it. Standing center left of the tree is Dr. Amorita Treganza, the first Miss Lemon Grove in 1928." (Courtesy of Helen Ofield.)

**A Christmas Tree Grows in San Diego Bay.** The USS *John Hancock*, CVA-19, was transferred from Bremerton, Washington, to San Diego in December 1954. A 60-foot tree from the Evergreen State was decorated and affixed to the number-one elevator. As the aircraft carrier pulled into North Island, the elevator slowly rose to create the illusion that a giant Christmas tree was growing from the Hancock's flight deck. (Courtesy of Harlan Demsien, Photographer's Mate Second Class, USN.)

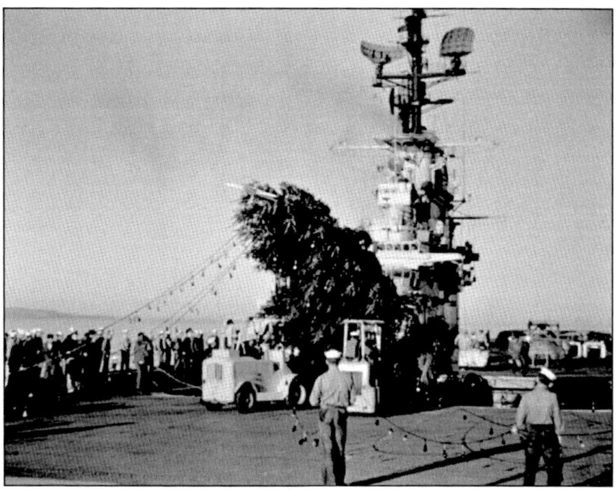

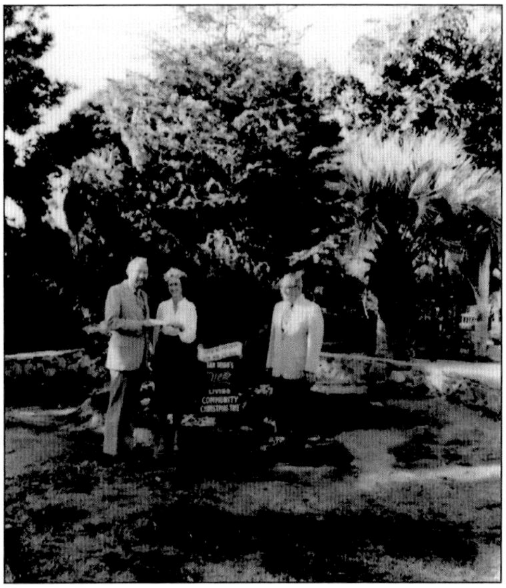

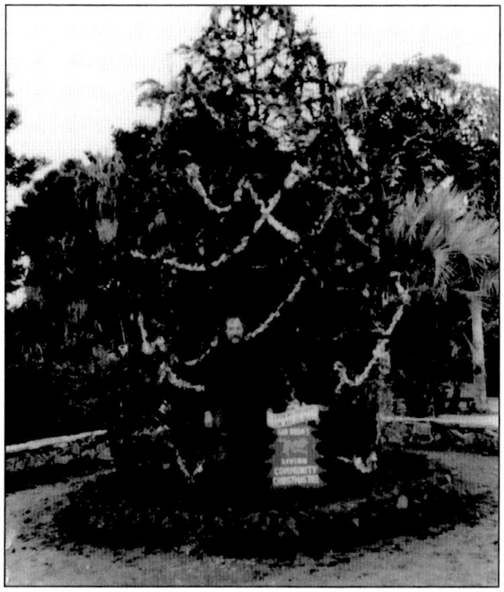

**Community Christmas Tree in Balboa Park.** In 1981, winter storms destroyed the Atlas Cedar that had been used as the community Christmas tree. Later that year, the Community Christmas Center Committee donated a transplanted Deodar Cedar and bronze plaque near the Organ Pavilion. At left, Al Gabbs is shown with city officials at the dedication ceremony and again at right, with the tree decorated for Christmas on the Prado. (Courtesy of the Community Christmas Center Committee.)

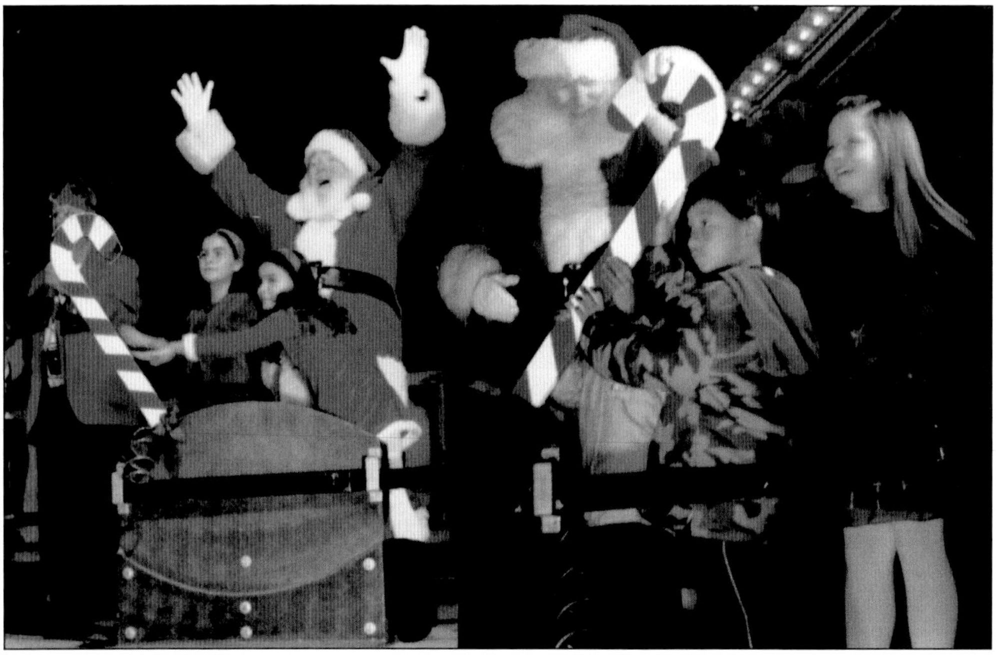

**Lighting the Community Christmas Tree in Balboa Park.** The Saturday after Thanksgiving, kids help Santa flip the switch and light the Community Christmas Tree. In 2004, days before his passing, 90-year-old Al Gabbs and his wife, Anna Belle, helped decorate the tree and flip the switch for the last time. Gabbs and J. Clark Chamberlain each bequeathed generous donations to perpetuate the Community Christmas Center for the enjoyment of all San Diegans.

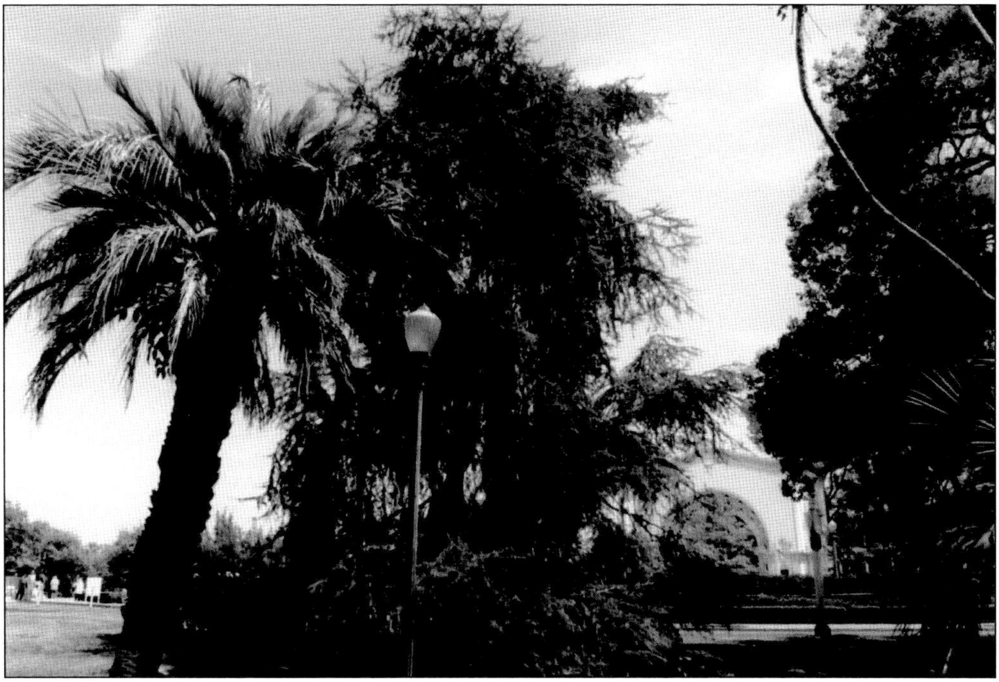

COMMUNITY CHRISTMAS TREE TODAY. *Cedrus deodaras* are commonly used as living Christmas trees. Though pyramidal when young, these evergreens mature into "flat-topped trees with broad-spreading horizontal branching." The tree has reached full maturity and many consider its non-pyramidal appearance to be a civic embarrassment. In 2012, city officials decided it was too old and fragile for decorations and lights.

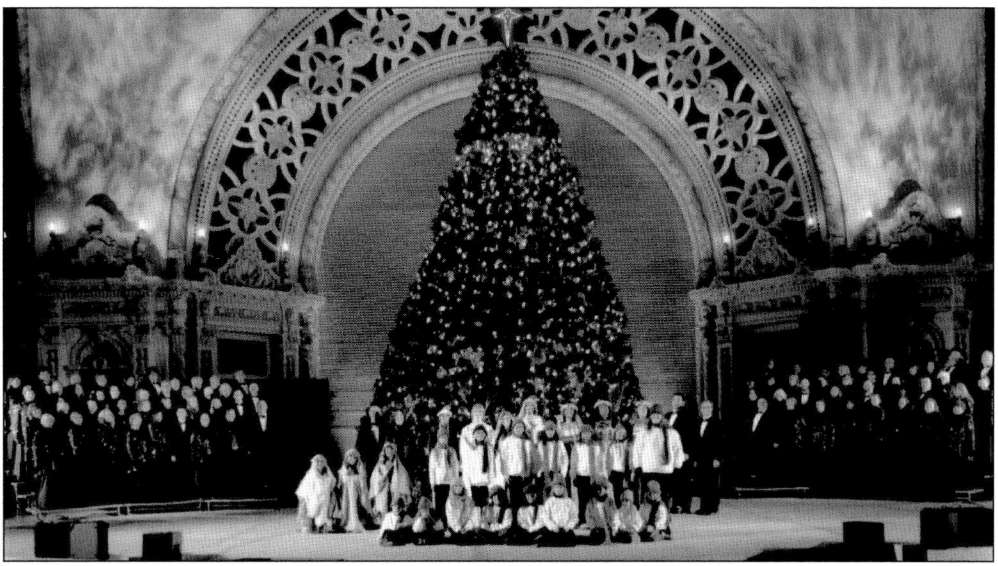

DEL CERRO BAPTIST CHRISTMAS STORY TREE. The Christmas Story Tree first appeared at the Del Cerro Baptist Church in 1976 and moved to the Spreckel's Organ Pavilion in 1986. It is a spectacular light show, with a 30-foot tree, 90-member choir (men in tuxedos, women in evening gowns), and live orchestra. "The choir and drama team present the story of Christmas in music and living scenes." (Courtesy of the Del Cerro Baptist Church.)

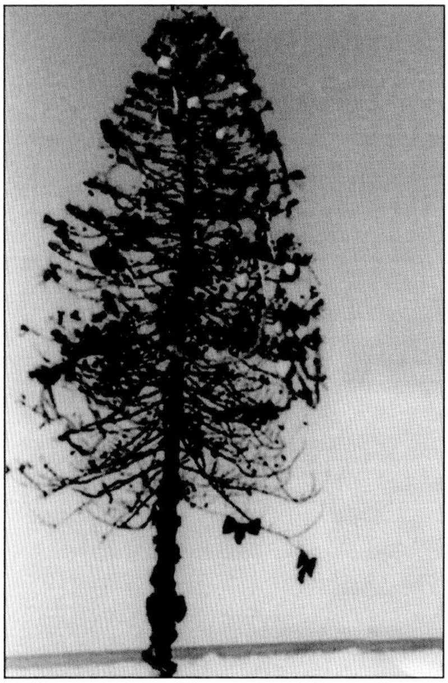

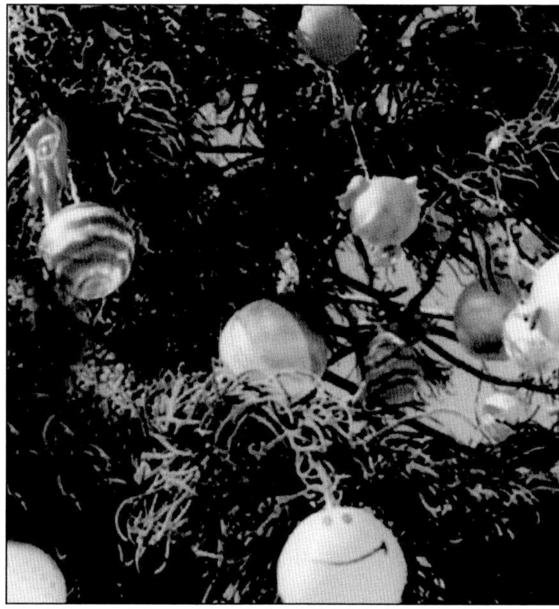

**OCEAN BEACH CHRISTMAS TREE.** The late Rich James is considered the father of the "OB Tree." According to legend, Rich and his brothers were drinking and discussing a Christmas tree for Ocean Beach in 1980. The more they drank, the bigger their ideas grew. Ocean Beach trees are meant to be nontraditional, like the sparse 1987 pine on the left, and it soon became tradition for residents to decorate them with beach balls. (Courtesy of Jean Lewin and Thais Jungblut.)

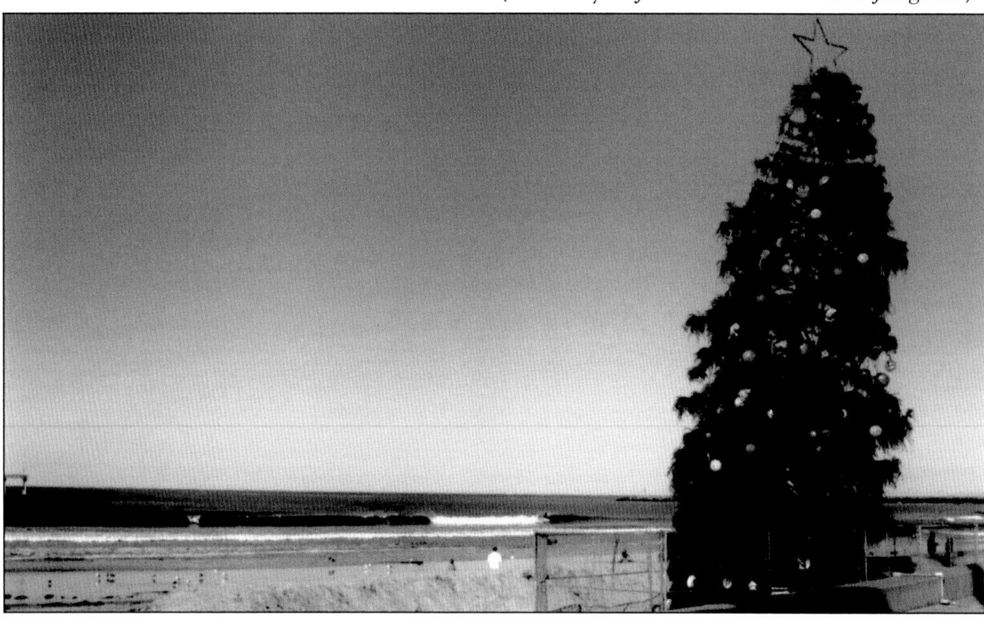

**HEY, THAT'S NOT OB ENOUGH!** Gretchen Newsom, president of the Ocean Beach Town Council, explains, "Whenever we do a tree, we want to find one that can be donated." They have to be tall. One year, there was a problem with a freeway overpass and boughs were lost in transit. However, branches are often cut to allow the trailer to negotiate tight turns on narrow city streets. People complained that the tree pictured was too perfect, and that it "wasn't OB enough." (Courtesy of Robert Jungblut.)

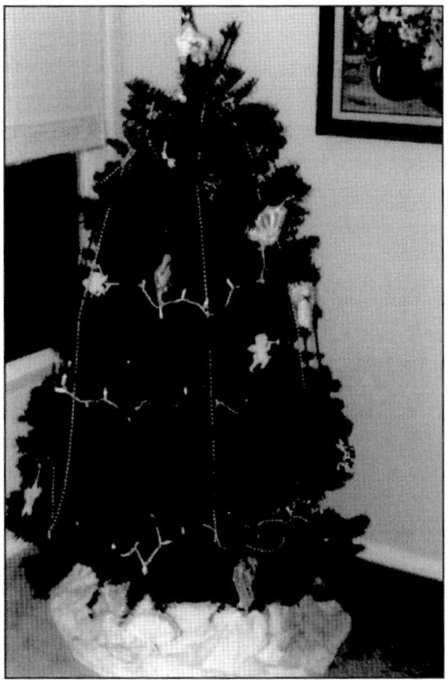 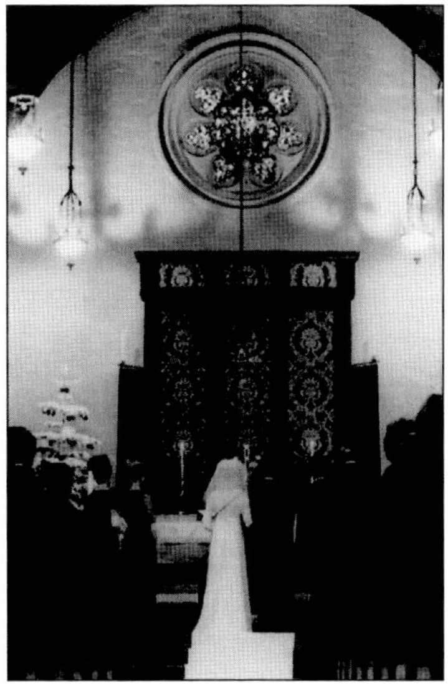

**Latvian Christmas Trees.** The National Christmas Tree Association recognizes Riga, Latvia, as the birthplace of the first decorated Christmas tree, in 1510. Despite claims that Hessian soldiers celebrated around the Christmas tree while Washington's troops crossed the Delaware in 1776, the Pennsylvania Dutch introduced the traditional Christmas tree to America in the early 19th century. The tree on the left is from the home of local Latvian native Janis Legzdins. At right is the 1966 Latvian Christmas Eve wedding of Vija and Arturs Burgelis, at Grace Lutheran Church. (Courtesy of Janis Legzdins.)

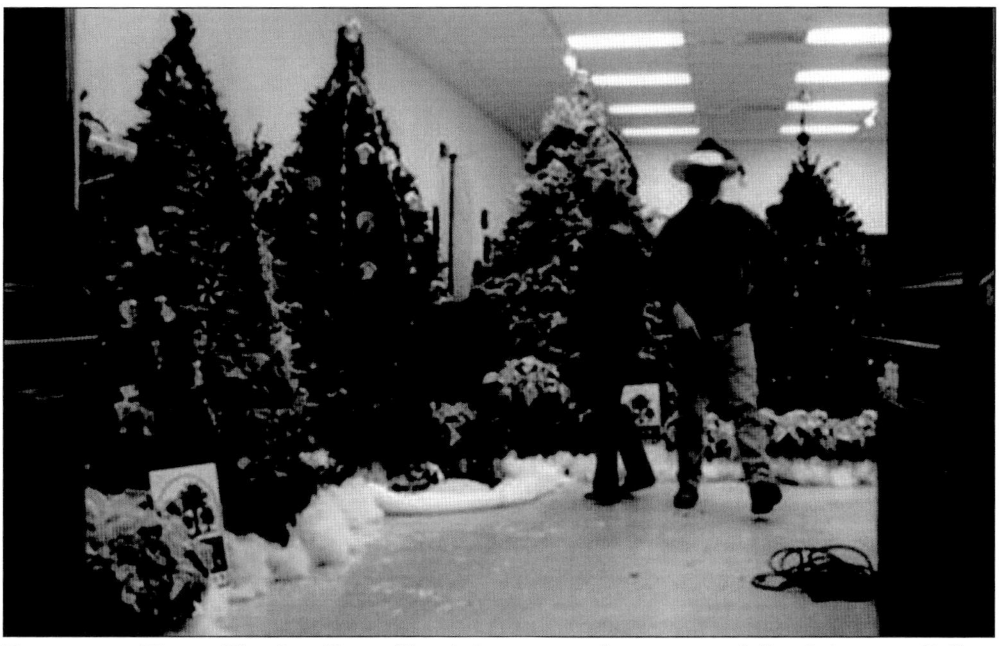

**Festival of Trees.** The San Diego Floral Association has organized floral shows in Balboa Park for 100 years. In 1978, their annual December show was one of the original attractions of Christmas on the Prado. It evolved into the Festival of Trees, at the Casa del Prado. Local garden clubs, schools, youth groups and nonprofit organizations decorate the trees. The Park's centennial celebration will feature "Holiday Trees of 1915 and Beyond." (Courtesy of Walter Andersen.)

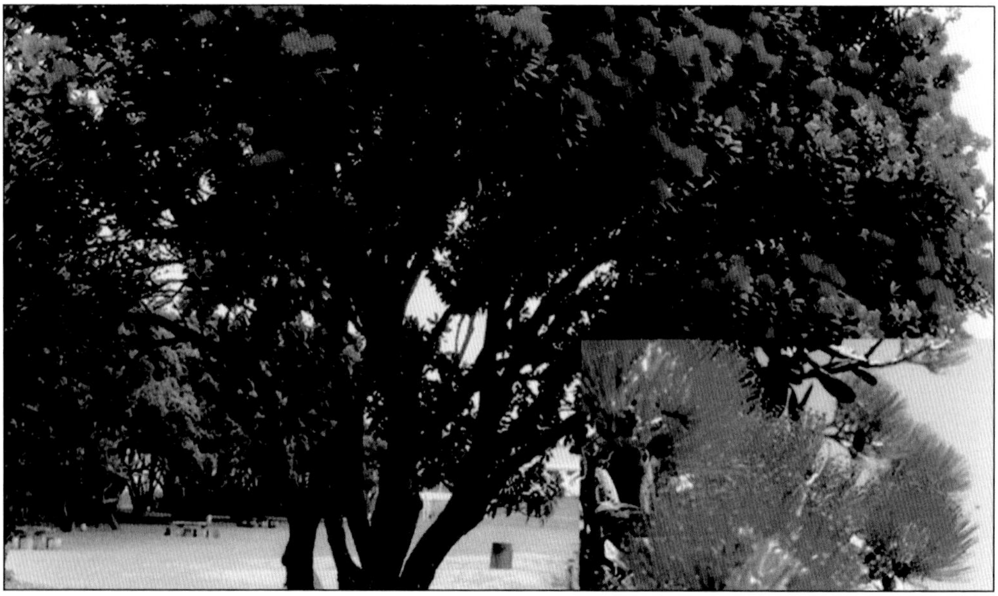

**New Zealand Christmas Tree.** Among the many trees that Kate Sessions planted in Balboa Park, one of the most colorful is the New Zealand Christmas tree. It is primarily found on the grounds of the San Diego Zoo. Kiwis don't decorate this tree at Yuletide, and its name comes from the brilliant canopy of bright red flowers that appear in late December. Because San Diego is in the northern hemisphere, our New Zealand Christmas trees bloom in late June. (Courtesy of Trevor Dickinson.)

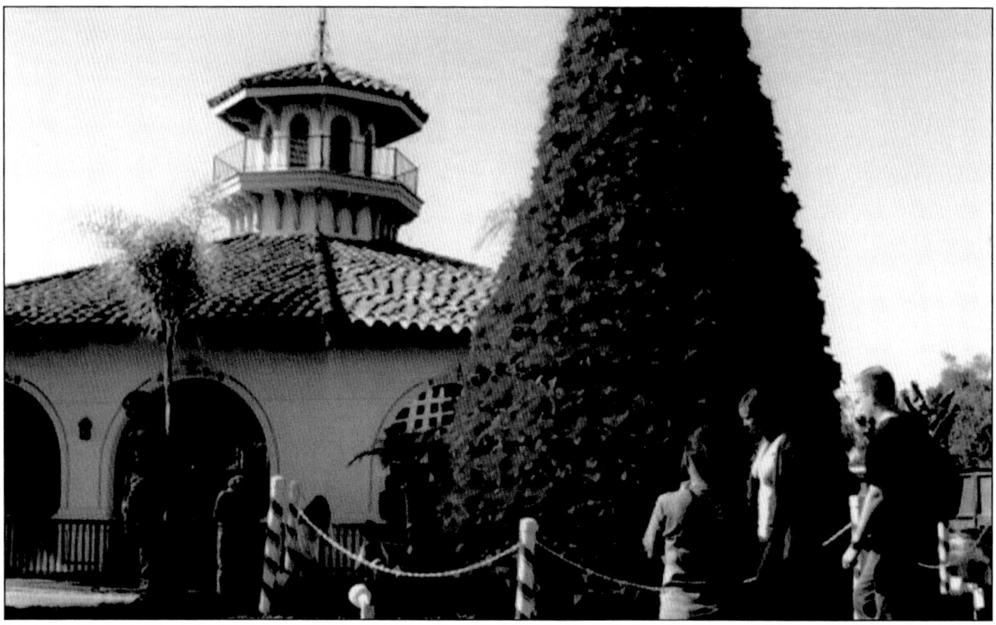

**Poinsettia Tree at Seaport Village.** One of the most spectacular Christmas trees in town is the giant poinsettia tree beside the Seaport Village carousel. Crafted from poinsettia plants wired to over 20 graduated concentric circles, the tree reaches over 20 feet in height. Each plant is on an individual drip irrigation system. It has been a holiday landmark since 2000. (Courtesy of coolsandiegosights.com.)

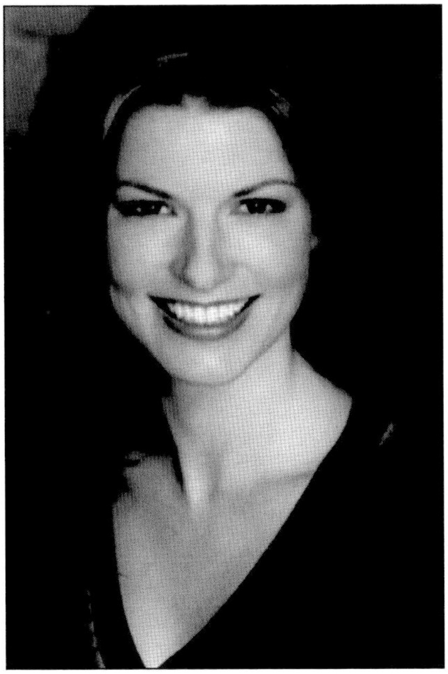

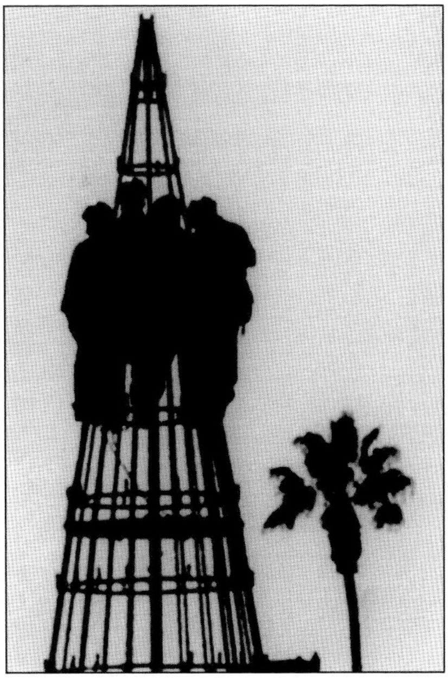

**Del Mar Christmas Tree.** Stuck in traffic on her way to work in early December 2011, NBC Channel 7 weather anchor Dagmar Midcap (left) captured this image of four silhouetted construction workers high atop a scaffold pyramid in Del Mar. They were preparing the structure for layers of decorations. Dagmar added, "The 'tree' sure does sparkle beautifully now. It reminded me a bit of 'the Charlie Brown' Tree . . . just needed a little bit of love." (Courtesy of Dagmar Midcap.)

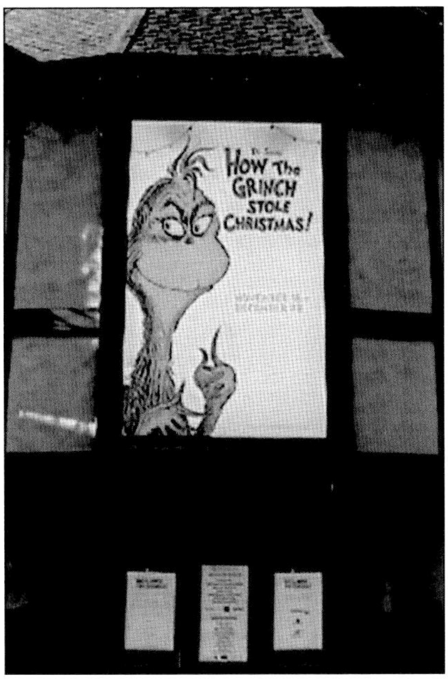


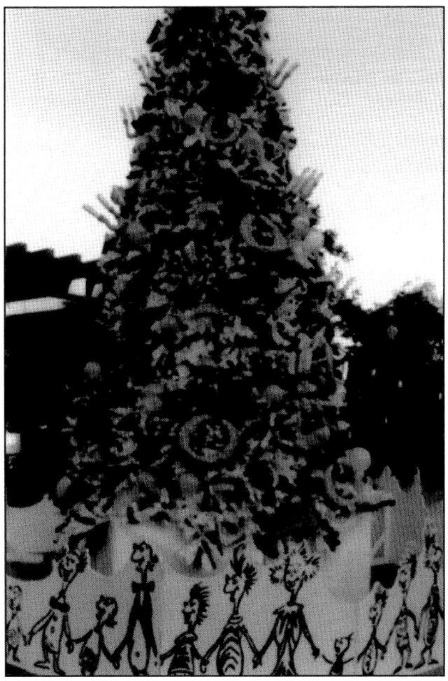

**Grinch Christmas Tree Lighting.** The Old Globe Theater's performance of Dr. Seuss's *How the Grinch Stole Christmas!* has been a staple of the holiday season in Balboa Park since 1997. The lighting of the Grinch Christmas Tree is held in mid-November. The smiling, singing residents of Whoville surround the base of this large, whimsical tree of cartoon candelabras, balls, wreaths, and red ribbon bows. (Courtesy of coolsandiegosights.com.)

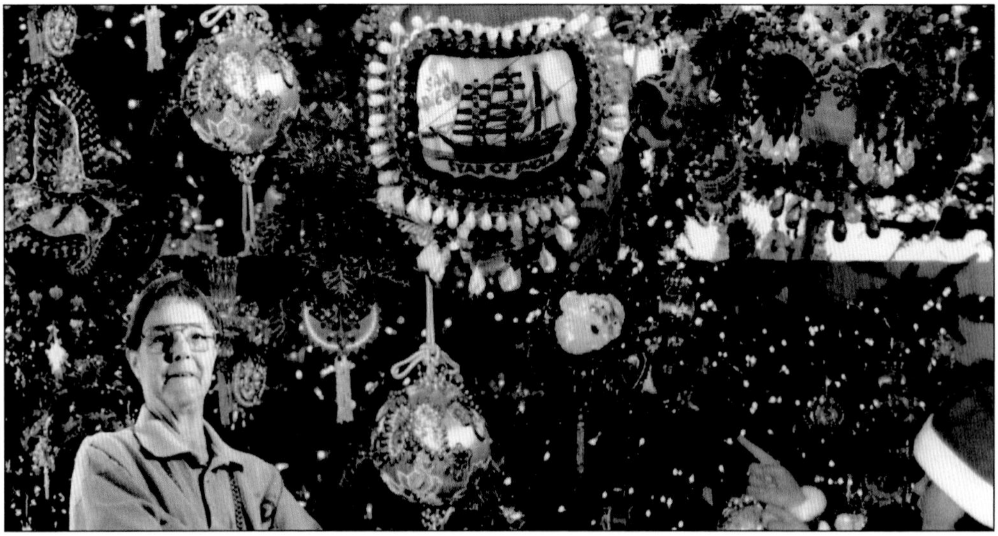

**The Hord-Schlappi Ornament Collection.** Florence Hord, wife of famed San Diego sculptor Donal Hord, was an accomplished artist in her own right. She began creating highly original Christmas ornaments in the 1930s. Florence was joined 30 years later by an enthusiastic elementary school teacher named Elizabeth Schlappi (pictured). Today, the Hord-Schlappi collection exceeds 2,000 ornaments. For the past 28 years, they have decorated what has been described as "the Lady Gaga of Christmas trees" for the Timken Gallery. (Courtesy of Elizabeth Schlappi.)

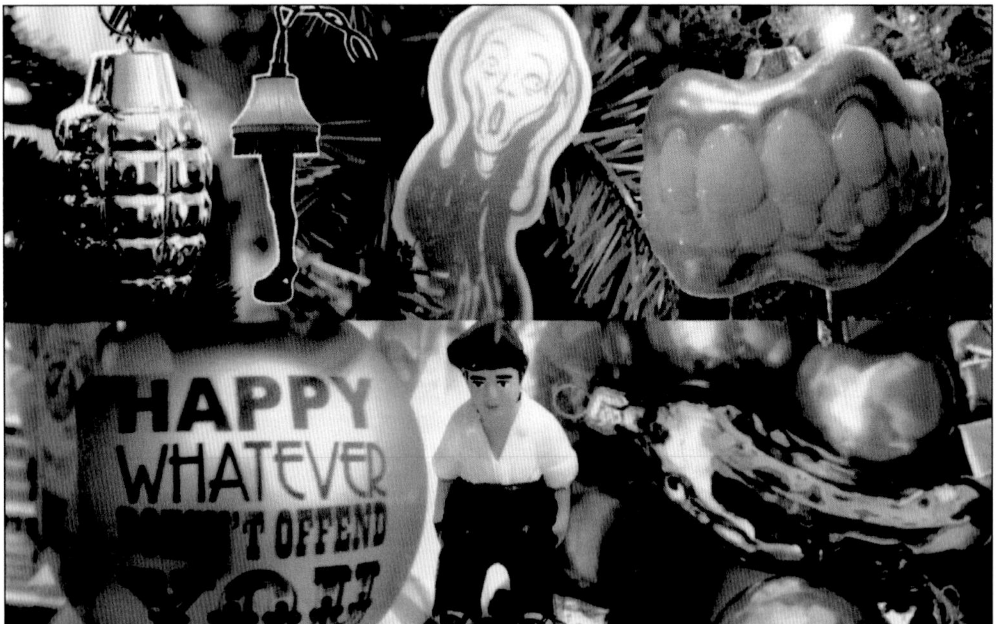


**Do You Have Any of These Ornaments on Your Tree?** The hand grenade ornament was sold at the Swedish Army Museum to benefit Christian Aid. The *A Christmas Story* leg lamp lights up. The Norwegian Embassy's Christmas Tree was once decorated with 700 ornaments of Edvard Munch's *The Scream*. Other odd ornaments include grandpa's teeth, the inoffensive Christmas ball ornament, and the Catalan Nativity Caganer. Finally, the lucky child who finds Weihnachtsgurke (German Christmas pickle) hidden on the tree gets a year of "good fortune."

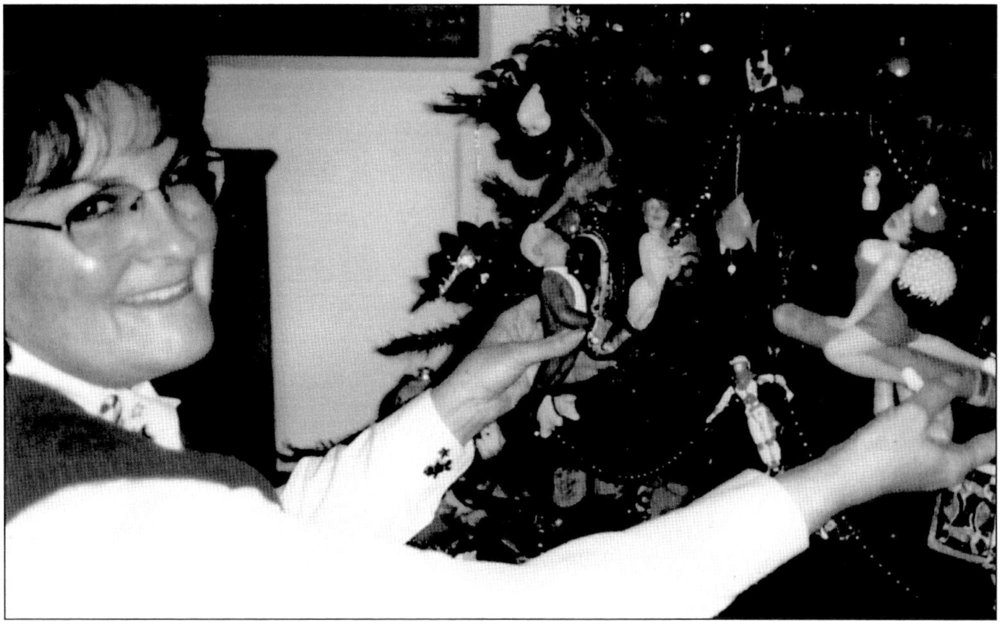

**Clinton Tree Ornaments.** Glen Crooks is best known for his magnificent San Diego landscapes. His work has been compared to the prominent early California impressionists Maurice Braun and Charles Reiffel, but Crooks can also be mischievous. These hilarious Christmas tree ornaments of Bill Clinton and Monica Lewinsky brought laughter to his circle of fellow liberal-minded friends at his 1998 Christmas party.

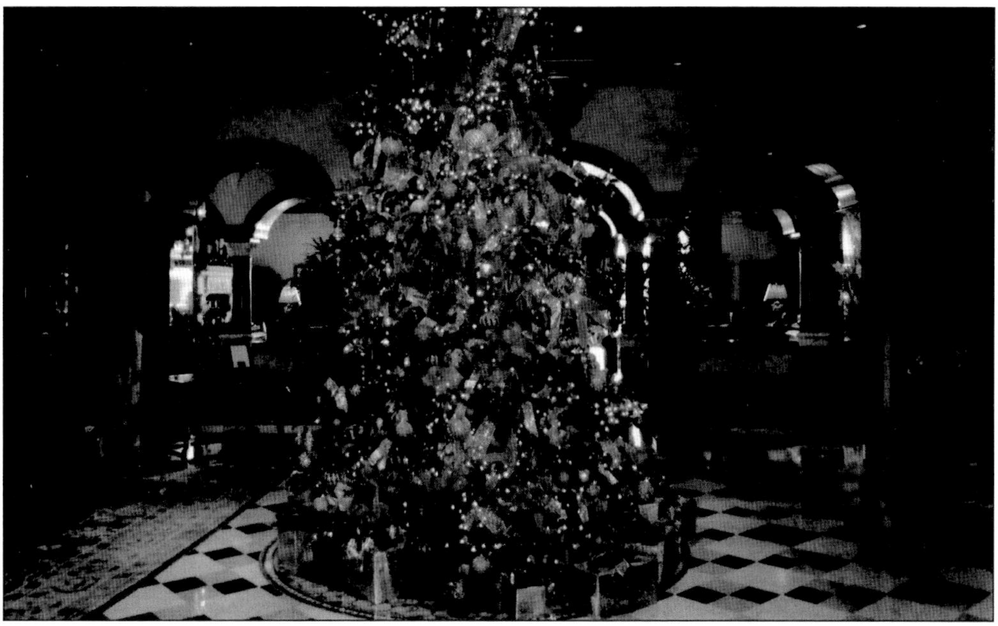

**The Grand Del Mar.** This elegant Christmas tree, decorated with 75 feet of ribbons and bows, 400 ornaments, and 10,000 lights, stands majestically in the main lobby of the Grand Del Mar Resort. A similar 18-foot tree, with 8,000 lights, can be seen in the outdoor Aria Pavilion. Ten smaller trees, each with 1,000 lights, are located throughout the property. The halls are decked, the season jolly, and everything about the Grand Del Mar is very grand.

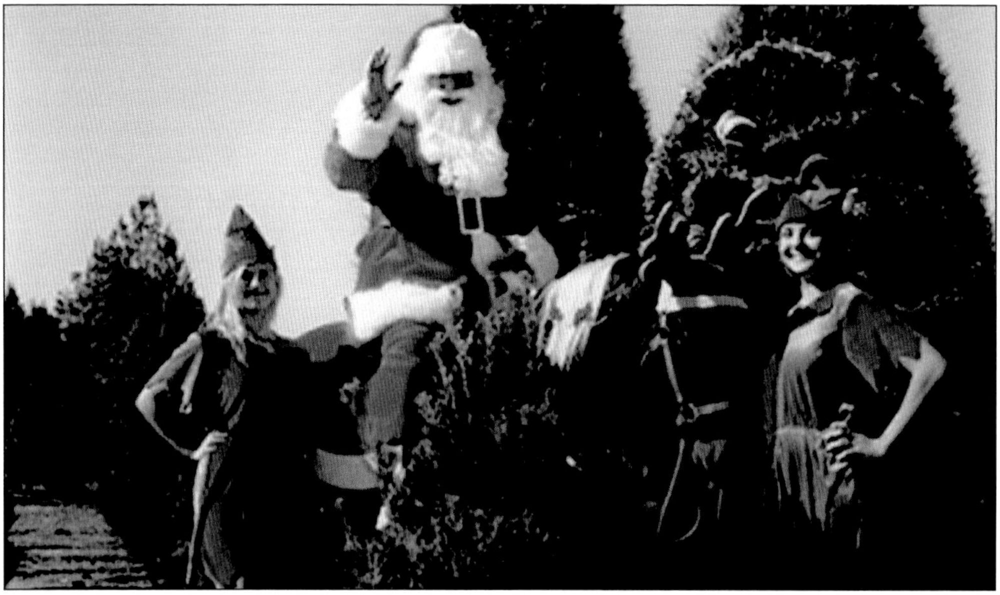

**Cut Your Own Tree.** For those who love the smell of pine and the tradition of cutting their own tree, Pine Tree Acres in Ramona is a destination. Only a handful of these family-owned enterprises, like Pine Tree Acres and Family Christmas Tree Farm in El Cajon, still remain. Pine Tree has been around for 27 years, and Family Christmas for over 40 years. One of the most innovative and respected tree farms was Nelson's Pine Patch (later known as the Pacific Tree Farm) in Chula Vista, which closed in 2006. (Courtesy of Pine Tree Acres.)

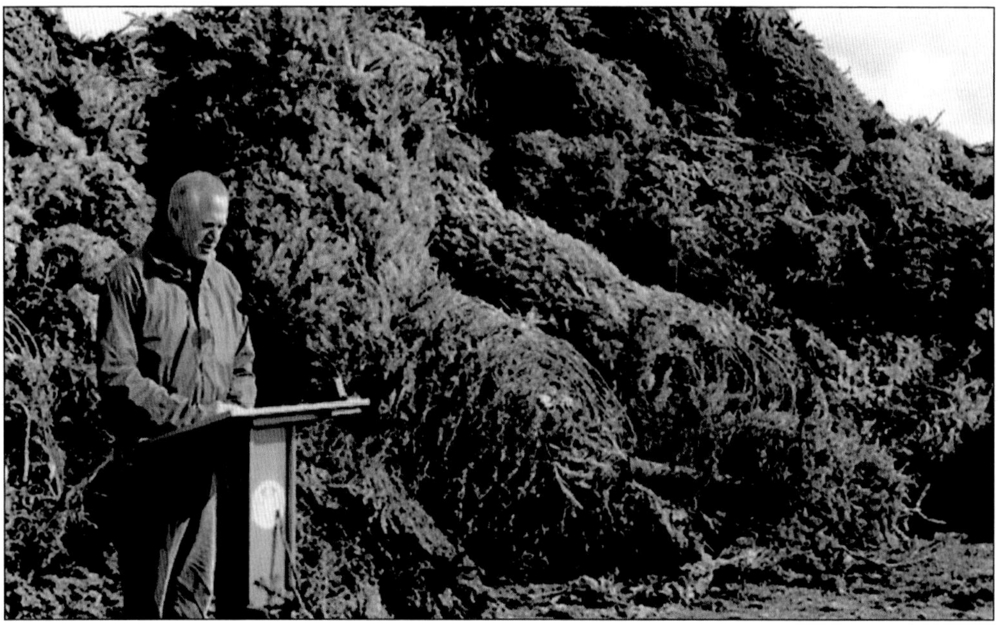

**The Christmas Tree Pile.** For over 40 years, the City of San Diego Environmental Services Department has ground up millions of Christmas trees and turned them to mulch and compost. ESD director Chris Gonaver is shown with a pile of trees waiting to be recycled at the Miramar Landfill. It is estimated that 93 percent of all real Christmas trees in the United States are recycled in similar programs. (Courtesy of Tom Fudge, KPBS.)

# *Five*

# SANTAS

*Merry Christmas from Sunny San Diego*

*December 25, 2011 Temperature: 70 Degrees*

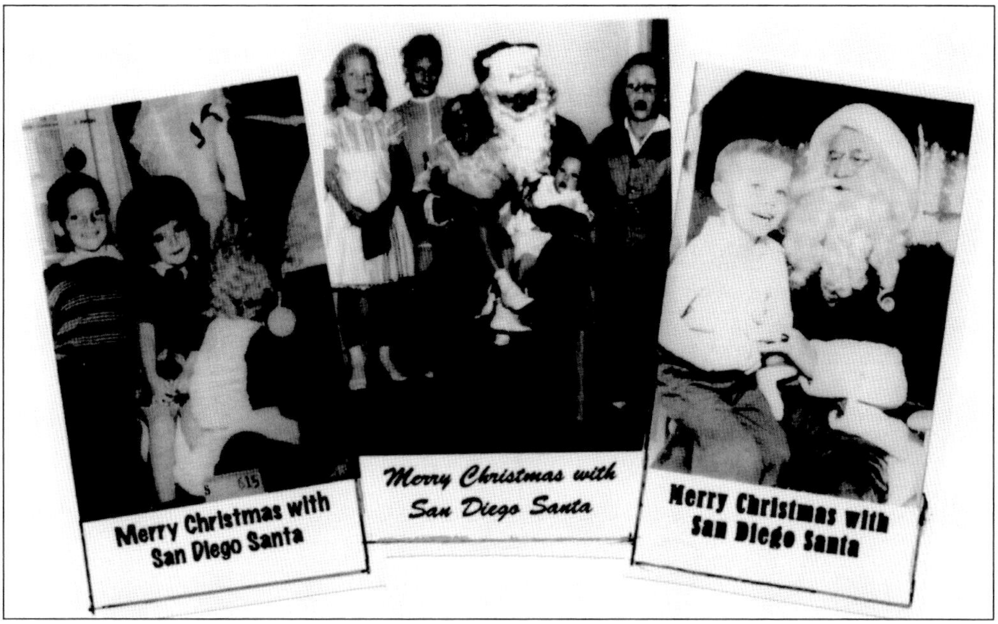


BLACK AND WHITE PICTURES WITH SANTA. At left, in Christmas 1953, eager Tommy (six years, two months) and tentative Rita (three years, 10 months) Gaffney visit with Santa at Walker-Scott's downtown department store. At center, in 1958, (from left to right) Katie, Mary, Eunice, Joanne, and Chuck Hornsby visited Santa while their father was stationed in San Diego with the Navy. At right, in the late 1940s, smiling Randy Seaver enjoyed posing with Santa at Marston's Department Store in downtown San Diego.

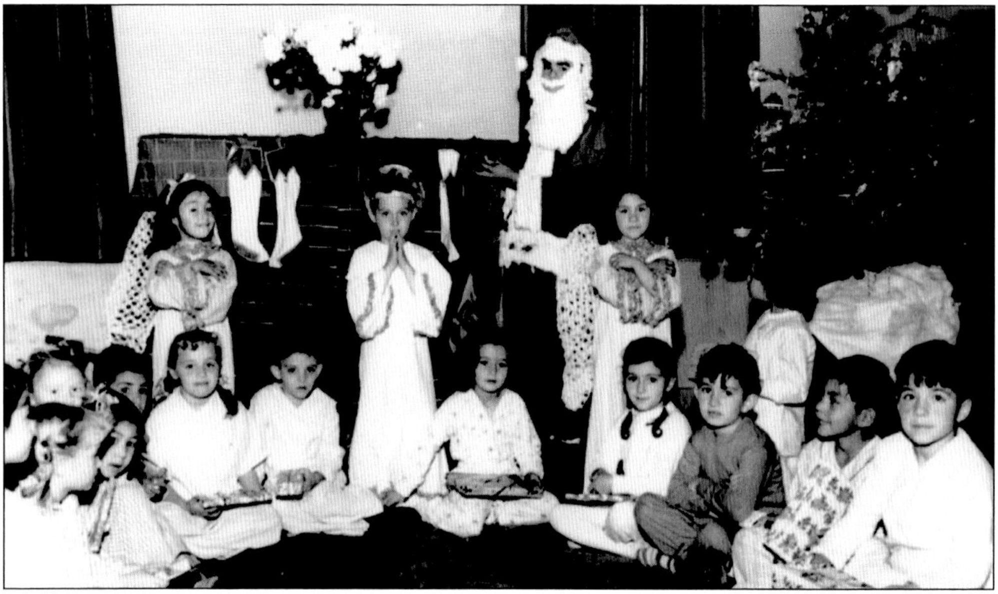

SANTA IN SAN YSIDRO. In the 1940s, the Our Lady of Mt. Carmel School needed a Santa for their Christmas program, so they enlisted the services of a former student—Chuck Velazquez. He remembered that one of the kids didn't believe a man with a white beard delivered gifts at Christmas. Chuck asked, "Then who brings the toys?" The child answered, "The Easter Bunny." Just a teenager at the time, Chuck also played for the San Ysidro Merchants baseball team, in the adult sandlot leagues. (Courtesy of Charles Velazquez.)

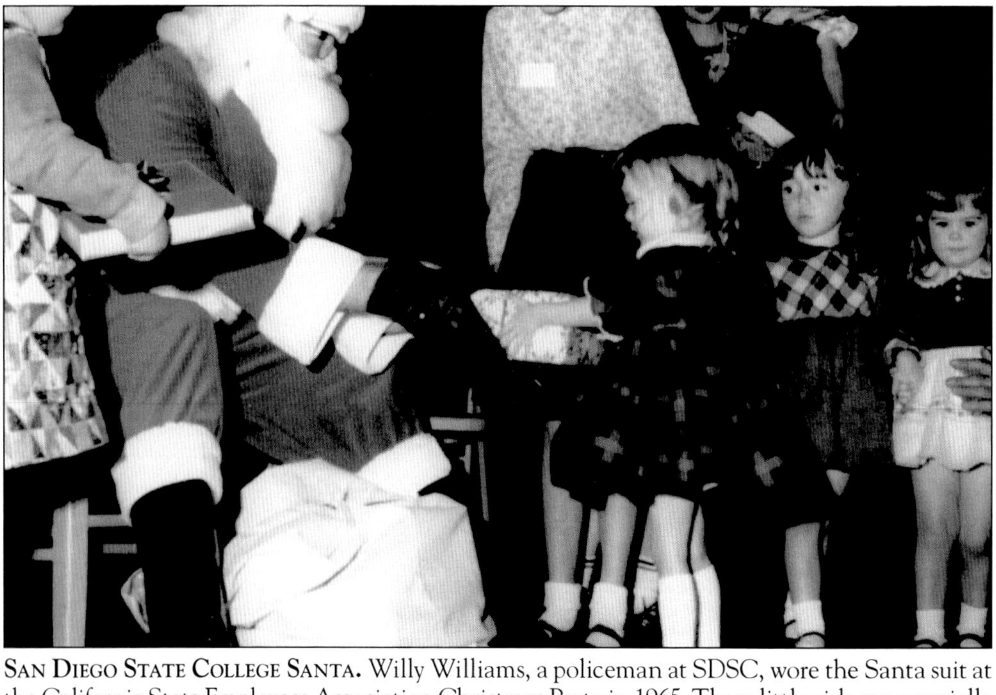

SAN DIEGO STATE COLLEGE SANTA. Willy Williams, a policeman at SDSC, wore the Santa suit at the California State Employees Association Christmas Party in 1965. These little girls are especially cute, with their long curls, fancy dresses, Mary Jane shoes, and white stockings. (Courtesy of the San Diego State University Library.)

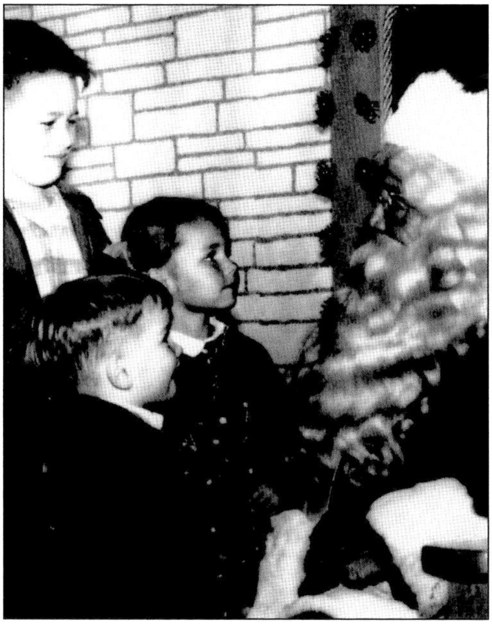

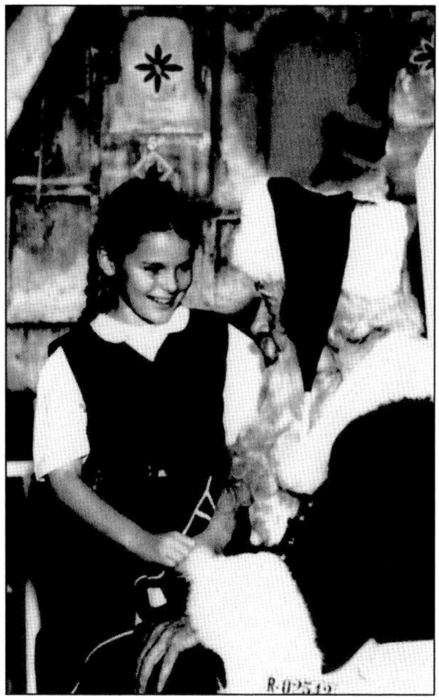

**Santa and Cousins.** The first year that Mission Valley Center opened in 1961, Eric Reis and his younger siblings, Sally and Mark, visited Santa Claus at the May Company. Their cousin, Veeda Lisle (right), remembers a long conversation with Santa in 1954. This image looks like a scene from *Miracle on 34th Street*, and pretty little Veeda grew up to be crowned Miss La Jolla in 1963. (Courtesy of Eric Reis and Veeda Lisle.)

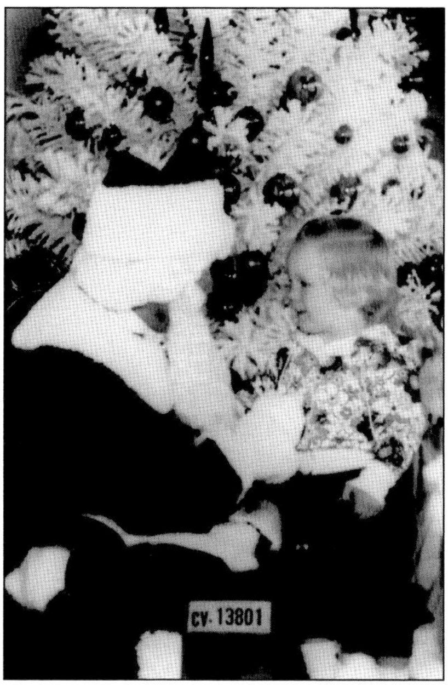


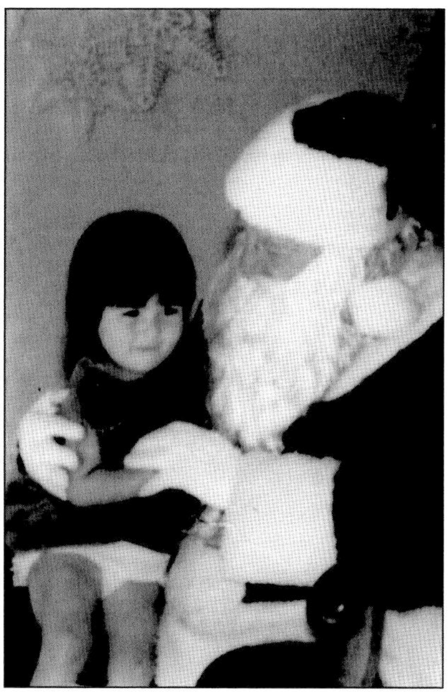

**Kodacolor and Santa Claus.** Color pictures were more expensive than black and white prints until the late 1960s, when color photography became affordable. At left, little Mary Oswell tells Santa what she would like for Christmas. Marcine Conrad is shy but composed as she sits on Santa's lap at right. Kids typically weren't afraid of Santa back then. The color may fade, but the memories remain bright. (Courtesy of Mary Oswell and Bob Conrad.)

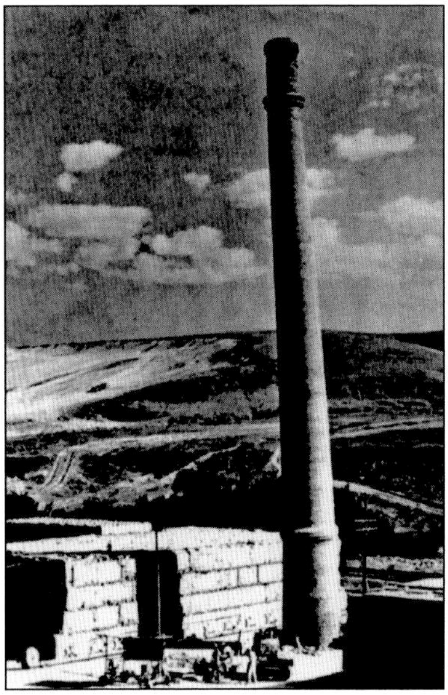

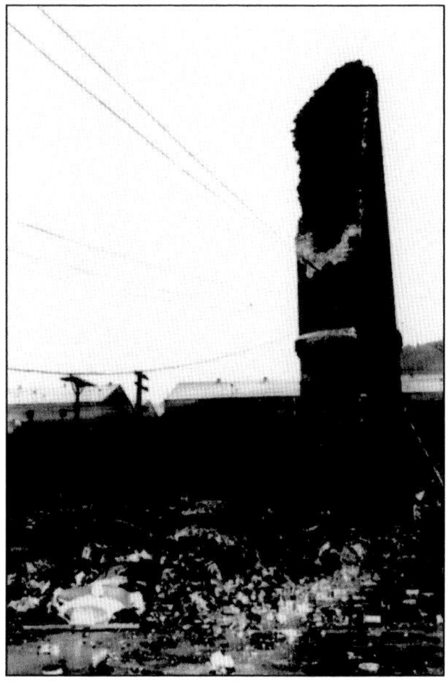

**Santa's Face Plant.** A helicopter would place a Santa figure on top of the Union Brick chimney during the Christmas season. Rose Canyon's landmark "Leaning Tower" smokestack stood eight feet off center, from 1888 until it was toppled by a winter windstorm in 1962. Pacific Beach Historical Society founder John Fry humorously refers to the image on the right as "Santa's face plant." Get out your magnifying glass to see poor Santa Claus, facedown in the rubble. (Courtesy of the Pacific Beach Historical Society.)

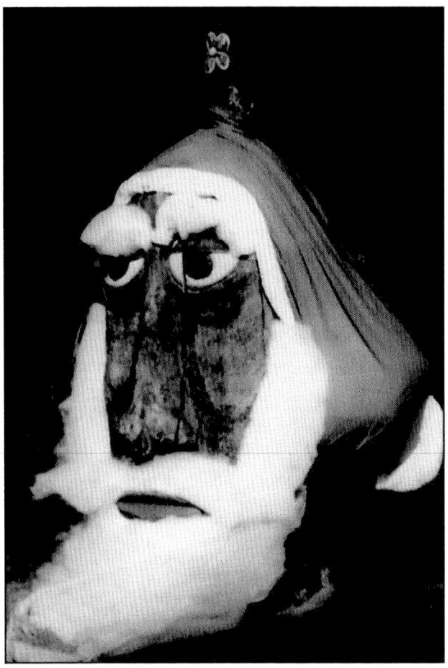

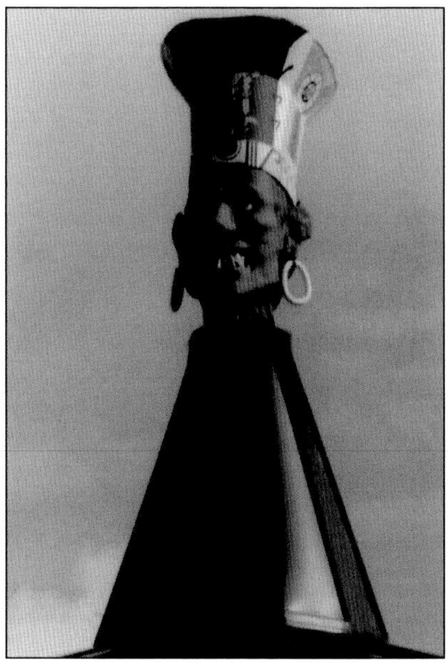

**Mr. Bali Hai Does Santa.** Since the 1950s, San Diego's most famous tiki, Mr. Bali Hai, has stood silently at the entrance of the Bali Hai restaurant. In 1958, he was disguised as Mr. Bali Hai Santa. The smiling tiki atop the roof is affectionately known as "The Goof" and, in the past, Christmas lights were strung around the base of his neck. During December, guests at the Bali Hai are greeted with "Mele Kalikimaka" which is Hawaiian for "Merry Christmas." (Courtesy of Larry Baumann.)

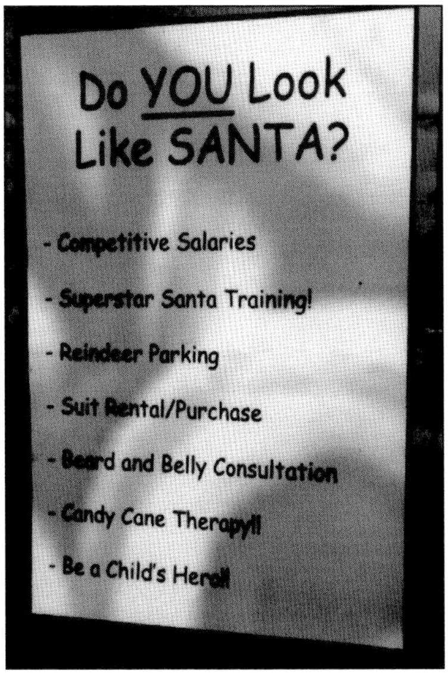


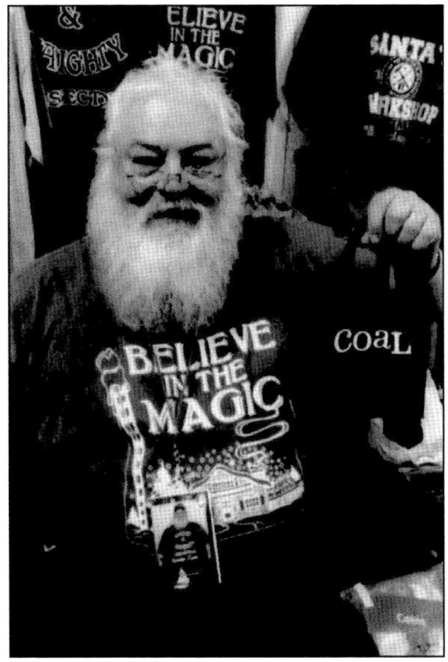


SAN DIEGO SANTA CLAUS CONVENTION. In 2012, the Fraternal Order of Real Bearded Santas held their annual national convention in laidback San Diego. The organization had split from the Amalgamated Order of Real Bearded Santas in 2008 after accusations of mismanagement, which translates to one thing: *money*. The media had a field day covering Santa fisticuffs and the true meaning of Christmas. (Courtesy of intenseindividuals.com.)

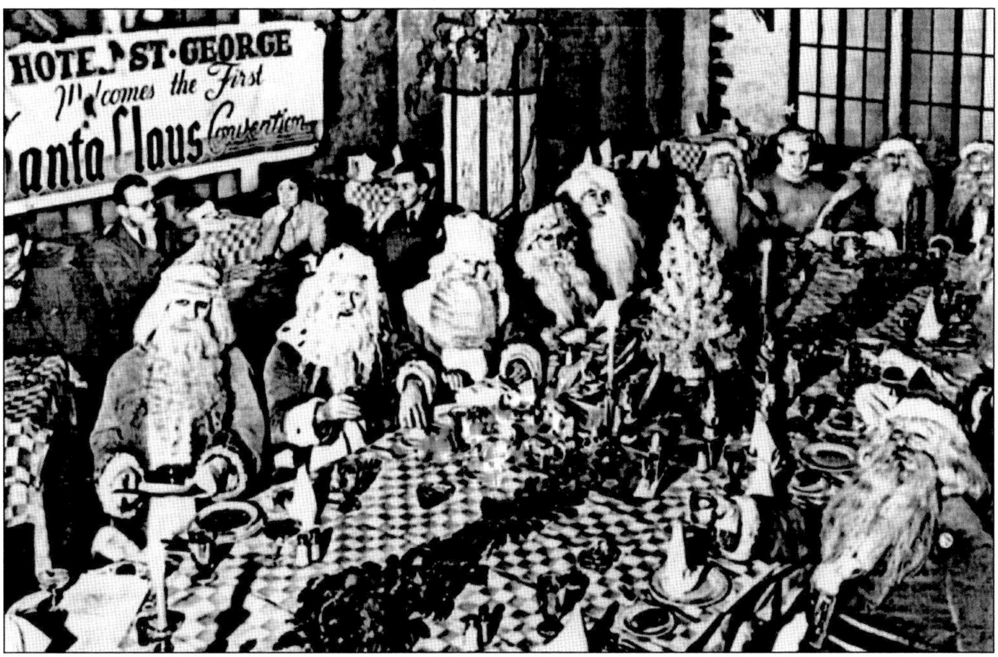


FIRST SANTA CONVENTION. In 1937, the Benevolent Order of Santa Claus was founded by department store Santas, including legendary Macy's Santa Charles W. Howard. Their first convention was held in 1939, at the Hotel St. George in New York City. Controversial issues, such as proper beard length and padded Santas, were at the top of the agenda. Fat Santas didn't want skinny Santas wearing pillows to take their jobs. (Courtesy of Phillip L. Wenz, Santa Claus Oath Foundation.)

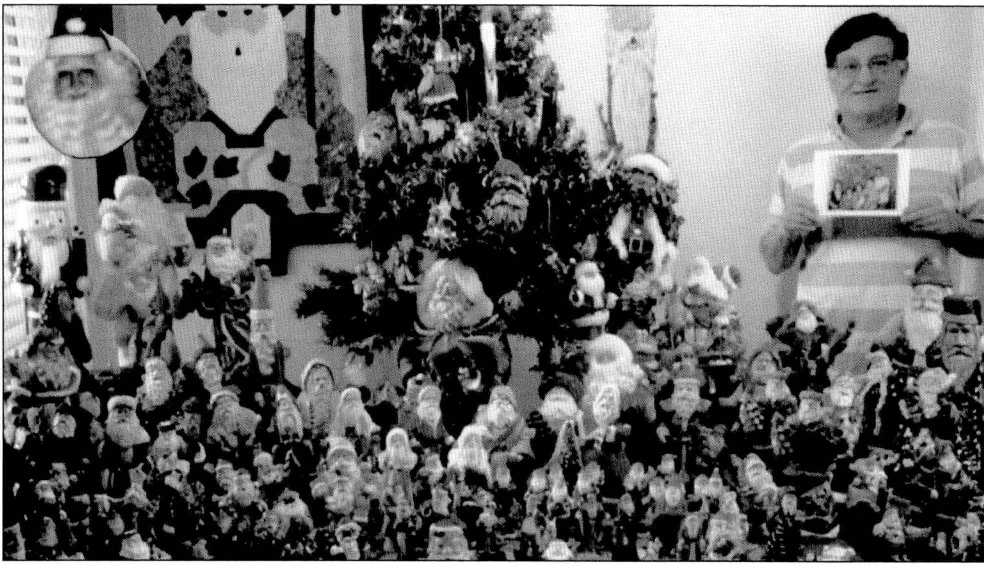

**I'm Gonna Be Santa When I Grow Up.** For years, Jim Crow, custodian at St. Mary's Catholic Church in National City, played Santa Claus for the students. Tony Valdez remembers that, as a little boy, he wanted to be Santa when he grew up. Here, he is shown holding a photograph of his first Santa at age six, while standing beside half of his Santa collection. Tony did grow up to be Santa (insert, upper left) for his family, and the kids at St. Mary's as well. (Courtesy of Tony Valdez.)

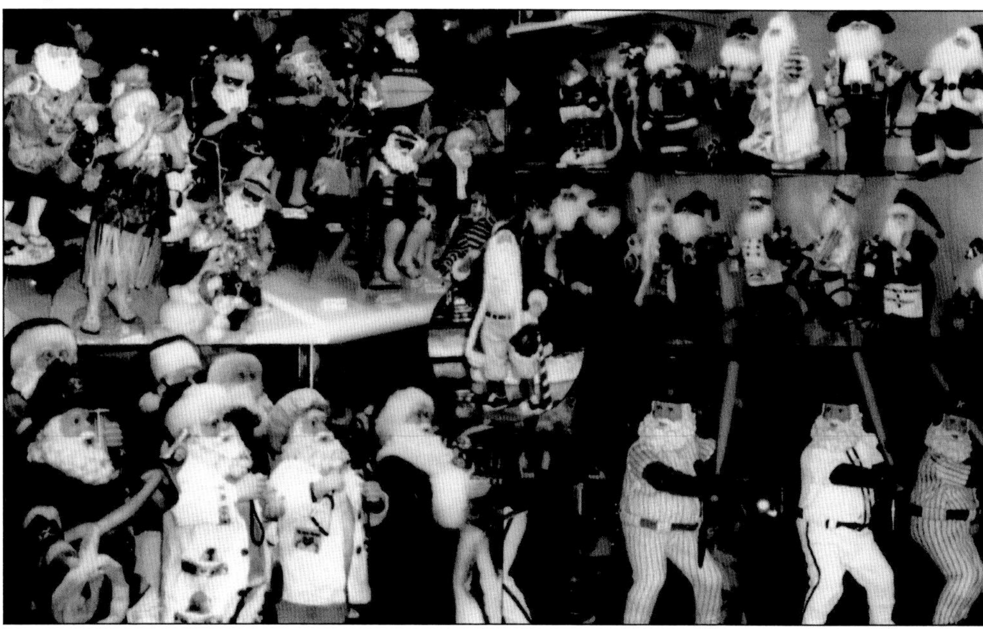

**San Diego's Largest Selection of Collectible Santa Figures.** City Lights' Year Round Christmas & Collectibles Emporium, in Bay Park, is headquarters for all the top artists and brand names of collectible Santas, including Barcana, Byers' Choice, Christopher Radko, Department 56, Disney, Foundations, Heart of Christmas, Jim Shore, Heartwood Creek, Karen Didion, Lemax, Lynn Haney, Mark Roberts, Old World Xmas, Pipka, Possible Dreams, Prizm, Roman, and Russian Gift, among others.

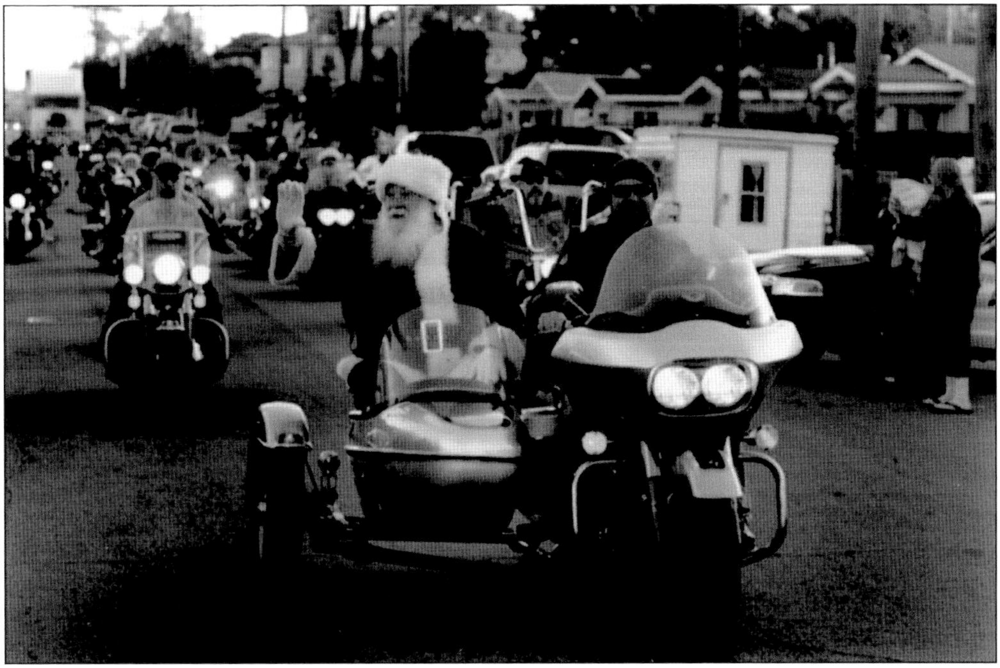

**Frank King's Christmas for Kids.** Some people become Santa Claus without knowing it. Frank King was such a man. In the 1970s, he began fixing bikes to give to underprivileged kids in his National City neighborhood at Christmastime. In the late 1970s, a motorcycle enthusiast named Snowman joined his efforts. Frank has since passed away, but the Boozefighters Motorcycle Club, among others, continue the tradition. They even have a parade with a biker Santa. (Courtesy of Snowman.)

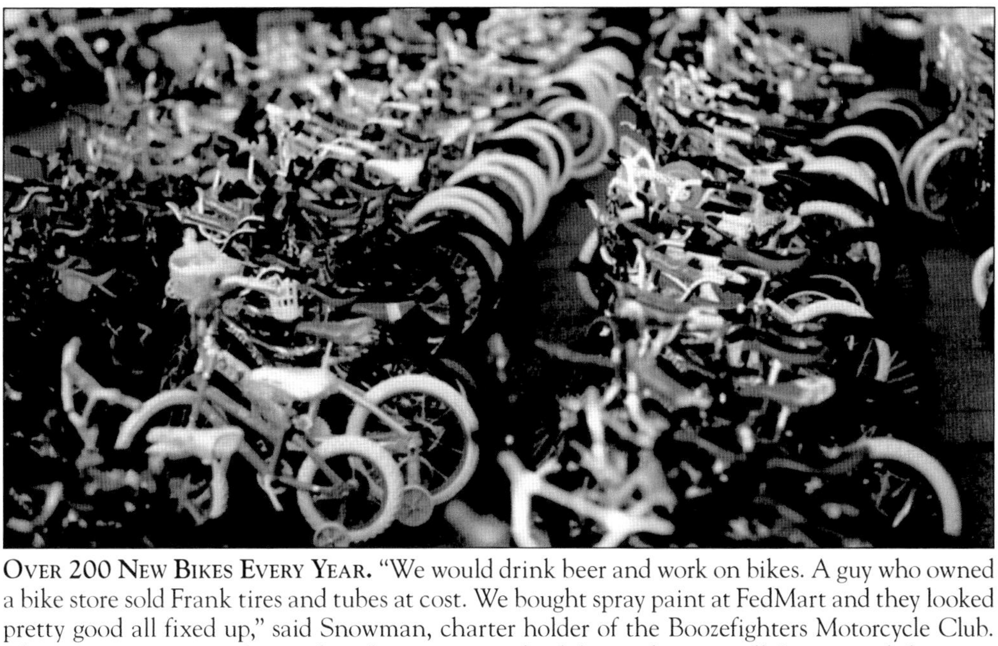

**Over 200 New Bikes Every Year.** "We would drink beer and work on bikes. A guy who owned a bike store sold Frank tires and tubes at cost. We bought spray paint at FedMart and they looked pretty good all fixed up," said Snowman, charter holder of the Boozefighters Motorcycle Club. They may not wear red suits, but these motorcycle club members are all Santas and they give away over 200 new bikes every year. (Courtesy of Snowman.)

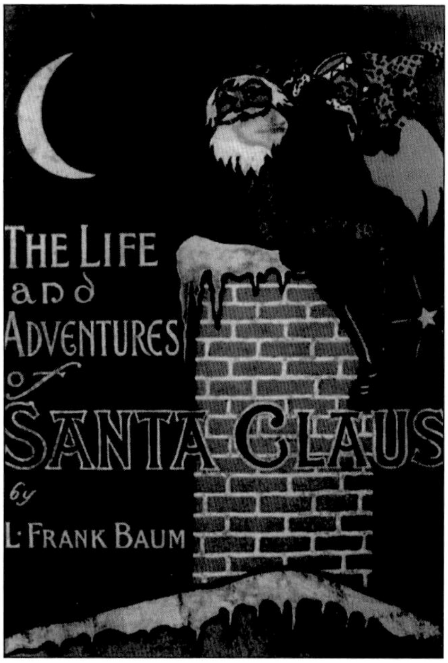


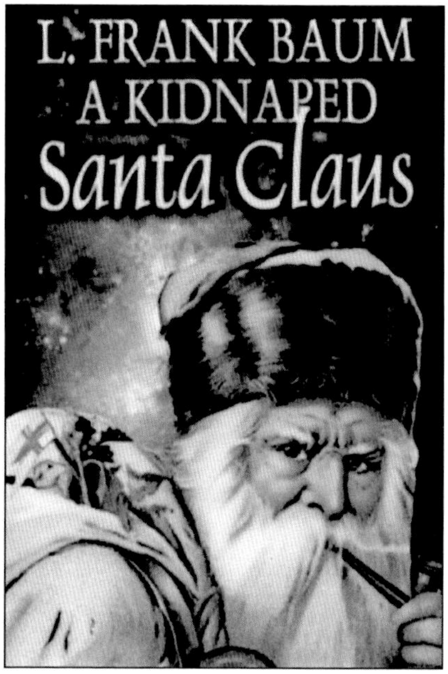


**SANTA CLAUS BOOKS.** In the early 1900s, L. Frank Baum, author of *The Wonderful Wizard of Oz*, spent his winters in La Jolla and Coronado. It was during this time that he wrote *The Life and Adventures of Santa Claus* (1902) and *A Kidnapped Santa Claus* (1904). Santa's sleigh was pulled by a team of five pairs of reindeer, which Baum named Glossie, Flossie, Racer, Pacer, Reckless, Speckless, Fearless, Peerless, Ready, and Steady.

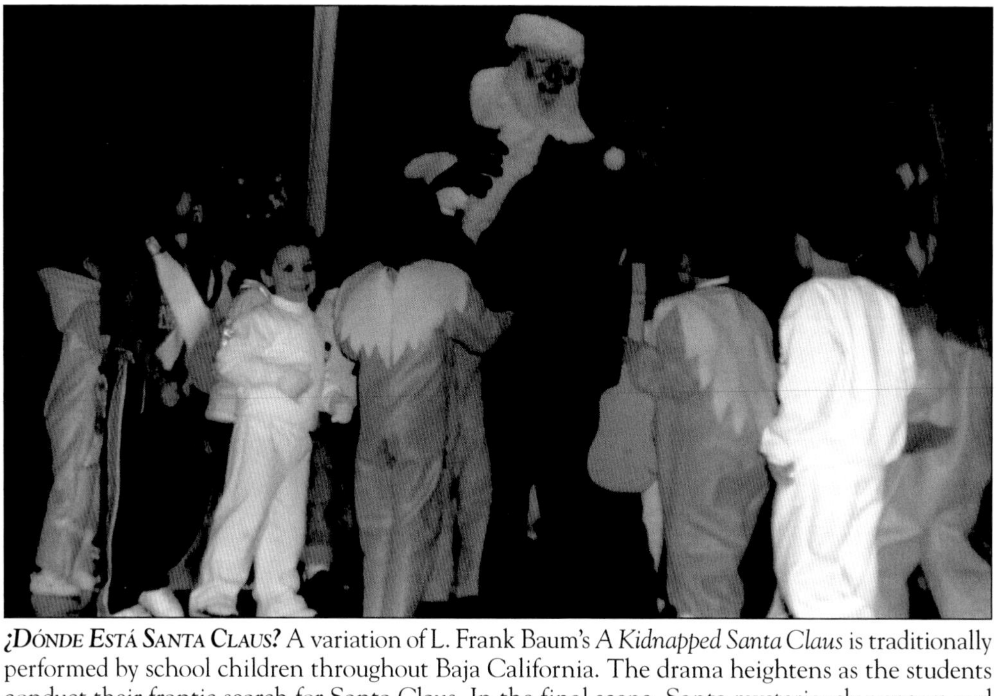

**¿DÓNDE ESTÁ SANTA CLAUS?** A variation of L. Frank Baum's *A Kidnapped Santa Claus* is traditionally performed by school children throughout Baja California. The drama heightens as the students conduct their frantic search for Santa Claus. In the final scene, Santa mysteriously appears and gives candy to all of the children. Many consider *A Kidnapped Santa Claus* to be one of the most beautiful stories that the *The Wonderful Wizard of Oz* author published.

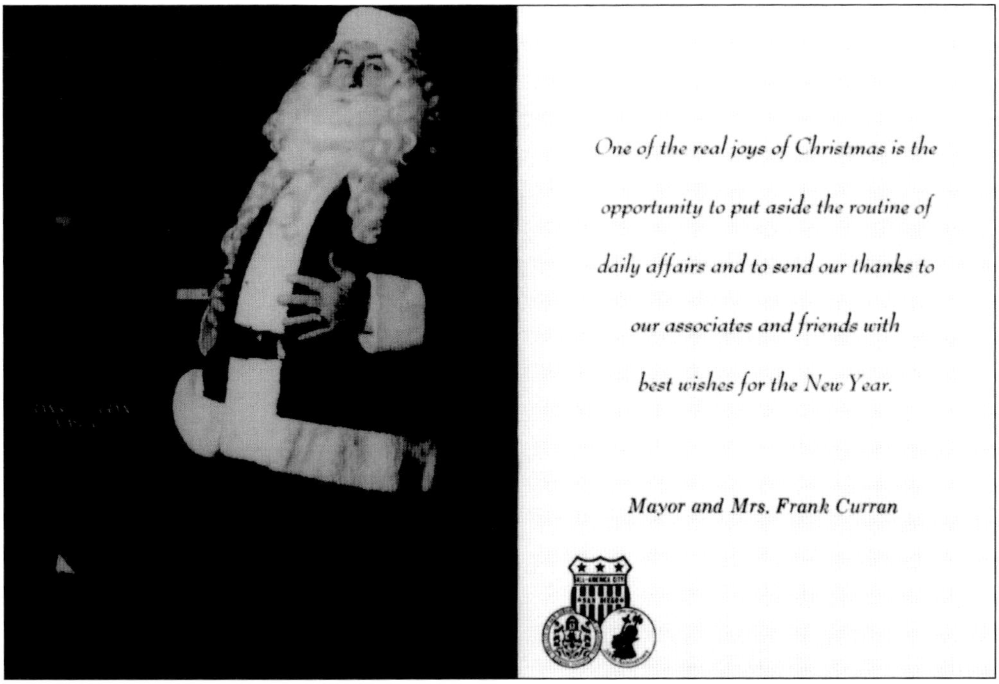


**CHRISTMAS THANKS FROM MAYOR AND MRS. CURRAN.** Frank Curran served as mayor of San Diego from 1963 until 1971. Frank died in 1992, and his widow, Florence, died in 2000. The Currans were childless, so their entire estate, estimated to be worth $1 million was given to San Diego City College. It is the largest gift the college ever received. Curran Plaza is named in honor of the school's Santa Claus. (Courtesy of Kathy Curran.)

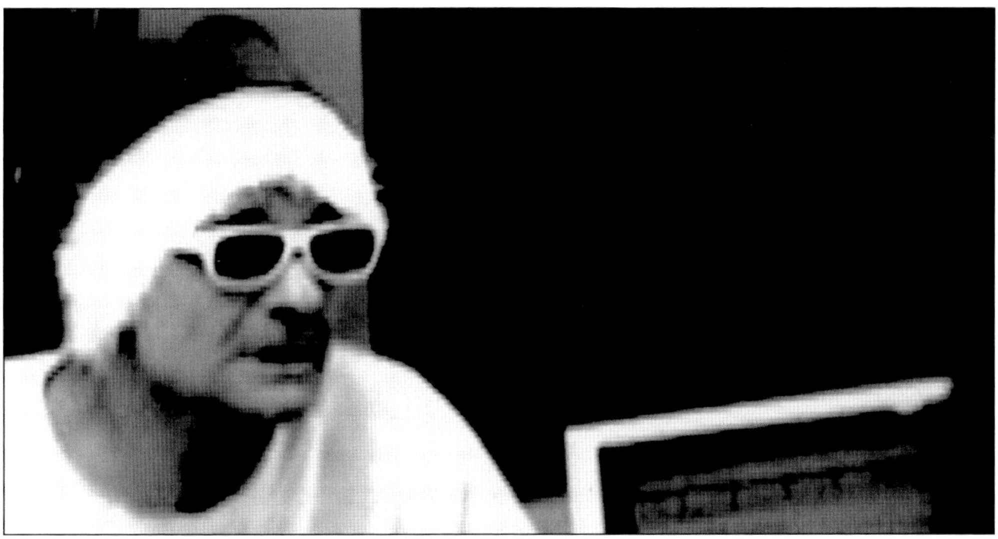

**WANTED BY THE FBI: SANTA CLAUS.** In 2011, this benighted man in Santa cap and white-rimmed sunglasses threatened an Encinitas bank teller with a gun and a tale of financial woe. Over the years, many criminals have disguised themselves as Santa Claus. In 2001, a terminated San Diego police officer wearing a red cap and a fake white beard robbed a Mission Valley bank. This Bad Santa was apprehended following pursuit by a security guard, police helicopter, and patrol officers.

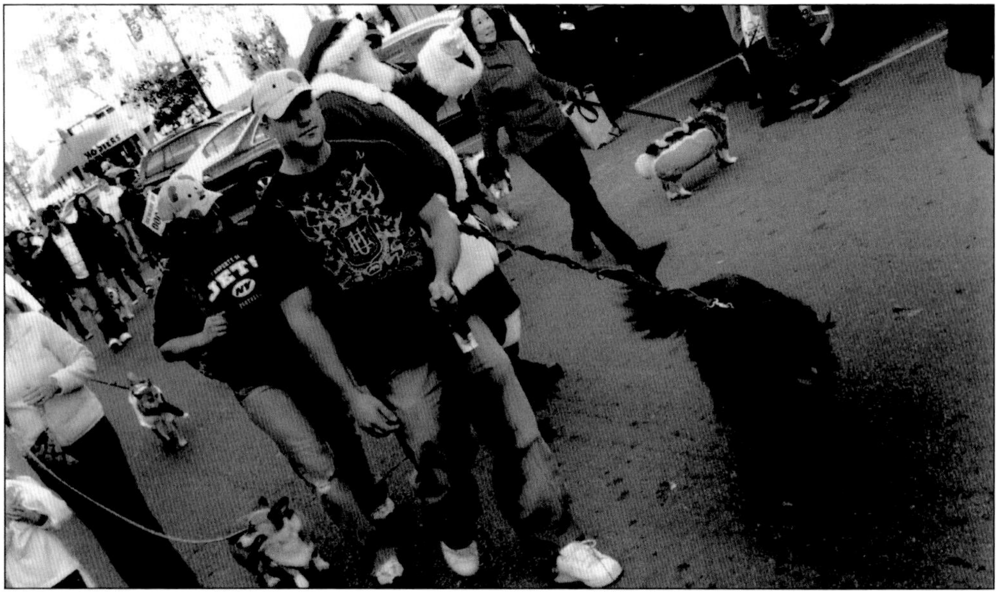

**GASLAMP HOLIDAY PET PARADE.** San Diego loves the opportunity to dress their pets for a parade. There are nine categories for the costume competition of the Gaslamp Holiday Pet Parade, including "Best Costume Made Out of Duct Tape" (Ace Hardware is a parade sponsor). Santa was skeptical when told a dog took this picture during the 2008 parade. (Nowadays, dogs actually have their own cameras.) After the parade, Santa handed out more dog biscuits than candy canes at the GQHS William Heath Davis Home.

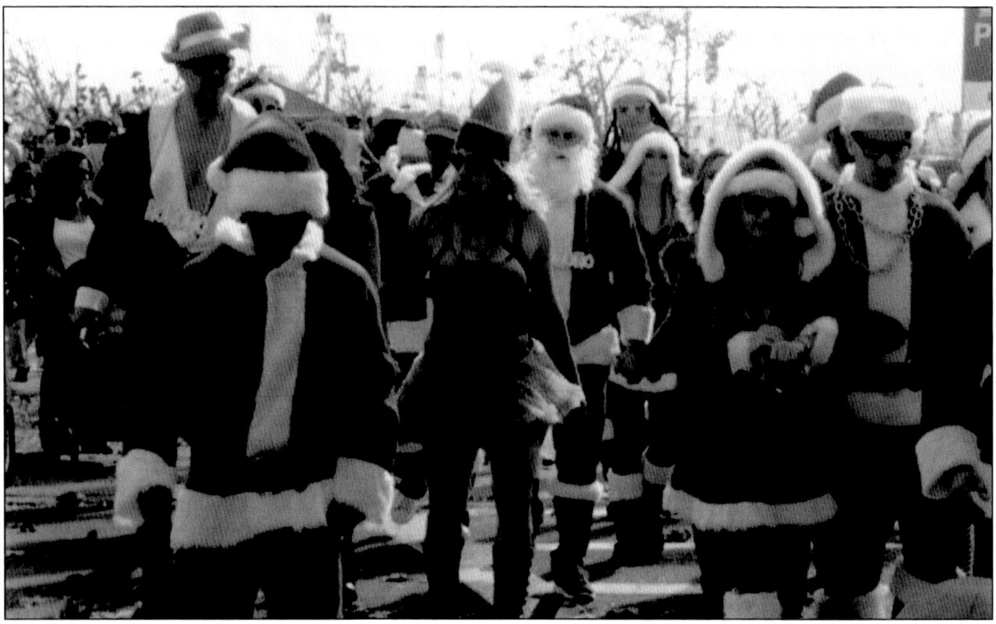

**SANTACON.** Members of San Francisco's Cacophony Society, who wanted to have fun dressed as Santa Claus, held the first SantaCon in 1994. SantaCon has spread to 339 cities in 47 countries, but the event earned a bad name in New York City for drunken behavior. San Diego has two, possibly three SantaCons: The Gaslamp, another for the hipsters of North Park, and (perhaps) Ocean Beach. Problems have not been reported. (Courtesy of coolsandiegosights.com.)

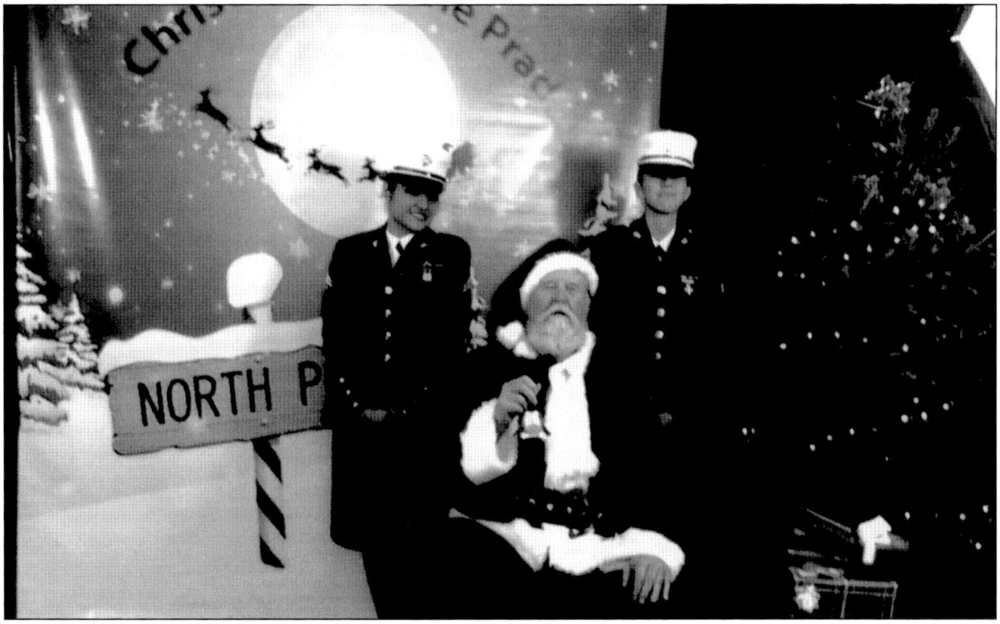


**San Diego Children's Coalition.** In 2009, several local Kiwanis and Lions clubs formed the Children's Coalition. In 2014, they celebrated their first Christmas on the Prado in Balboa Park, with the Marine Corps Toys for Tots campaign. Former Marine Doug Beckham traded his dress blues for the red suit. Doug has also volunteered as Santa at Ronald McDonald House and the Linda Vista Recreation Center Christmas Breakfast. (Courtesy of Al Demoran.)

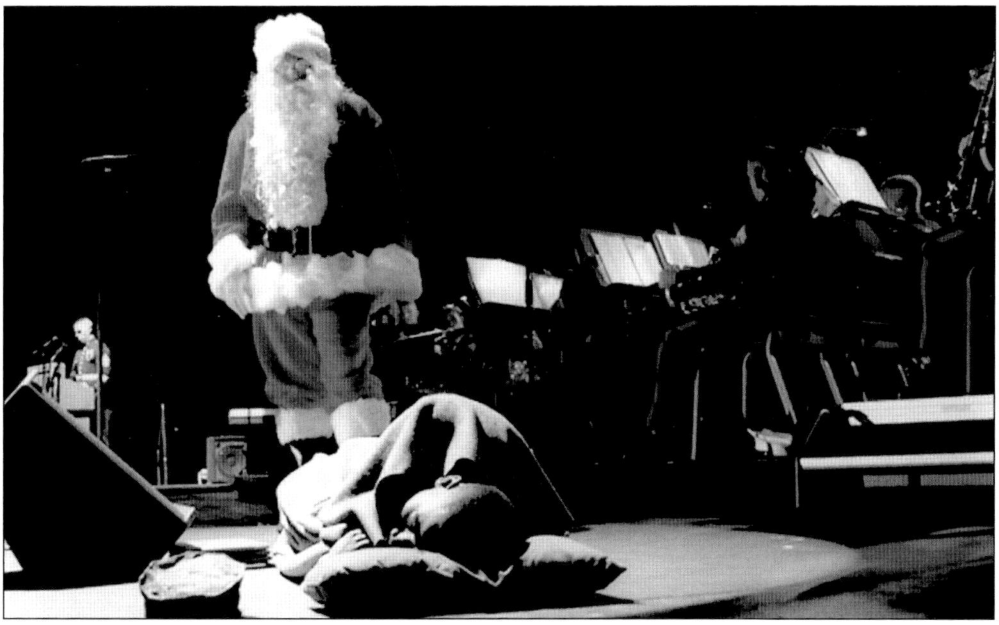

**Carry On, Santa, It's Christmas Day, All Secure.** "Merry Christmas, My Friend" was penned by Marine L.Cpl. James M. Schmidt in 1986. It was recited and performed during the Marine Corps Recruit Depot Holiday Concert and Tree Lighting Ceremony in 2010. The most quoted line from the poem is from this passage: "But half asleep he rolled over, and in a voice clean and pure, said, 'Carry on, Santa, it's Christmas Day, all secure." (Courtesy of MCRD San Diego.)

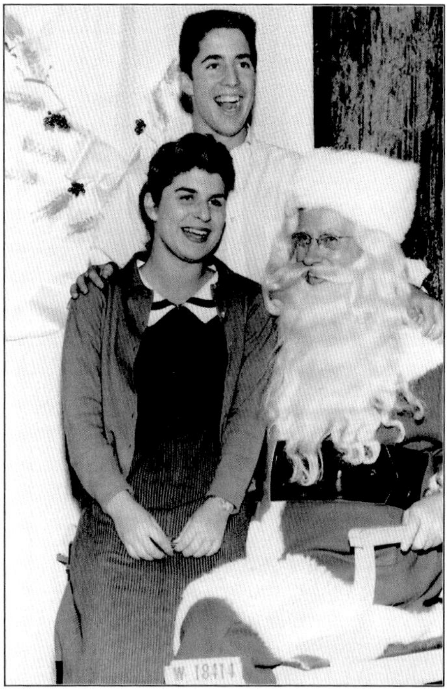

**Santa's Little Helper.** While a student at San Diego High School, Wendy (Palmer) Gay worked as Santa's photographer at the downtown Walker-Scott department store. She is shown in 1954 with her younger brother, Scott Palmer, and Santa. The public was unaware that one of Walker-Scott's Santas was a light-complected African American. According to Wendy, he was a jovial man and all the kids loved him. (Courtesy of Wendy Gay.)

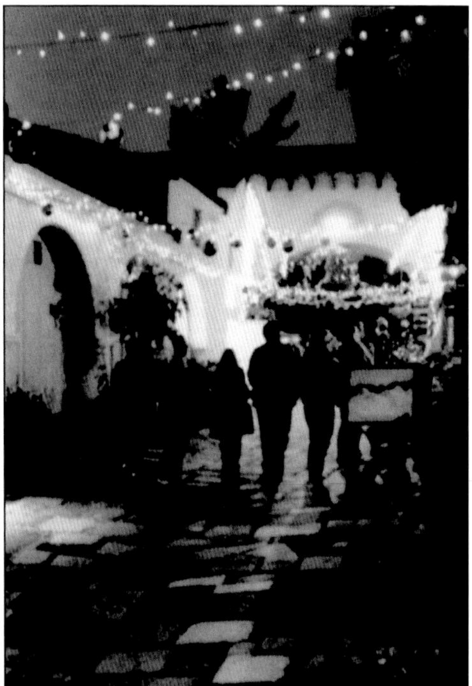

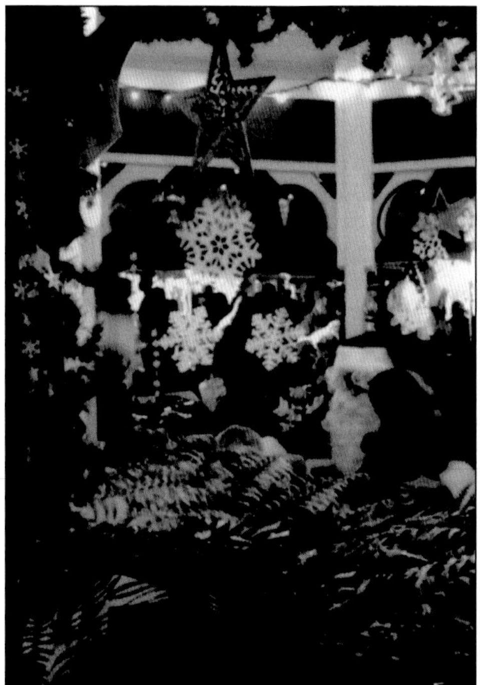

**Santa Claus in Spanish Village.** There are 37 studios and 250 artists in cozy, colorful Spanish Village. They "deck the halls for the holidays and Santa Claus comes to town." Vincent van Gogh's "Café Terrace at Night" and J.C. Leyendecker's Santa Claus covers for the *Saturday Evening Post* come together to capture the spirit of December nights in Spanish Village. It was Leyendecker who gave us the modern image of a robust, jolly Santa. (Courtesy of Victoria Ward.)

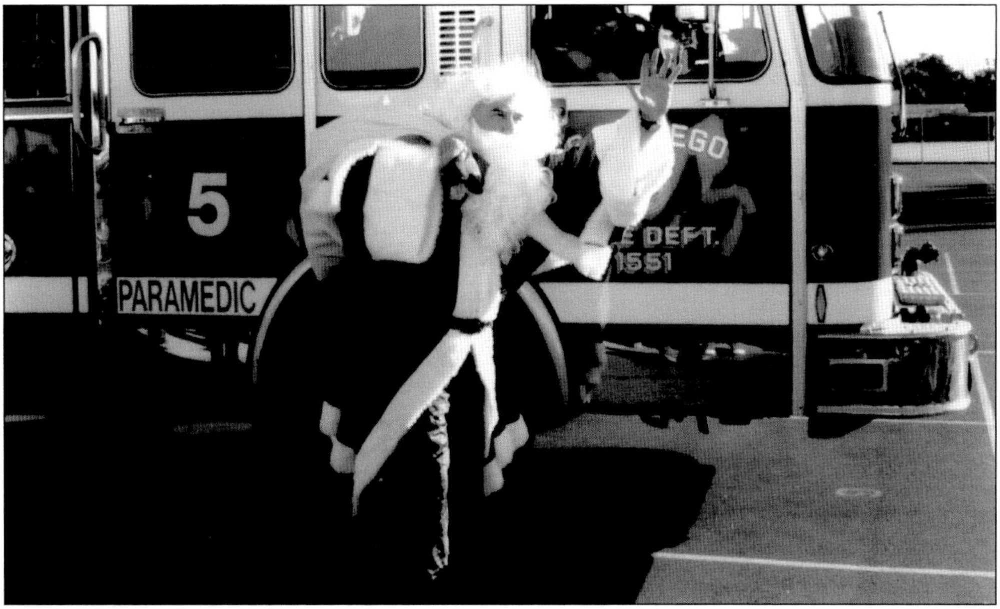


**IRISH YOU A MERRY CHRISTMAS SAN DIEGO.** Irish Outreach sponsored an Irish Christmas gala for the students and families of Roosevelt Middle School in 2014. The event featured Irish dancers, musicians, and athletes, Madigan the Magician, and Edward the Irish Wolfhound. Dinner was served to 250 people. The highlight of the day was the arrival, via fire truck, of the green Santa O'Claus, Mick Ward (shown), proprietor of The Ould Sod Pub, who was delivered by members of the San Diego Firefighters Emerald Society.

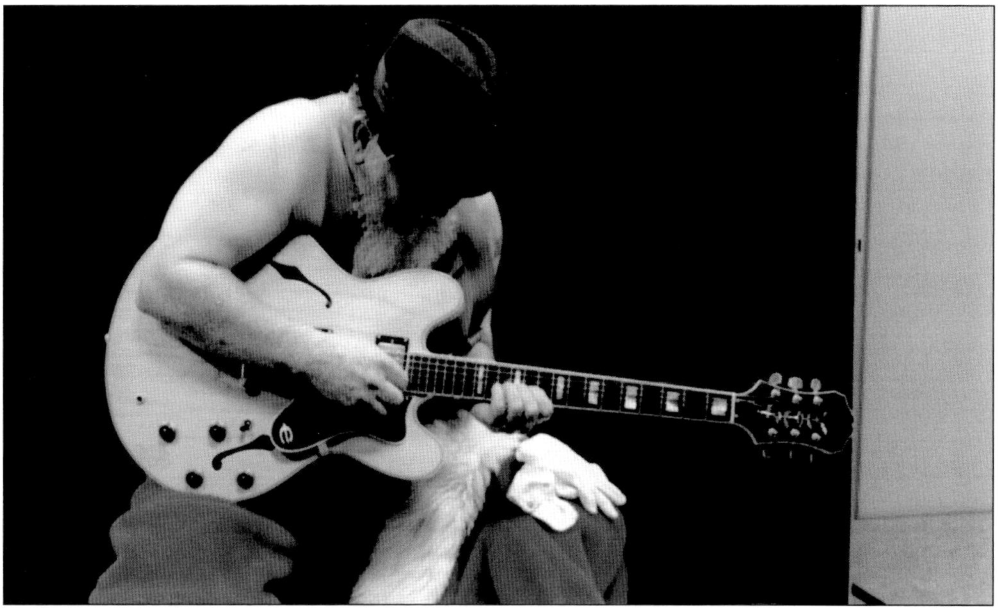

**BEEFCAKE SANTA.** For over 10 years, Drum Macomber—a former El Cajon Citizen of the Year—has been a volunteer Santa Claus for the El Cajon Mother Goose Parade, St. Madeline Sophie's Center, Home of Guiding Hands, El Cajon Animal Shelter, East County Toy Drive, and The Spirit of Liberty Foundation. He is shown having some fun as a rock and roll Santa at the Reuben H. Fleet Science Center, during their 2013 guitar exhibition. (Courtesy of Drum Macomber.)

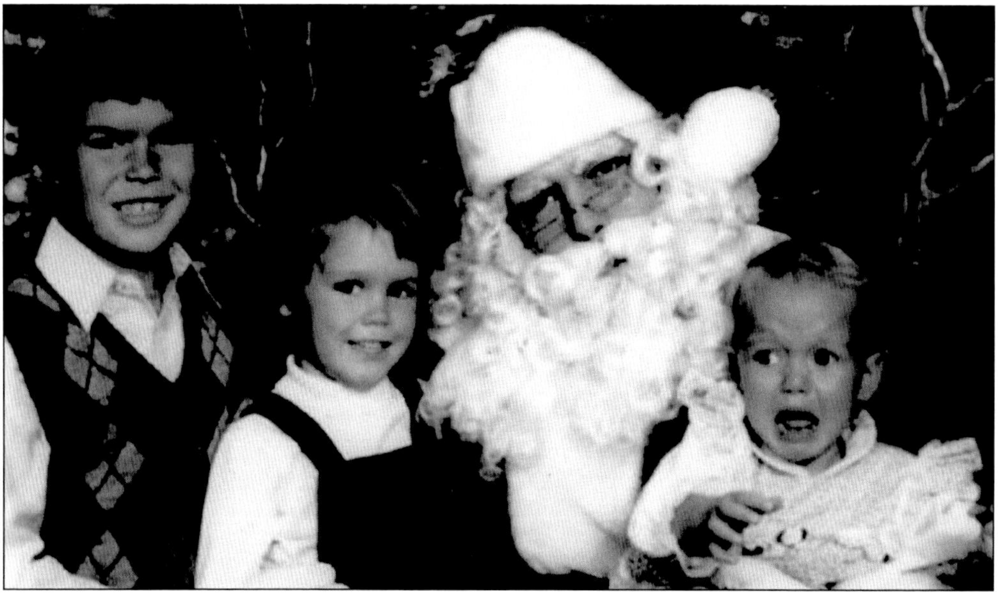

**Scared of Santa.** In 2011, Russ Keltner's 1984 picture of his kids with Santa won third place in the UT San Diego Scared of Santa contest. The caption was, "Russell and Ryan Keltner seemed to like Santa. Their sister Lynnae just freaked out." Lynnae was only two-and-a-half and doesn't remember the photo session. "I have fond memories of Santa and Christmas is my favorite time of year," says Lynnae. "The family puts the picture on display every year and everybody gets a kick out of it." (Courtesy of Russ Keltner.)

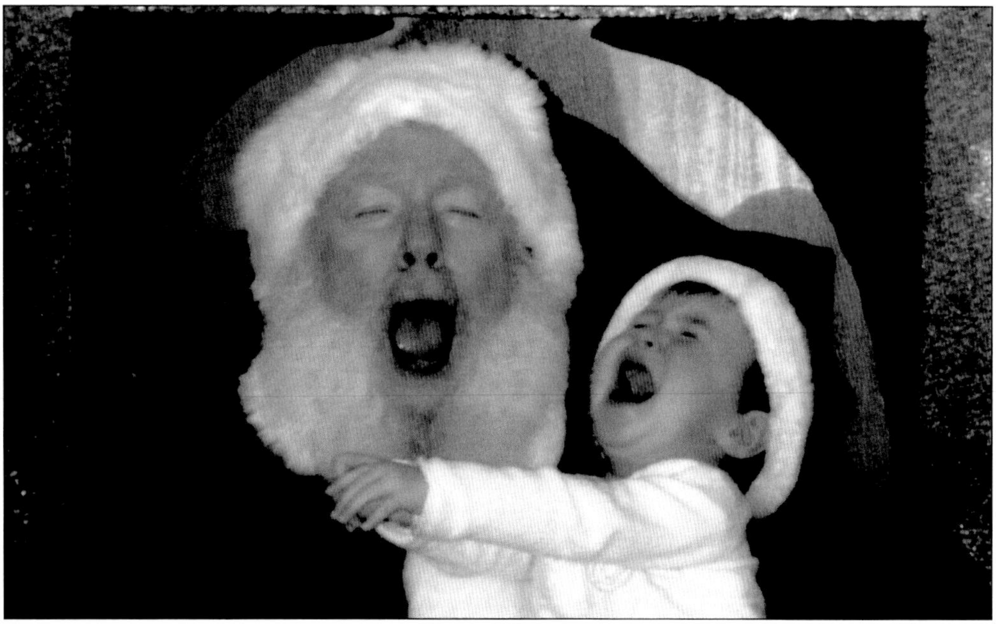

**Scared of Santa, Fourth Place.** Don King entered this photograph, titled, "Crying Santa," in the same UT contest. The picture placed fourth, from over 200 entries. It bothers the author when kids are afraid of Santa, and he suggests parents hold their child while the parent sits on his lap. Some parents like crying pictures and shoot too many poses, but occasionally—depending on the parents—the author will have fun by crying along with the child.

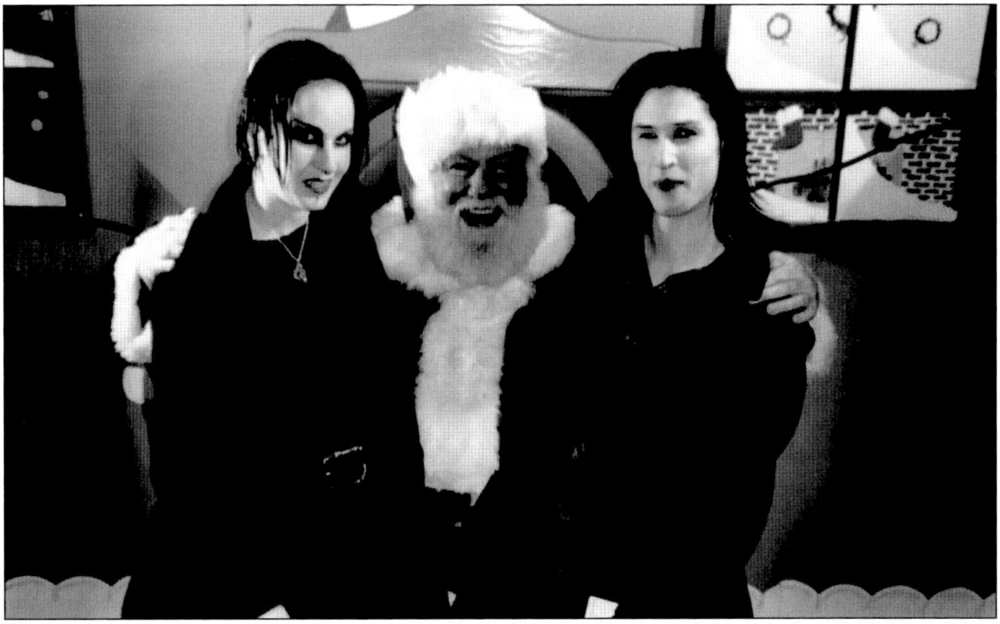

**THEY APPEARED OUT OF THE NIGHT.** At 8:00 p.m., the author moves behind the Gingerbread House, to prevent the lights from interfering with the stage performances at the Spreckels Organ Pavilion. In 2003, two vampires with long, sharp canine teeth appeared out of the night and sat on Santa's lap. One of them, Don Henrie (right), would be appearing in a new TV reality series, *Mad, Mad House.*

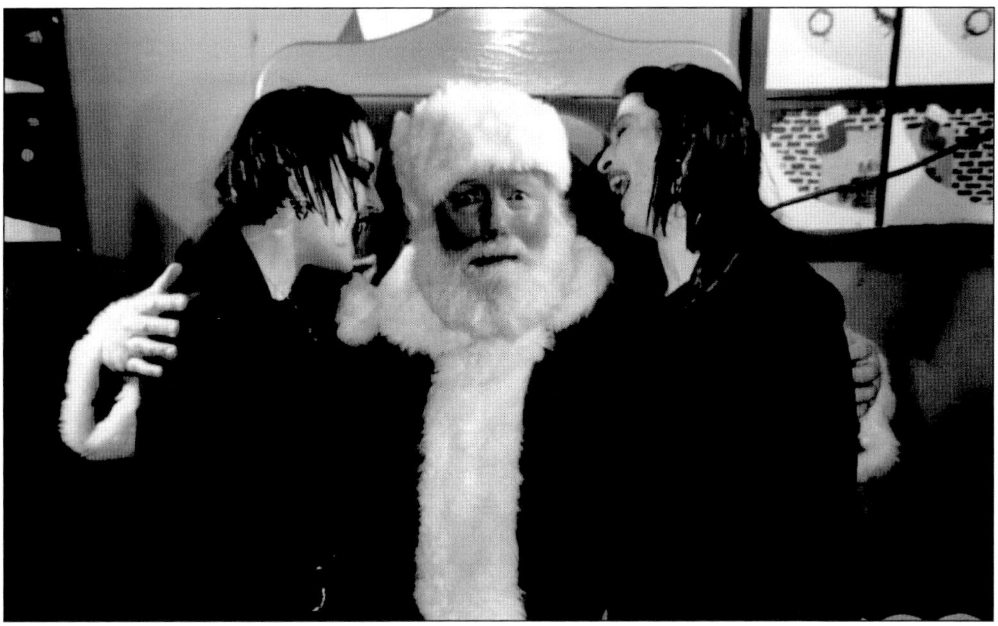

**"WE REALLY WANT A PICTURE BITING SANTA."** After a relatively conventional conversation and smiling portrait with Santa, Vampire Don whispered, "We really want a picture biting Santa." The author agreed to a show of their fangs, but warned against biting. Although *Mad, Mad House* would later be panned as a "bad, bad show," Don and his girlfriend were a couple of very likeable vampires.

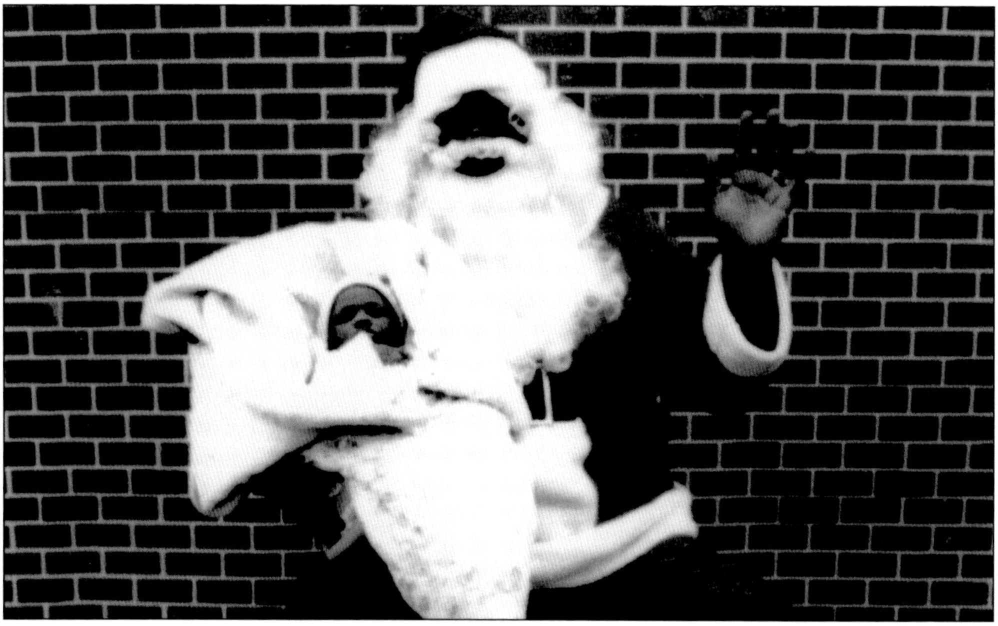

**Black Santa.** In the 1970s, Bob "Hubba Jubba" Moss recognized the need for Black Santa in San Diego. He advertised his services in the newspaper, as this would be an opportunity to earn a few extra bucks during the holiday season. The most memorable party he attended was in Santee. Moss rang the doorbell. The man who answered the door was as shocked as Santa—Hubba had been hired to hand out gifts at a Hells Angels Christmas party. (Courtesy of Bob Moss.)

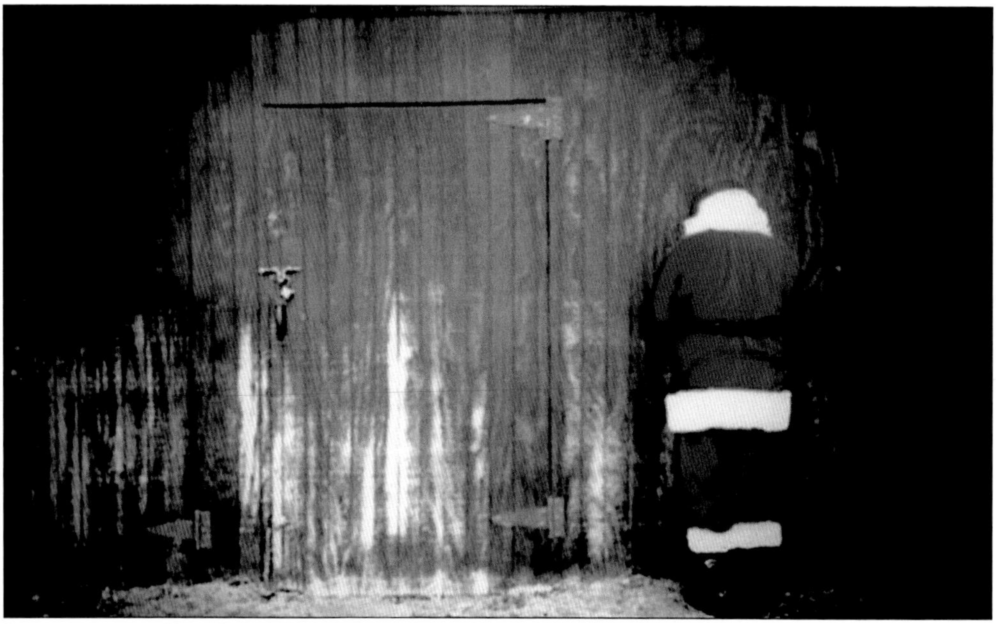

**Santa and the Red Barn.** For over 20 years, Bill Lansville wore the red suit to family get-togethers in Chula Vista, San Diego, and Poway. After the Navy chief retired and relocated to Barstow, the mayor convinced him to ride on a float as Santa Claus in the town's annual Halloween parade. Larry Halstead was inspired to compose and photograph this artistic image of Santa Bill and a red barn. Lansville's friends haven't stopped laughing. (Courtesy of Bill Lansville.)

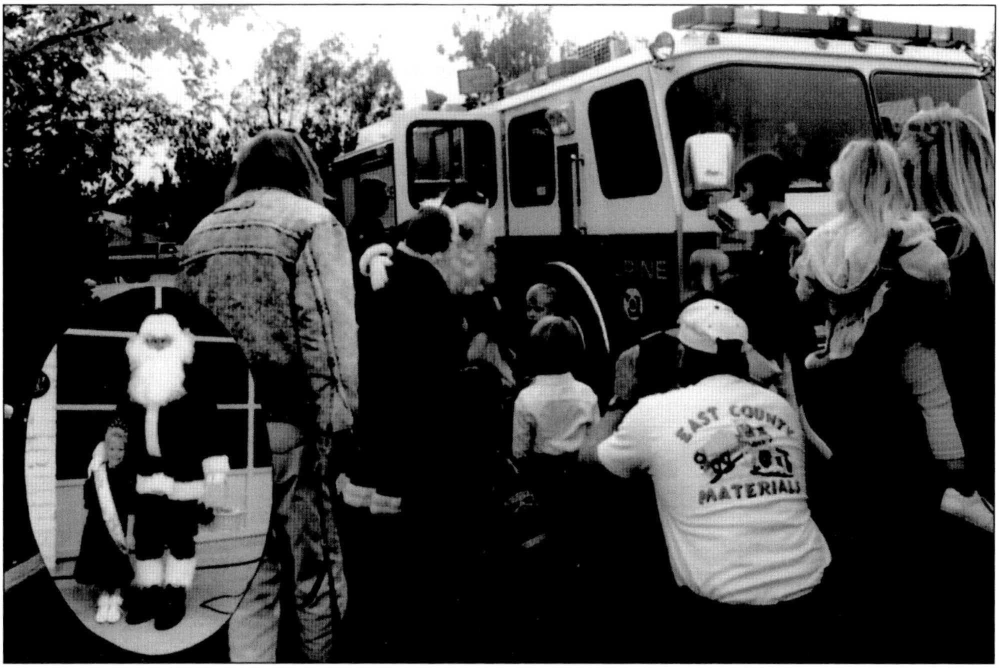


**SANTA VISITS ALPINE IN 1994.** Everybody wants to ride in a fire truck, including Mr. and Mrs. Claus. Santa David Bruce (insert) is shown with Little Miss Alpine of 1994. It was the little Mexican children who made a lasting impression on Bruce. "The boys had their white shirts buttoned to the top; the girls wore pretty dresses. They were so happy, so well-behaved and appreciative." (Courtesy of David Bruce.)

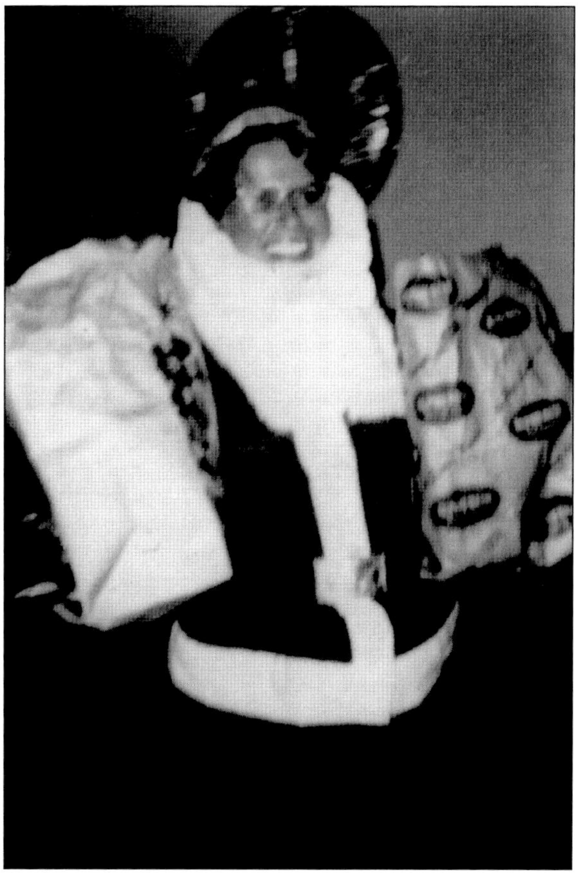

**WEAR THE RED SUIT, GO TO JAIL.** In 1972, Sheila Mura found herself in a bit of a predicament on the morning of the Department of Vocational Rehab Christmas Party. She was responsible for the event, but Santa called in sick. Nobody else was willing to fill the role, so Sheila good-naturedly volunteered to wear the red suit and beard. Lucky for her that she was in California. According to urban legend, women in Minnesota can be sentenced to 30 days in jail for impersonating Santa Claus. (Courtesy of Sheila Mura.)

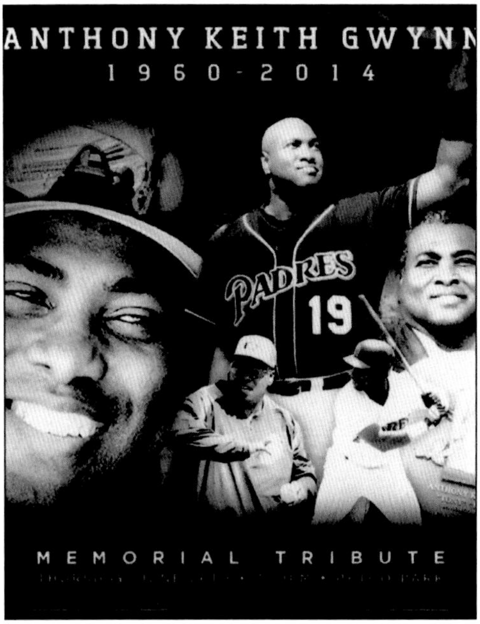


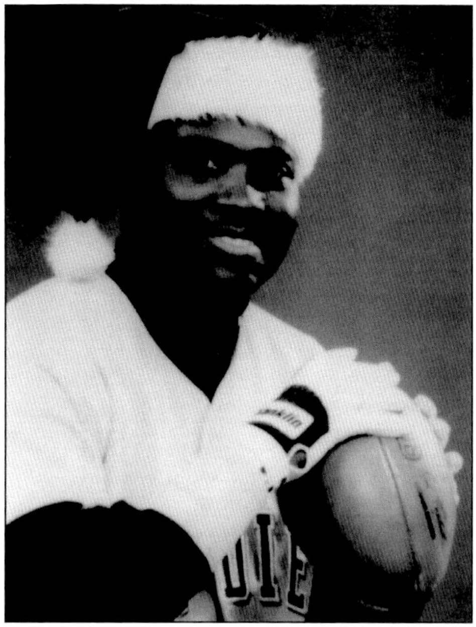

**Santa Claus in a Baseball Uniform.** In 2014, San Diego mourned the loss of "Mr. Padre," Tony Gwynn. At a memorial tribute at Petco Park, he was described as "Santa Claus in a baseball uniform." Dodgers broadcaster Vin Scully was asked to describe Tony in one word. That was easy: "Jolly." Tony used the photo on the right for his Christmas card in the 1990s. San Diego loved Tony Gwynn just as they love Santa Claus. (Courtesy of the San Diego Hall of Champions.)

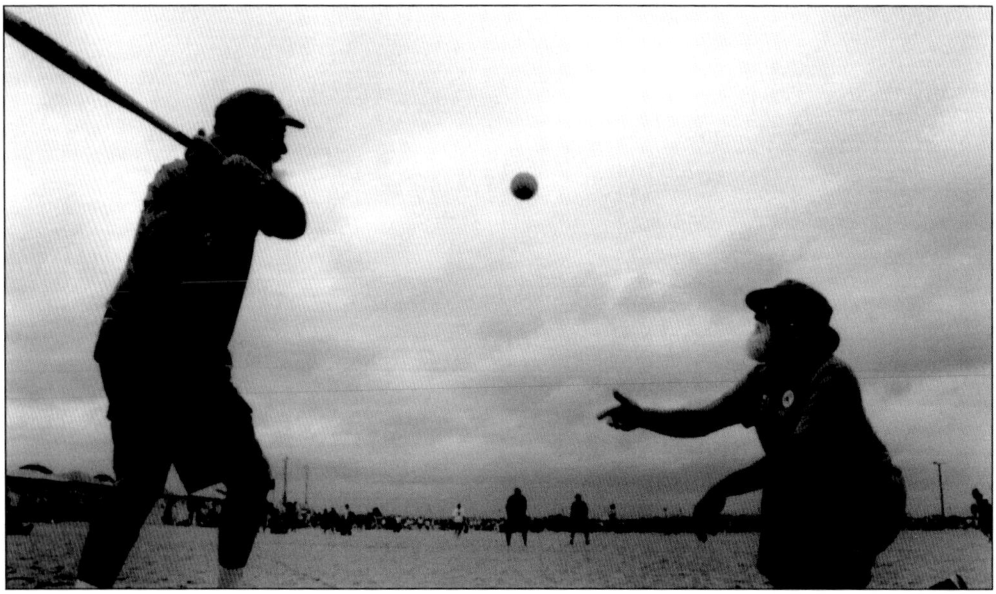

**Santas United in the War on Childhood Obesity.** A team with that name participated in the 61st Annual OMBAC World Championship Over-The-Line Tournament, on Fiesta Island. Their captain, Richard Eckfield (left), identifies himself as "Sustainable Santa." He appears at farmers' markets throughout the North County and tells kids to eat their vegetables. "If you eat junk food, you're gonna die," is a line from his song, "Santa's Got Some Food Rules for You." (Courtesy of Robert J. Trombley.)

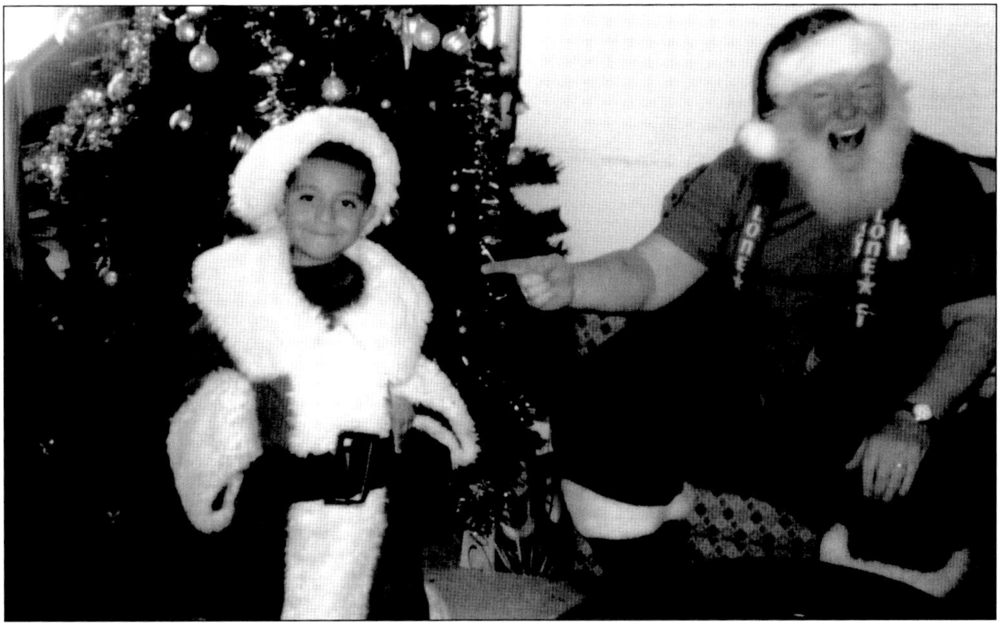

**San Diego Hospice.** Santa visited hospice kids and families in their homes from 2010 until San Diego Hospice declared bankruptcy in 2013. This little boy told the author that he wanted to be Santa Claus when he grew up. The author asked, "Why wait," and removed his cap, coat, and belt. The boy wanted to give Christmas gifts to others. Reflecting on those three years, they were the most painful, yet rewarding of the author's Santa experiences.

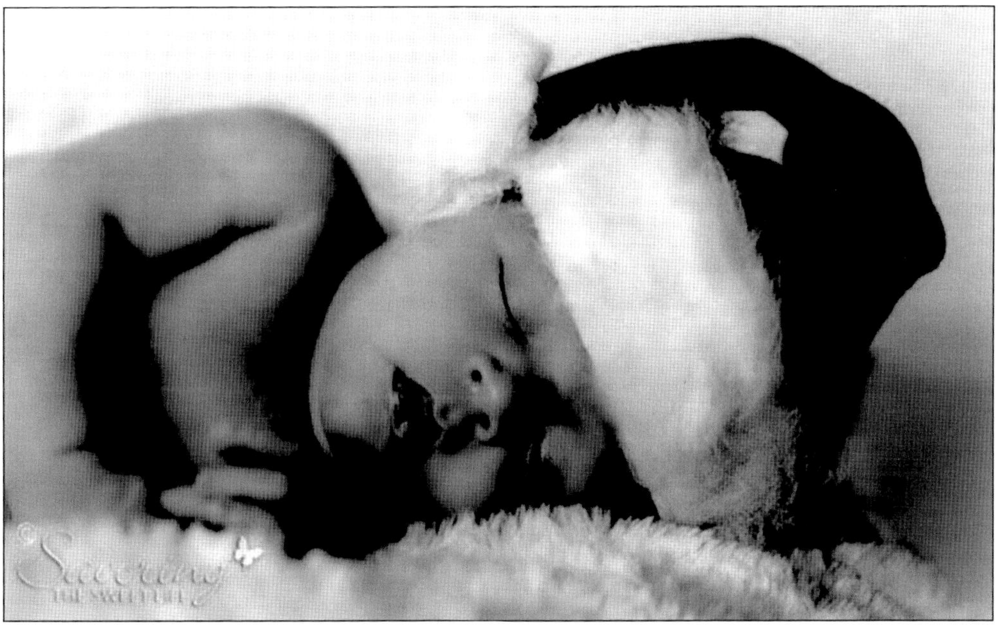

**The Santa Babe.** Christmas is the celebration of birth. A time of joy and hope. The history of Christmas in San Diego began with the birth of Salvador Ignacio Linares, the Christmas Babe. Pictured is little Aidan Bush, a modern San Diego "Santa Babe." May the sweet innocence of a sleeping newborn put a smile on your face and fill your heart with joy and hope for the future. (Courtesy of Pam Davis, Savoring the Sweet Life Photography.)